Higher Education in India

Higher Education in India

The Changing Scenario

Edited by
S.L. SHARMA
B.S. GHUMAN
SHITAL PARKASH

RAWAT PUBLICATIONS
Jaipur • New Delhi • Bangalore • Guwahati • Kolkata

ISBN 978-81-316-0651-3

Reprinted, 2018

Published under the auspices of Senior Citizens' Council for Human Resource Development, Chandigarh.

Published by
Prem Rawat for **Rawat Publications**
Satyam Apts, Sector 3, Jawahar Nagar, Jaipur 302 004 (India)
Phone: 0141 265 1748 / 7006 Fax: 0141 265 1748
E-mail: info@rawatbooks.com
Website: www.rawatbooks.com

New Delhi Office
4858/24, Ansari Road, Daryaganj, New Delhi 110 002
Phone: 011 2326 3290

Also at *Bangalore, Guwahati* and *Kolkata*

Typeset by Rawat Computers, Jaipur
Printed at Chaman Enterprises, New Delhi

Contents

Contributors

Bedi, S.C., Campus Director, Rayat Technology Campus, Railmajra, Ropar, Punjab.

Chadha, G.K., Chief Executive Officer, South Asian University, Professor Emeritus and former Vice Chancellor, Jawahar Lal Nehru University, New Delhi.

Ghuman, B.S., Professor, Department of Public Administration, Panjab University, Chandigarh and former Dean of Arts, Panjab University, Chandigarh.

Ghuman, Ranjit Singh, Nehru SAIL Chair Professor, Centre for Research in Rural and Industrial Development, Chandigarh.

Gupta, Namita, Assistant Professor, Centre for Human Rights Duties, Panjab University, Chandigarh.

Gupta, Rajiv, Joint Commissioner-cum-Secretary, Municipal Corporation, Chandigarh.

Kaushik, S.P., former Chairman and Senior Professor, Department of Surgical Gastroenterology, Sanjay Gandhi Postgraduate Institute of Medical Sciences, Lucknow; former Professor and Head, Department of General Surgery, Government Medical College and Hospital, Chandigarh; and former Additional Professor of Surgery, Postgraduate Institute of Medical Education and Research, Chandigarh.

Mathur, B.P., IAAS (Retd.), former Dy. C.A.G., former Chairman, Audit Board of India and Director, National Institute of Financial Management, Faridabad.

Mathur, Kuldeep, former Rector and Professor of Political Science, Jawaharlal Nehru University, New Delhi; former Director, National Institute of Educational Planning and Administration, New Delhi; and former Professor of Political Science and Public Administration, Indian Institute of Public Administration, New Delhi.

Mathur, S.S., former Professor of Education, Panjab University, Chandigarh, and former Professor, Dean of Education and Head of the University Campus, Kumaoun University, Nainital.

Mehta, Akshat, Assistant Professor, Centre for Police Administration, Panjab University, Chandigarh.

Mohammad, Sohail, Junior Research Fellow (UGC), Department of Public Administration, Panjab University, Chandigarh.

Sethi, Asha, Professor, Institute for Development and Communication, Chandigarh.

Sethi, Jitendra, former Professor of English, Central Institute of English and Foreign Languages, Hyderabad.

Sharma, Puneet, President and CEO, Silverlining, Gurgaon.

Sharma, S.K., Professor Emeritus, Panjab University, Chandigarh.

Sharma, S.L., former Professor, Department of Sociology, and former Dean, Faculty of Arts, Panjab University, Chandigarh.

Singh, Ranjeet, Senior Research Fellow (UGC), Department of Public Administration, Panjab University, Chandigarh.

Singh, Veer, Professor Emeritus, Panjab University, Chandigarh; former Vice Chancellor, NALSAR University of Law, Hyderabad, and presently Director (Academics), Chandigarh Judicial Academy.

Tankeshwar, K., Professor, Centre for Computer Science and Applications, Panjab University, Chandigarh.

Remembering Professor Chander Mohan Bahl

(20 October 1946 – 13 March 2011)

Youngest of five siblings, Chander Mohan Bahl was born on 20 October 1946 at Lahore. After his M.Sc. (Honours School) in Mathematics from Panjab University, Chandigarh in 1970, he started his career in computer applications at Computer Centre Department of Mathematics, Panjab University. He got married to Mrs Bindu Bahl in 1973 and was blessed with two sons – Puneet Bahl and Sumit Bahl in 1975 and 1979 respectively. He was a caring son and a brother, a loving husband, a dedicated father, an affectionate grandfather and a true professional.

He has been a very popular teacher/ trainer and a great professional in computer science and applications. He worked on several platforms (PC-DOS, PC-Windows, VAX-VMS, SUN-Solaris, HP-UX and PC-Linux etc.) using a variety of development tools and application packages. During all these years, his major contributions have been in the areas of teaching, training, curriculum development, development of data processing systems, technology implementation and campus-wide network planning and management. He groomed the careers of a large number of students, research scholars, teachers, executives through Diploma/Master courses and training programmes in Computer Science and applications at Panjab University and elsewhere. He directed large number of projects from many prestigious institutions and has been formal and informal consultant to a number of organizations and individuals in the region. He helped all students, teachers, scholars and others whosoever came to the Computer Centre, Panjab University. He has been Chairman of the Department of Computer Science and Applications and Director of Computer Centre, Panjab University. He held eminent positions in a number of professional associations.

He was one of the architects of Senior Citizens' Council for Human Resource Development. With his support and guidance the Council was able to organize about 350 programmes, a number of national seminars on various subjects, published twenty books and have awarded 16 scholarships to meritorious students from poor families.

He joined Rayat-Bahra Group of Educational Institutions as Managing Director in 2003. He gave vision and a blue-print to Rayat-Bahra Group. It was his leadership and entrepreneurship of Mr Gurvinder Singh Bahra that it has developed into a major multi-disciplined educational group with more than 50 institutions, one university in Shimla, six multi-disciplinary campuses, international campuses in UK and USA, with more than 30,000 students and more than six thousand employees.

He was humble, helpful to everyone, passionate with his work, excellent human being and a "*Yaaron Ka Yaar*".

Anyone who came in contact with him has always been indebted to him in one or the other way and cherishes the memories of the time spent with him till date. He believed "They alone live who live for others".

Rayat-Bahra Group

- 5 CAMPUSES IN INDIA (4 in Punjab, 1 in Delhi-NCR)
- 1 UNIVERSITY IN INDIA (Himachal Pradesh)
- 2 INTERNATIONAL CAMPUSES (USA & UK)
- 1 SKILL DEVELOPMENT CENTRE
- 1 ENTREPRENEURSHIP DEVELOPMENT CENTRE
- 50+ INSTITUTES
- 30,000+ FULL TIME STUDENTS
- 6,000+ EMPLOYEES

Rayat-Bahra Group of Institutes

Rayat-Bahra Group was established in 2001 with Rayat Engineering Institute at Ropar (Punjab) by two young men – S. Nirmal Singh Rayat and S. Gurvinder Singh Bahra with Professor Chander Mohan Bahl as Managing Director. Together they saw a dream of creating a state-of-the-art educational hub. Within 14 years, the group has emerged as one of the largest educational group of institutions in northern India. Indeed its a dream come true. Today it has six multi-disciplinary campuses at Ropar, Mohali, Hoshiarpur, Patiala, and Sonepat – Haryana in NCR, one university in Shimla, international campuses in USA and UK, one Skill Development Centre and one Entrepreneurship Development Centre comprising more than fifty institutes, more than 30,000 full time students and more than 6,000 employees.

Mission

Within a vibrant, ever-challenging and supportive learning environment, the Rayat-Bahra Group discovers, disseminates, and applies new knowledge through teaching and learning, research and creative activity, community involvement, and partnerships. The Rayat-Bahra Group grooms individuals for the day-to-day challenges of life by developing their intrinsic human abilities and in turn provide a skilled human resource for the job market, who would contribute to the advancement of knowledge in the larger perspective. Rayat-Bahra Group, would thus, become a channel for giving a national and international voice to innovation and ultimately play a lead role in placing India on the global forefront.

Vision

To provide value-based and affordable education to those who are keen to learn, discover, explore and to develop the talents of those who are desirous of outstanding achievements in all fields, thus building one of the world's great educational set-up for the 'Good of All'.

Values

Teaching and Learning

The group believes that learning is central to everything that we do. We recognized that we are a community of learners who discover, interpret, apply and transmit knowledge. We aim at creating new technologies for the 'Good of All'.

Excellence

We believe that the promotion of personal and academic excellence provides a foundation for institutional quality. We are committed to achieving the highest standards through ongoing assessment and continuous quality improvement.

Human Dignity and Respect

We believe that wisdom, sound judgment, acceptance and respect for other persons, cultures and ideas are characteristics of an educated person. We seek to demonstrate, through all programmes, activities and services, an appreciation of human diversity and an atmosphere of mutual respect and support for individual differences.

Diversity

We believe that cultural diversity enriches learning experience and promotes respect and understanding. We welcome qualified learners of varying interests, abilities, backgrounds and expectations and are committed to create an exclusive educational environment that provides exceptional opportunities for all learners. We seek to attract, serve and retain a highly qualified and diverse student body, faculty and staff, and to make special effort to provide access to educational opportunities for non-traditional and under-represented population.

Scholarship and Intellectual Freedom

We believe that intellectual and creative freedom support scholarship and advance the learning process. We promote, encourage and support personal and academic freedom. We seek to provide an environment that fosters knowledge development and creative learning experience through intellectual and cultural exchange.

Public Engagement

We believe in public engagement activities which seek to educate and inform. This mutually beneficial relationship is an important tool for building a common ground. We aspire to develop regional, national and international partnership that allows us to serve our stakeholders more effectively. This would provide increased learning opportunities for our students, faculty and staff.

Leadership and Participatory Decision-Making

We believe that effective organizations are characterized by visionary leadership and participatory decision-making at all levels. We are committed to create and support an environment that fosters open communication and innovative approaches to change.

Integrity

We believe that integrity is critical to our continued success and institutional effectiveness. We expect and support the highest level of personal, intellectual, academic, financial and operational integrity within the universal community.

Guiding Principles

Accessibility

An inclusive community of learners that provides educational opportunities to any qualified individual who wishes to participate.

Relevance

Programmes designed to broaden perspectives, heighten awareness, deepen understanding, establish disciplined habits of thought, respond to changes in the workplace and society, and to help develop individuals become informed and responsible citizens.

Responsiveness (to change)

A learning community that is responsive to economic, social and political change. As an agent of change, the institutes explore new alternatives, recognize constraints and make wise institutional choices.

Flexibility

While recognizing that various constituencies have different needs, academic programmes, activities and services are flexible so that people have the opportunity to participate and to achieve their goals.

Collaboration

All programmes, activities and services work collectively to solve problems, provide greater efficiencies and expand learning opportunities. Collaboration extends beyond the institution to colleagues, communities and other related institutions.

Accountability

The institution has consistent policies and procedures to endure accountability at all levels. All members of the institution community are accountable for their actions and decisions.

Affordability

Qualified individuals who desire to participate in our academic programmes are not discouraged from doing so because of financial resources.

Governance

Rayat-Bahra Group of institutions is a self-financing set up where every institution has board members that comprise representatives of the public, staff, faculty, and students. Overall governance follows a corporate hierarchical structure with due freedom to perform as per the portfolios assigned to the team of directors and managers at different levels of organization. Team work, delegation of authority, a sense of ownership and transparency are the hallmarks of Rayat-Bahra Group.

Innovating Excellence et al.

In a fast-paced, continually shifting environment, resilience to change is often the single most important factor that distinguishes the one who succeeds from the one who fails. In order to build the students who have the ability to thrive on change, they must develop the capacity to experiment and eventually learn to create new vistas of knowledge from their own learning. Rayat-Bahra has taken a resolve to facilitate learning through participation and encourage students to venture into uncharted waters. As such, we promote our students to innovate learning in equal quantum from their successes as well as failures.

At Rayat-Bahra, we are making a sincere effort to meticulously weave all factors in the external and internal environment of our institutions, so that the professionals being groomed at our institutes, always have an edge over their competitors in the world. We sincerely hope and desire that every single student, entering any of Rayat-Bahra Institutes at any stage of his learning, should be enabled and empowered enough so that he/she is assured of best and rewarding career opportunities. At Rayat-Bahra, dreams are realized at optimum level.

Rayat-Bahra Group has now attained a stage when our academicians and educational managers, working 24x7, are ready to collaborate with their counterparts in the world. This would help to facilitate the learning community of the country to develop their competencies in order to derive 'innovative excellence'.

All this has been achieved with the vision, guidance and leadership provided by our esteemed Professor Chander Mohan Bahl. He has been our friend, guide and philosopher. We shall ever be indebted to him for his contribution not only to Rayat-Bahra Group but personally, to us as well. We shall always try to follow he path shown by him and imbibe some of his qualities in ourselves.

S. Nirmal Singh Rayat
President, Rayat-Bahra Group

S. Gurvinder Singh Bahra
Chairman, Rayat-Bahra Group

Introduction

The Changing Scenario of Higher Education

The purpose of this introductory essay is three-fold: (a) to highlight the major currents of change in Indian higher education; (b) to provide abstracts of the papers comprising the volume; and (c) to deliberate on some of the common concerns reflected in various contributions.

Currents of Change

Recent years have witnessed huge transition in the field of tertiary education in India. This is manifest from such developments as exponential growth of educational institutions and student enrolments, rapid rise of private enterprise and glocal campuses, great surge of technical and professional institutions, growing trend of public-private partnerships, widening inequities in access to education, and deteriorating standards of education and research.

The number of universities has grown three-fold increasing from 184 in 1990–91 to 556 in 2010–11 and of colleges six-fold from 5,748 to 33,623 during the same period. Similarly, the number of students enroled has also soared three times, increasing from 4.9 million in 1990–91 to 14.6 million in 2008–09 (Ernst and Young, 2011). This signifies a stupendous growth by any measure. Little wonder, India has emerged as a country with the third largest higher education system, next only to USA and China. Lest we feel unduly elated about it, we need to know that we have yet to go a long way. Our achievements are far short of our requirements, especially in comparison with the developed nations.

Another key development is the phenomenal rise of private educational institutions. Not a new phenomenon, we have had the presence of private institutions in the past too. However, earlier, they were managed by foundations, trusts, societies and were largely aided institutions. Recent decades have witnessed an upsurge of unaided private colleges and universities owned and managed by individuals and business entities. The share of unaided private institutions in tertiary education shot up from 43 per cent of the total institutions in 2001 to 63 per cent in 2006 and of student enrolment from 33 per cent to 52 per cent (ibid.). A large number of private universities have as well come up accounting for 22.63 per cent of the total universities during 2005–07 (Chadha, 2013). Private colleges have sprung up all around making 44.67 per cent of all the colleges during the same period. So spectacular has been their growth that it has literally transformed the educational landscape of the country from the one dotted by sparsely located colleges to the one booming with private campuses. No doubt, private institutions have helped immensely to improve access to higher education, but this expansion has excluded sizeable number of students belonging to lower strata of society due to exorbitant fee structure. With a view to make education imparted by private institutions all-inclusive, the government is planning to set up Independent Regulatory Commission for regulating fee structure as well as quality of higher education.

The globalization of higher education is yet another growing trend. For the last many years Indian students have been going abroad to get foreign degrees. Recently many of the foreign institutions have opened their campuses in India. They are offering vocational courses in collaboration with their Indian affiliates. Given the growing number of young Indians who aspire for a foreign degree but cannot afford to go abroad, such institutions find a ready market here. The foreign universities target such glocal students as a part of their global expansion plans. These institutes range from internationally renowned to not so renowned. While their Indian collaborators highlight 'world-class curricula' and the provision of 'study abroad' programmes for students with higher GPA, their faculty remain largely Indian which is viewed by some as a weakness. However, their selling point is the offer of 'global experience' at 'local' cost. Their tuition fee in India is much less than what is charged abroad. It is still far more than that of the reputed Indian institutions. Their degree nevertheless carries foreign brand value. In the interest of quality of education the Indian government proposes to allow 100 per cent foreign direct investment (FDI) in higher education under the Foreign Education Provider (Regulation) Bill which is yet to be passed by the parliament. The purpose of the bill is to regulate the working of the foreign campuses in India for quality as well as social equity. To ensure the latter goal, the bill seeks to make reservation mandatory in such institutions.

Another distinguishing feature of the current scenario is the meteoric rise of technical and professional institutions. Their number has grown considerably over the past few decades. Take, for example, the case of engineering institutions. Their number has soared from a mere 38 in 1947 with the total 2,500 seats to as many as 1,500 with 583 lakh seats in 2007 (Chhapla, 2013). In the last few years their number has more than doubled to 3,800 with annual intake capacity of 1.7 million. In the last one year, i.e. 2012, India added a total of 1.3 lakh new seats in various engineering colleges as reported by S.S. Mantha, Chairman of the All India Council of Technical Education. A similar boom has also occurred in other domains of technical and professional education. This has happened largely due to increasing penetration of private sector in technical and professional disciplines. Consequently, private institutions account for a disproportionately large share of professional enrolment. According to one source, as high as 78 per cent of professional enrloment was in private institutions in 2006 as against only 22 per cent in public institutions (Agarwal, 2006). A discipline-wise breakdown of enrolment in 2006–07 further indicates as huge as 91–95 per cent enrolment in engineering, physiotherapy, hotel management and pharmacy, while it ranged in between 62–68 per cent in the disciplines of computer applications, management, architecture and technical education. In the courses like medicine and dentistry, it ranged between 50–59 per cent (Ernst and Young, 2011).

The rise of private enterprise in higher education has no doubt helped address the need for expansion, as gross enrolment ratio (GER) has gone up from 6 per cent in 1990 to 18 per cent in 2010. However, it still falls short of the world average at 27 per cent, leave alone the developed nations like USA and Russia at 95 per cent and 76 per cent respectively (World Bank, 2010). On the flip side, the upsurge of private sector has aggravated the problem of equity and quality. The problem of unequal access is evident from the glaring disparities in GER between rural and urban areas and across the diverse social strata, apart from other groups. For example, the GER for rural areas is disproportionately low at 11 per cent compared to 30 per cent for urban areas. Similarly, it is 11.6 per cent for the Scheduled Castes, 7.7 per cent for the Scheduled Tribes and 14.8 per cent for the Other Backward Classes against 20 per cent for others (Planning Commission, 2012). These disparities have been widened in part by privatization of education which is apparently marked by a strain of commercialization. The government's noble, though unrealistic, intention of declaring education as not-for-profit zone aside, private entrepreneurs have devised dubious ways of profit multiplication by way of capitation fee, donations, development funds and other charges. This has turned education from a 'public good' to a 'private commodity'. In effect, it has limited the reach of the poor and socially disadvantaged to technical and professional education.

Yet another development, though distressing, is the decline in the quality of education. Not known for any world-class standards earlier too, the quality has dipped further in recent years. This is clear from various available reports, including those of NAAC, UGC, equivalence studies, ranking surveys and recruiters' appraisals. Of the 3,492 colleges, which constitute 17 per cent of the total accredited by the NAAC until 2008, only 9 per cent scored grade 'A', 69 per cent grade 'B' and 23 per cent grade 'C'. Of about 16,000 colleges under UGC purview only 5,813 (or 36%) met the minimum standards and qualified for UGC grants, 100 colleges (or 0.6%) recognized for potential excellence and 250 colleges (or 1.6%) as autonomous colleges (UGC report, 2008). As for equivalence assessment, our Bachelor's degree is undervalued in developed parts of the world including USA and Europe. For example, in The Netherlands our Honors Bachelor's degree is treated as equivalent to only two years of university education, with the exception of an Honors Bachelor's degree with first class distinction (Graded 'A' by NAAC) which is recognized as equivalent to a Dutch 'WO'. More compelling evidence is advanced by international ranking surveys which reveal an embarrassingly low rating of our tertiary education in comparison with other nations. Not one of our educational institutions features among the top 200 of the world. The Government of India has taken cognizance that none of the Indian universities has a brand name in term of quality. It has constituted an 18-member committee to examine about the low ranking of the Indian universities and suggest strategy to improve it. Finally, the employers' recruitment surveys also accord low employability value to Indian graduates, except for graduates of some premier institutes. For improving employability of graduates the central government has taken two new initiatives. First, all the technical institutions have been advised to adopt the National Vocational Education Qualification Framework (NVEQF) to develop a unified national approach for linking academic and workplace standards. Secondly, the government has decided to set up 200 community colleges across the country on pilot basis. The two-fold mandate of community colleges is (i) equipping students with skills aligned to job market and re-skilling displaced workforce, and (ii) promoting students' upward mobility to higher education through Associate Degree Programmes.

A number of factors account for the unenviable quality of our higher education. These include: the system of affiliating universities with huge numbers of affiliated colleges; poor, inadequate and deficient infrastructure and equipments; lack of regular and qualified faculty; outdated, inflexible and irrelevant curriculum; monologues and boring pedagogy; deficient testing procedures; lack of quality research and innovation; bureaucratic controls and lack of professional and financial autonomy; and lack of internal quality control and assessment. For addressing some of these factors the Indian government has initiated a flagship programme, known as Rashtriya Uchttar Siksha Abhiyan (RUSA), on the pattern of Sarva Shiksha Abhiyan (SSA) and Rashtriya Madhyamik Shiksha Abhiyan (RMSA).

Since the above traits allegedly characterize the private institutions more than the public ones, the blame of declining quality is laid on the door of the former. Not confined to India, this allegation against the private institutions is widespread across developing countries. Umpteen evidence of it is cited by Goel (2013). For example, some private universities in Bangladesh are allegedly selling certificates, easy-to-get degrees, substandard teaching, poor infrastructure and high tuition fee, etc (Naser, 2008; Mazumdar, 2012). In Africa, such universities are dubbed as "'briefcase universities' delivering degrees with no real value, though costly"(Ngosi, cited in, Kyama, 2012). In India, many of the private institutions are popularly called 'teaching shops' concerned as they are with 'profitability' rather than 'quality'. Not surprisingly, a large number of them are faced with the prospects of closure and quite a few have already shut down according to the available reports, 32 professional colleges have closed down in just one state (*Times of India*, May 28, 2012), 63 management institutes across the country are on the verge of closing down (*Times of India*, February 19, 2012), and as many as 1,500 business schools are likely to close down within the next two years (Ganguly, 2010). The reported low credibility of many private institutions for quality notwithstanding, it will be unfair to malign the image of all private institutions on this count. Some private institutions provide 'examples of excellent teaching and quality education' as rightly stated by Goel (2012).

Themes and Issues

Since the book is about the changing contours of tertiary education in India, it deals with the above delineated changes in some depth and details. It is a product of a national seminar organized by the Senior Citizens' Council for HRD, in collaboration with the Department of Public Administration, Panjab University, Chandigarh and ICSSR North-West Regional Centre, Chandigarh, in April 2013. The seminar was organized in memory of Late Shri Chander Mohan Bahl (1946–2011), an eminent computer professional, a great visionary and institution builder. The volume comprises select papers presented there. While each paper highlights a specific facet of educational change, it is arranged along with others in such a manner that it makes an integral part of the overall theme of the book. The book is organized in four major thematic parts, viz., public and private sector in higher education, technical and professional education, public-private partnership, and other facets of education. The first section deals with the rise of private enterprise in higher education and its fallouts. The second section focuses on technical and professional stream, especially in engineering, medical, legal and management education, and illustrates their domain-specific trends, issues and challenges. The third section brings together the papers reflecting on the models of public-private partnership, including the academic-industry interaction. The fourth section discusses some other potentially influential developments such as Right to Education (RTE) and e-governance in educational institutions.

The book opens with S.L. Sharma's paper providing a comparative analysis of the quality of education delivered by private and public institutions. He begins with the poser: what has private sector done to quality of education? Has it led to quality upgradation or its dilution? To answer the question, he advances a three-part criterion of quality education comprising quality assurance factors, quality performance factors and quality outcome factors. In light of this criterion and the findings of the available studies, he finds private schools faring better than government schools. Conceding the role of students' family background and support, a competing hypothesis advanced by some researchers, he attributes it primarily to the better work put in by teachers in the private schools. Accordingly, he maintains that school type matters. However, private education does not have the same edge over public institutions at all levels. At the level of higher education, the situation gets reversed: the public universities and colleges outperform their private counterparts. This, however, presents a stark contrast to the situation in some of the developed nations where private institutions figure among the world-class centres. Sharma attributes the tardy performance of our institutions to their crass business motive and their use of unethical practices. The quality of our overall educational system, including that of public institutions, is no significantly better either. For improving the quality, Sharma lays major stress on investing in faculty development, among other things.

In the next piece, B.S. Ghuman focuses on privatization and globalization of higher education. With its gross enrolment ratio (GER) at 18 per cent, India figures at the bottom of the ten select countries. In respect of privatization of higher education, Ghuman shows that in 2012 out of 33,682 institutions of higher learning, 20,121 were privately-owned and managed, which constitute 62.41 per cent of the total. Private institutions have boomed mainly in the field of 'sunrise' disciplines such as engineering and management. Viewing privatization as not an unmixed blessing, Ghuman underlines its following worrisome consequences: unequal access and exclusion, low quality, malpractices and corruption. Most worrisome of all, he maintains, is marginalization of social sciences and humanities in the wake of privatization. Turning to globalization,

Ghuman refers to the trend of penetration of foreign educational institutions in India in collaboration with their local affiliates. He notes that there are around 150 foreign education institutions in various parts of India having 12,000 students. The trend is likely to gather strength once the government allows 100 per cent FDI in education.

The third paper sketches the changing role of private enterprise in higher education. In his paper S.S. Mathur observes that privatization has had a long history in India and that it is not entirely a new phenomenon. What is new about it is its enormous expansion in the past couple of decades. More important than that is its changing character in recent times. Earlier, the private sector patronized the field of education driven largely by missionary and noble considerations. Today, it has become mercenary. Citing a couple of case studies of private universities from the states of Chhattisgarh and Maharashtra, Mathur illustrates the nefarious role played by political and commercial interests in the field of higher education. He shares his personal experiences of how attempts were made to lure him by offering cash and gold and simultaneously to scare him by showing loaded pistol to influence his decision to recommend grant of affiliation. Nothing can document the unscrupulous role of private sector more authentically than this.

Concerned over the current developments, B.P. Mathur expresses his dismay at the misdirection of higher education. Posing the query: 'whither higher education in India?' he laments its poor standards and lack of concern for character-building. In his view, education should aim at producing young men and women of knowledge, character and values. Falling short of this great vision, higher education in India seems to have lost its track and instead acquired a constrained vision of producing manpower for infinite economic growth. Its emphasis has shifted from knowledge and values to information and skills, from character-building to career training, and from comprehensive human development to human capital formation. To stem the tide, Mathur urges upon the policy makers to arrest the vitiating trend of trivialization of education and take earnest steps to restore its ennobling mission.

Focusing on the need for proper regulation of higher education, B.S. Ghuman, Ranjeet Singh and Sohail Mohammed offer a brief account of the composition and functions of the regulatory bodies. For purposes of performance appraisal, however, they select a few major bodies such as the University Grants Commission (UGC), the All India Council for Technical Education (AICTE) and the Medical Council of India (MCI). The UGC comes under scanner for its inefficient working and governance deficiencies, the AICTE for its questionable approval of many institutions of doubtful integrity as well as non-recognition of a few credible premier institutes, and MCI for relaxing norms in favour of many private institutions for considerations other than merit. In view of this, the authors commend the proposed move of the government to set up a National Commission of Higher Education and Research (NCHER).

In view of the paramount importance of economic growth in the present era of globalization and also of technical and professional education for economic growth, the second section encompasses papers on technical and professional education. In his persuasive paper G.K. Chadha foregrounds the crucial importance of education for raising quality workforce for the development of knowledge economy in India. Fully aware of the composite concept of quality of workforce and of the inadequacy of relying on education alone as its surrogate, for heuristic purposes, however, the author still takes education as a critical minimum measure of it. On this simplistic yardstick too, he finds the profile of India's workforce below the mark, especially in agriculture, construction, mining-querying, despite the significant improvement in some other sectors in the last two decades. In view of the emerging knowledge-based innovations in the new agriculture, industry and services, he underlines the need for developing a skilled, productive and flexible labour force. And for this, he maintains that education holds the key.

S.C. Bedi, in his paper, reflects on the state of engineering education. He observes that our engineering education suffers from imbalances of all sorts, viz., imbalance between the regions, between quantity and quality, private and public, physical and intellectual and inter-branch, etc. Providing a SWOT analysis of the technical education system, the author offers critical reflections on the role of the regulatory bodies. He urges upon them to do self-introspection and transform themselves from punitive to nurturing agencies.

Not all is well with our medical education either. It suffers from all sorts of maladies: shortage and sale of medical seats, substandard infrastructure and equipment, old and unrevised curriculum, compromised quality of faculty and students, rise of unethical practices and poor standards of training. For the same reason, in the next chapter, S.P. Kaushik expresses his concern over the pathetic and decrepit state of medical education in India. He attributes the above ills to the policy of reservation, indiscriminate privatization and increasing bureaucratization. Reservations have also led to decline in the quality of students and faculty, privatization to making a business of medical education, and bureaucratization to erosion of autonomy and integrity of medical professionals. Highlighting the shortage of doctors which in his estimate stands at one doctor for 10,000 patients as against the norm of one doctor for 1,000 patients, the author underscores the need for boosting the provision of medical education. In fact, the latest available data reveals that there is only one government medical college for over 35,000 people today. Taking the private medical colleges together with government colleges, it comes to one seat for 26,042 people – far short of the WHO standard of one seat for every 600 people. In view of his intense concern for quality, Kaushik too offers some valuable suggestions to tone up the standards of medical education.

Reflecting on the legal education, Veer Singh in his article traces its growth in India through four phases: colonial, early post-Independence, pre-globalization and era of globalization. For a detailed treatment he focuses on the fourth phase because it is in this phase that legal education came of age. It began with the establishment of a new category of National Law Schools in 1987 and also witnessed rise of law universities and law colleges, apart from departments of laws as parts of multi-faculty universities. It also saw proliferation of private law colleges which, according to the author, has adversely affected the quality of legal education due to excessive commercialization. Singh, however, commends the emerging trends of diversification of legal education in response to the needs of the era of globalization. Concerned over the institutional variations in the quality of legal education, he offers some valuable suggestions for achieving uniformity of high standards across the country. In this regard, he underlines the importance of founding legal education upon the knowledge of social sciences and incorporating the new technical advances.

In the next paper, Puneet Sharma reflects on the state of management education and deciphers the challenges and issues which it faces. He sketches the growth of management education in post-Independence era in two phases: pre-liberalization and post-liberalization. In so doing, he shows how liberalization has leveraged the growth of management education and changed its complexion remarkably. In his view, the current scenario of management education suffers from quality deficits which in large part are caused by mushrooming of private management institutes. Viewing quality education as a function of inputs, processes and outputs, Sharma finds our management education leaving something to be desired on all the three. On the front of inputs, he maintains that neither the student selection is based on aptitude nor is the faculty always proficient. The curriculum is unthinkingly borrowed from the West and is often out of sync with the Indian business reality. The same is the case with the processes which lack the culture of interaction, experiential learning, real-life exposure, Indian content and case studies, research inputs and skill developing instructions. No wonder, a large many of our management graduates fall short of the expectations of the industry and fail to find jobs commensurate with their qualifications. As it is, Sharma finds management education in India deficient on many counts, especially diversification, innovation, glocalization, research and, above all, practical training. He views them as challenges for the Indian management education. In addition, he also discusses certain critical issues such as defining a suitable model of management education for India, striving for professional excellence in bureaucratic setting, and reconciling business interests with the ethics of corporate social responsibility (CSR).

The last paper of this section by Ranjit Singh Ghuman brings to the fore the imbalances and inequities in higher education, particularly in its technical and professional stream. Based on a comprehensive survey of higher education in Punjab, Ghuman advances substantial evidence of it. Tracing the imbalances that have appeared in the last two decades, he shows how more of the colleges have sprung up in urban than in rural areas, how the private educational institutions have proliferated vis-à-vis the public institutions, and how the technical professional stream has registered greater expansion than the liberal arts stream. Similarly, in respect of social inequities, he documents how rural students, particularly SCs and OBCs, are woefully under-represented in higher education, especially in technical-professional courses, in comparison with urban, non-SCs and non-OBCs. Examining the economic cost of technical and professional education, Ghuman attributes the under-representation of rural students in general and SC and OBC students in particular to their inability to pay. In light of this, he finds the goal of inclusive education a distant dream.

The move towards public-private partnership (PPP) in the field of education is another notable trend of our times. Given its crucial importance, the third section of the book is devoted to it. In his paper, Kuldeep Mathur underscores the key policy significance of PPP for provisioning education to the people at large. He briefly discusses the initiatives taken by the governmental and the non-governmental organizations (NGOs) towards promoting it at the level of school education. For the higher education, he stresses the need for promoting collaboration between university and industry in the field of research.

Public-private partnership can take various forms in the field of higher education. Dealing with them in their essay, B.S. Ghuman, Akshat Mehta and Ranjeet Singh cite the following four models: basic infrastructure, outsourcing, equity, and reserve outsourcing. They find the outsourcing and the equity models more suitable for higher education in India. Easy to envisage, the PPP models are often hard to manage for reasons of difficulties of harmonizing the interests of the public and private entities. In addition, their interests have also to be reconciled with the larger objectives of equity, access and quality. The authors offer some policy suggestions too to streamline the prevailing PPP models and smoothen their operations.

Picking on the industry-institute partnership, S.K. Sharma advances a new paradigm in technical education. He briefly describes the growth of technical education in India and expresses his concern at the recent decline in its quality. Based on a comparison of the Indian engineering institutions with select international universities, he observes that even our premier institutes score lower on major quality indicators than the institutes in USA and China. In respect of the average institutions, the less said the better. He blames it on the recent indiscriminate expansion of technical education under the sponsorship of private sector. In addition he attributes it to the lack of industry-institute association too. He faults the engineering institutes for their failure to involve industry and other user agencies in developing curriculum and criticizes industry for its lack of seriousness in delivering practical training. To fix the flawed system of engineering education, he stresses the need for closer industry-institute collaboration, and setting up industry liaison cells and technical business incubators.

In the next paper Namita Gupta and Rajiv Gupta examine the existing modes of industry-academy interactions with a view to finding out those which are viewed as more beneficial by the academy. Based on an empirical study of four engineering institutions, two of them public universities and two private colleges, in and around Chandigarh, the authors find student internship, exchange of resource persons and consortium R&D projects as favourites of the engineering institutes. Further, they also note certain lacunae in the operations of such programmes. These include lack of efficiency in the planning and management of practical training, low level of participation by industry in curriculum development, and the indifference of industry to invest in R&D.

The last part of the book deals with some other facets/developments that have the potential to significantly influence the future course of higher education in India. The Right to Education Act, 2009 (RTE) is one such development. Education is not just for a privileged few any more. The RTE mandates it for every child in the age group of 6–14 regardless of caste, class, creed, gender and community. Asha Sethi, in her paper, provides an idea about the provisions of the Act, the problems in its implementation and the ways to overcome them. She finds its objectives of providing free and compulsory education to all children too ambitious in view of the staggering deficiencies and pathetic conditions of schools; its input norms of infrastructure and faculty too demanding for both the government and the private schools; and its concerns for learning outcomes too feeble in view of the provisions of automatic promotions to next class without any board examination. With the expiry of the three-year compliance period on 31 March 2013 and failure of a large number of schools to meet the input norms, her observations have proved right. A number of reports, including the one by Child Rights and You (CRY), have revealed that not all is well with the RTE after the expiry of the deadline of its compliance period (cited in *Times of India*, 27 June 2013). Even the official data shows that 40 per cent primary schools suffer from teacher shortage, 33 per cent lack girls' toilets and 39 per cent lack the ramps for children with disabilities (cited in *Times of India*, 28 September 2013). As a result, a large number of low budget private schools are faced with prospects of closure because of undue emphasis on infrastructure norms rather than learning outcomes. Yet, the mission is noble enough to be realized. For the same reason, the author offers some constructive suggestions to expedite its success.

The advent of information technology (IT) and its use in education is another recent development with a potential to influence the future of education. It has already begun impacting our education system in a number of significant ways such as widening educational access, scalability and quality. Identifying some of these effects of IT, K. Tankeshwar focuses on the state of e-governance in educational institutions. Based on the observations gathered through websites and his personal interactions, the author provides a comparative view of e-governance in the government and private institutions, and maintains that private institutions score over government institutions in switching over to e-governance. He finds age of the personnel and timings of their education as big factors affecting their disposition to e-governance: the seniors in rank and age and those graduated before 1985 (the era of no personal computer) being less computer savvy.

In the last paper of the book, Jitendra Sethi underlines the imperative importance of English for educational development. Proceeding from this premise, he advances strong advocacy for enhancing proficiency in English. To achieve this end, he suggests two measures: (a) to adopt English as a medium of instruction from an early stage; and (b) to institute public-private partnership in imparting education. The PPP model that he suggests is the one in which the public sector is expected to finance and private sector to manage the institutes under an independent body comprising representatives of both.

Addressing the Concerns

From the above four major concerns have appeared in the changing scenario of higher education: commercialization and corruption, uneven access, marginalization of human and social sciences, and falling standards. These are reflected in almost all the contributions. As such, they are too compelling to let go unaddressed.

It is widely held that privatization of higher education carries with it a grain of commercialization. This is validated by the manner in which private sector has conducted itself in the field of education. With the opening of educational field, the private entrepreneurs jumped on the bandwagon in a big way, perceiving in it a lucrative business opportunity. For the same reason, they targeted technical and professional education where they saw huge demand and money. Nothing wrong with that since privatization is all about profit. However, the wrong emerged when many of them did not shy away from taking recourse to foul means to multiply their profits *ad infinitum*. That is where commercialization and corruption crept in. The private players alone are not to blame for it. The unrealistic and unreasonable policy of government to declare education as a not-for-profit zone and the unscrupulous ways of its regulatory bodies are equally to blame. Whatever the reasons, it has produced some serious distortions such as robbing education of its noble mission of human development, rendering it inaccessible to the poor and the deprived, and diluting its quality.

Till a few decades back, education used to be viewed as a noble profession. Not any more. It has now got infected with devious practices. Many of the private institutions are known to indulge in all kinds of malpractices including corruption, fleecing, duping, cheating, playing games, flouting norms and compromising with standards. They indulge in corruption for securing approvals and accreditations; in fleecing, duping and cheating students and their parents by showing them rosy dreams; in playing games with regulatory bodies for flouting norms of infrastructure, admissions, faculty recruitment and payment, and professional standards. Little wonder, education has earned the ignoble distinction of featuring among the corrupt most sectors. Nothing could be more disastrous than this. How can one expect delivery of high quality education, leave aside value-based instructions, from institutions raised on foundations of corruption and maintained by unprofessional and unethical practices.

There are two ways to look at the possible role of private sector in the field of education. One, to view it as an efficient and credible agency to raise high class institutions. Two, to view it as an agency having low credibility for it. The former is derived from the experience of the US, UK and some other developed nations where it has raised some world-class institutions having ultramodern infrastructure and hi-tech equipment, advanced curriculum, creative pedagogy and innovative research. Given that experience, one would have expected the private sector in India too to have raised institutions of high repute. But, that was not to be for reasons of the kinds of private entrepreneurs who came forward to patronize the field of education. No wonder, private universities and colleges here carry by and large a low credibility, honourable exceptions apart.

But this has to change. To provide change, we should devise enlightened policies and adopt the best practices followed by the reputed private institutions in advanced countries. For this it is necessary to urgently review our policy of defining the field of education as a not-for-profit zone. The policy is patently unrealistic and unworkable. It needs to be revised to allow the private sector to earn a reasonable margin of profit on its educational ventures. This may attract credible corporate houses to invest in higher education which is as much in their interest as in public interest. Needless to say that they too need competent manpower for running and promoting their industry and business. Here is an opportunity for them to shape the kind of human resource that they need. More importantly, here they also get a handsome opportunity to perform their corporate social responsibility (CSR). The reasonable margin of profit may be decided in consultation with the credible corporate houses. Given the advanced methods of cost computation, it should not be difficult to do so. Simultaneously, the government needs to set its own regulatory bodies in order and to reorient them to play more of a constructive than a restrictive role.

From a sociological angle, a problematic consequence of privatization of education is the glaring disparities in the enrolment ratios of various socio-economic groups. The current GER for the SCs, for instance, is at 7.7 per cent as against 18 per cent for the general population. Though not so low for the STs at 11.6 per cent, it is still low enough in comparison with that of the general population. This imbalance gets more glaring between rural and urban areas with 11.1 per cent for rural as against 30 per cent for urban. Thus, privatization has rendered higher education more inaccessible to the youth of lower socio-economic strata than those of the other sections. This runs counter to the avowed goal of inclusive education and therefore calls for measures to contain it. One of the ways to do so is to provide for differential fee structure for the youth of the poor and the prosperous sections. The private educational institutions may be required to provide admission to a reasonable number of students of socially disadvantaged and economically deprived sections at a minimum fee affordable by them. The balance of fee for such students may be compensated to the institutions by the government so as not to deprive the institution of its approved margin of profit. In granting admission to such students, the institution may not be required to relax the merit criteria for them. Similarly, for tackling the problem of under-representation of rural students in higher education, government may inspire private sector to launch higher education institutions in rural areas by offering to them some attractive incentives. Such institutions have to give preference to rural students in their admissions, though without compromising the eligibility criteria and the principle of merit. To meet the merit deficit, if any, the rural institutions may be allowed to run summer classes or preparatory coaching programmes for applicants from rural areas. This may be done at government expense.

Appreciative of the wisdom of human and social sciences for developing wholesome personality and society, some enlightened businessmen and intellectuals have come together to launch new ventures to restore the noble status and glory of liberal arts. It is indeed heartening to note, as reported by Mukul (2013), that at least two such ventures are in the offing: Ashoka University (AU) in Kundli, Haryana and Shiv Nadar University (SNU) in Noida. Besides being quite ambitious projects, they share in common at least three major concerns: no-profit norm, stress on humanities and social sciences and world-class standards. This is a commendable development and it signifies a paradigm shift in the role of private sector in education. At any rate, the industry, state as well as larger society need the insights of social sciences to tackle emerging problems and challenges and to strive for wholesome development. The state, therefore, needs to do more to promote development of human and social sciences by creating job opportunities for their graduates. Simultaneously, the educational authorities and professional bodies of these disciplines should do their bit to develop market-oriented applied courses so as to enhance the job capabilities of their graduates.

Much concern has recently been expressed in civil and intellectual circles, including the present collection, over the quality of Indian education in the light of international rankings. Like in previous years, in 2013 too, no Indian university features among the top 200 of the world in the Times Higher Education Survey (THES). Panjab University has emerged as the highest ranked Indian institution, though bracketed with the institutions in the rank category of 225–250. The question then is: how to improve the quality of our education to a level where couple of our institutions make it to the top 10 elite club? One way to do so is to figure out what all makes a world-class university. A world-class university is not simply an institution of high quality education and research but one with a capacity to excel in global competition. The excelling capacity of an institution is judged by the leading ranking agencies like Times Higher Education (THE) and Shanghai Iiao Tong University (SITU) by the methodologies that they have devised. The parameters used by the two are largely common except that THE privileges international outlook and combines both subjective and objective criteria, while SITU relies exclusively on objective criteria.

Questions have been raised about the concept of world-class universities as a uniform standard in view of their 'elite Western bias' as well as about the serious limitations of the existing ranking methodologies. Without entering into that controversy here, it may be rewarding to look into what distinguishes them from the regular universities. Some of their distinctive traits are as follows: talented students, highly accomplished faculty, innovative curriculum, creative teaching, excellence in research, academic freedom, institutional and professional autonomy, and a vibrant intellectual culture, besides an international outlook. These certainly are also some of the key indicators of quality education. We would, therefore, do well to cultivate these key attributes of quality for infusing excellence in our institutions of higher learning.

In order to do so, three agencies need to come together to make concerted and coordinated efforts: government, private sector and academic institutions. Government, both at centre and state levels, need to accord top priority to promoting quality of education, provide a favourable policy environment and a supportive regulatory mechanism, and necessary funds. It must review some of its existing policies to which repeated references have been made earlier, incentivise credible corporates to set up institutions of excellence, upgrade educational institutions with potential for excellence, and substantially reduce bureaucratic controls to provide for institutional and professional autonomy. For sure, the government is doing its bit but not enough. It needs to do more.

The private players must rise above their shortsighted approach of making a business of education. In fact, they need to realize that they cannot survive for long in the field of education with their rapacious business mentality. The quality conscious Indian youth is getting increasingly disillusioned with the dubious ways and dismal performance of many a private institution. As a result, they are deserting such institutions. The dwindling numbers of students in private institutions and the consequent closure of a number of them are proof enough of it. This signals the need for quality assurance if the private institutions have to survive in the changing scenario. Happily, some signs of this realization dawning upon the private sector are in sight. According to recent reports, some private entrepreneurs have announced to undertake such a ground venture (*The Economic Times*, 27 September 2013).

The most vital role, however, is to be played by the educational institutions themselves. Ironically, it is the internal structures and cultures of the educational institutions which in large part are responsible for the indifferent quality of education. Their leaders lack an institutional vision, academic professionals a measure of intellectual integrity and researchers a concern for excellence. Most important of all, their heads lack a will to fill even the sanctioned faculty positions, let alone other things. Needless to say that teachers constitute the backbone of any educational system. They hold the key to most other attributes of quality education, including the standard of curriculum, teaching and research. An educational institution can be just about as good as the quality of its teachers. Does anybody care for this simple truism? It does not seem so. Otherwise our educational institutions would not have been languishing at 40 per cent vacant faculty positions, a large many temporary teachers, and swelling number of guest lecturers, most of them blatantly underpaid. It is simply ridiculous to expect quality education in view of these ground realities. This calls for serious heart searching on the part of all concerned, especially the institutional authorities who need to set their own house in order. They should also set their priorities right and urgently fill all the vacant faculty positions with competent teachers. In addition, they need to give a push to faculty development programmes so as to upgrade the quality of the existing faculty.

The destination is clear: to build quality institutions which "contribute to the advancement of knowledge through research, teach with the most innovative curriculum and pedagogical methods ... and produce graduates who stand out" (Salmi, 2009). The roadmap is clear: government to provide for requisite resources and supportive policy environment, private sector to come forward to build institutions of excellence in its own interests as well as in the interests of larger society, and educational institutions to shake out of their slumber and do whatever they can to enhance the quality of education. Over to the agencies concerned to rise to the occasion.

References

Agarwal, P. 2006. 'Higher Education in India: The Need for Change'. Working Paper 180. Indian Council for Research on International Economic Relations.

Chadha, G.K. 2013. 'Higher Education for India's Future Development: Some Views of an Economist' (unpublished). ICSSR Regional Centre, Panjab University, Chandigarh.

Chhapla, Hemali. 2013. 'Greek Tragedy: Plot Weakens'. *Times of India,* 4 August.

Ernst and Young. 2011. *Private Sector Participation in Indian Higher Education.* FICCI Higher Education Summit, 2011.

Ganguly, S. 2010. 'Why Over 1500 B-Schools in India Would Shut Down in the Next Two Years' (cited in Ved Goel, 2013).

Goel, Ved. 2013. 'Access, Equity and Quality in Private Higher Education'. *Commonwealth Partnership in Education,* TSO (former HMSO).

Kyama, R. 2012. 'Private Universities Helping to Meet Student Demand', *University World Views,* Issue 236.

Mazumdar, Q.H. 2012. 'Private Higher Education in Bangladesh: Quality or Profitability?', *Daily News*, Dhaka, 12 January.

Mukul, Akshaya. 2013. 'Paradigm Shift in Private Education', *Times of India*, 28 October.

Naser, Abu. 2008. *Education Quality of Private Universities in Bangladesh: Faculty Resources and Infrastructure Perspective* (cited in Ved Goel, 2013).

Planning Commission. 2012. *Twelfth Five Year Plan 2012–2017, Social Sectors*, Volume 3, New Delhi.

Salmi, Jamil. 2009. *The Challenge of Establishing World-Class Universities*. The World Bank. Washington D.C.

Thorat, Sukhdeo. 2008. *Higher Education in India: Issues Related to Expansion, Inclusiveness, Quality and Finance*. University Grants Commission, New Delhi.

World Bank. 2010. Retrieved from http://dataworldbank.org/indicator/SFTERENRR, last accessed online 23 April 2013.

Part I

Public and Private Sectors in Higher Education

1

Quality of Education

Private and Public

S.L. SHARMA

'Expansion, excellence and inclusion' have emerged as the three critical concerns of education in India, as rightly underlined by the National Knowledge Commission. To meet the challenge of expansion, the Indian state provided for greater participation of private sector in education in the wake of economic reforms. Consequently, private sector ventured into the field of education in a big way leading to mushrooming of private education institutions all around. The private sector has penetrated especially the technical and professional streams because of huge demand for them. As a result, recent years have witnessed a massive growth of unaided private higher education institutions and student enrolment in them. According to a recent report (E&Y, 2011), the share of private institutions increased from 43 per cent in 2001 to 63 per cent in 2006 and their student enrolment grew from 33 per cent to 52 per cent during the same period.

The rise of private enterprise in education has no doubt made education accessible to a much larger number of people than before. However, it has done so only for those who can afford to pay its high cost in the form of capitation fee, donations and other spurious charges, besides greatly enhanced tuition fee. For the same reason, it has not much benefited the Scheduled Castes and the poor. If anything, it has discriminated against them by restricting their access to education. This is evident from the significantly low enrolment ratio of the Scheduled Castes at 10.2 per cent and the Scheduled Tribes at 4.4 per cent, as against the gross enrolment ratio (GER) of the general population at 16 per cent, as revealed by the first-ever countrywide Survey of Higher Education (2012). Similar inequities in school enrolment have been revealed by a longitudinal study which shows government schools as the only option for the 'poorest of the poor' with over 70 per cent of the sampled students belonging to households from the bottom two quartiles (Singh, 2013).

Indiscriminate expansion of education, especially private institutions, is also believed to have adversely impacted the quality of education, particularly of higher education. Expressing his lament at the dismal quality of education, Najeeb Jung, the Vice Chancellor of Jamia Millia Islamia, says, '[In] the private universities, there is no commitment to higher education, they are only charging a fee, where is the quality' (cited in Mathur, 2013). Many others hold the same view which, of course, is vehemently contested by the votaries of the private sector. The latter, on the contrary, maintain that the private sector participation in education has contributed to the improvement in the quality standards of education. Jhingan (2011), for instance, observes: 'the private sector can be credited with the establishment of some globally renowned institutions that have established state-of-the-art infrastructure and impart world class education. Going forward, the role of the private sector can be expected to assume greater significance in establishing quality higher education institutions.' Given these divergent views, it calls for a deeper probe.

Quality education is not an option, nor a choice: it is a critical condition for development – economic, human and civil. More than ever before, it has gained in special significance in the present era of globalization which is an era of intense global competition for excellence. For the same reason, it is necessary to accord serious attention to the state of quality of our education and the factors that affect it with special reference to the bearing of private sector on it.

This paper attempts to do precisely that. It seeks to address the emerging quality concerns in education with a focus on a comparative view of private and public institutions. More pointedly, it seeks to reflect on the following posers.

(i) Do private schools deliver better quality education than public (government) schools?
(ii) Do private colleges/universities deliver better quality education than government/aided colleges and public universities?
(iii) What is the state of quality of education on the whole, regardless of private and public domains?
(iv) How to enhance quality of our education to make it globally competitive?

For a systematic examination of the above questions, it is necessary to begin by identifying the parameters of quality education. The following section attempts to figure them out.

Parameters of Quality Education

Efforts have been made by quality control agencies as well as independent researchers to devise parameters of quality education. These have been cast largely in terms of quality assurance factors such as infrastructure, faculty, curriculum, etc. The present author has shown it elsewhere (Sharma, 2004) while reviewing the parameters used by National Assessment and Accreditation Council (NAAC). Quality assurance factors represent at best quality inputs, not quality outputs. For the same reason, the National Board of Accreditation, a quality control agency for higher technical education, has recently revised its procedure from infrastructure-based to outcome-based measures.

For a comprehensive mapping of quality education, it may be rewarding to formulate benchmark in terms of a three-part criterion: quality assurance, quality performance and quality outcome measures. Quality assurance factors include infrastructure, faculty, student selectivity, curriculum, etc. which virtually constitute the necessary conditions for quality education. As important as these, there are the performance factors which serve as sufficient conditions. These include the quality of teaching and research, of learning and testing, of intellectual interactions within and outside the classrooms, and of new visions and experimentations. In short, performance measures are about the quality of work put in by the teachers, students, researchers and all concerned.

Finally, like the quality of any product or service, the quality of education needs to be judged by its outcomes. It may not always be easy to measure the outcomes of education. Part of the reason for it is that education is not the same kind of service as others: it is a service with a difference. While others are services for gratis, education is a life-shaping service. A more important reason seems to be the lack of consensus about the overall purpose of education. There have appeared two broad visions about the purpose of education which for want of better terms may be called intrinsic and instrumental. The intrinsic view of education envisages it as a mechanism of training the intellect for its own sake. The instrumental view of education projects it as a mechanism of training the intellect for a profession, industry or market. Since it is hard to operationalize the intrinsic view of education, most efforts have focussed on the instrumental outcomes. Such outcomes have been looked at in two ways: (a) in terms of immediate cognitive and career gains and (b) in terms of long-term attitudinal gains. Some of the widely used indicators of the former are results, pass percentages, percentage of merit holders and placements, etc. Depending on the level of education, the cognitive gains may range from knowledge of three r's (reading, writing and arithmetic) to instilling ability of analytical, critical and creative thinking. In terms of long-term gains, the attitudinal changes have been judged in terms of development of discriminatory ability to tell the virtue from vice, right from the wrong and fair from the foul. This is what is signified by Malcolm S. Forbes' oft-cited statement: 'The purpose of education is to convert an empty mind into an open mind.' That precisely is the goal of education according to our tradition as well which expects it, 'Lead me from darkness to light, from evil to good'. That is what true education is all about as it aims at qualitative transformation of consciousness, i.e. its emancipation from ignorance and prejudices.

By way of further elaboration of the long-term outcomes of education, I can do no better than cite the broad vision statement of education envisaged by the International Commission on Education (1996) popularly known as Delors Commission. This Commission highlights the following four goals of education: to impart learning to know, to do, to live together and to be. In this light, quality education is expected to instil the four capabilities as spelt out below:

1. to think logically, analytically, critically and laterally
2. to eke out an honourable living by learning occupational skills and work experience
3. to realize one's potential for self-development in terms of physical, intellectual, emotional, aesthetic and moral attainment through educational experience
4. to acquire discriminatory capability to appreciate and imbibe the emerging values of our times such as concern for ecology, equality, civility, harmony and cultural pluralism.

For a comprehensive assessment of quality of education, both the short and long-term outcomes need to be taken into consideration, besides, of course, those stipulated by the education institution itself.

The above noted three measures of quality education are both independent of one another and yet closely dependent on each other. It may be the case that we have one of them in place but not the other. For instance, we may have quality assurance factors in place and yet no quality outcomes. The three are, nevertheless, so closely interrelated that one weak link in the chain is enough to affect the end-product. Hence, the significance of taking care of each one of them singly as well as jointly. Taken together, they make a complete and credible criterion of quality education.

School Type Matters

Studies from several parts of the world, especially developing countries (Jimenez et al., 1988, 1991a, 1991b; Jimenez and Cox, 1990; Aslam, 2003; Newhouse and Beegle, 2005) show that private schools deliver better quality education than government schools. Several studies from India, including Kingdon (1996) and Young Lives cited by Singh (2013) have as well reported the same trend. Kingdon found private schools scoring over government schools on quality as well as in efficiency. Young Lives study as well reported better performance of private school students than those of government schools. Some other studies (Murthy, 1977; Sharma, 1979), have observed that private schools deliver better not only an cognitive outcomes but also on attitudinal change. Murthy found students of convent schools scoring significantly higher than those of government schools. Sharma discovered type of school to be a powerful predictor of student modernity, with students of missionary schools outperforming those of government schools.

Recently, this view has come under critical scrutiny. It has been contested by a number of studies on the basis of their deeper probe. A major study (Braun et al., 2006) conducted by the US Department of Education is particularly instructive in this regard. Based on a comparison of private and public schools, like other previous studies, it initially found private schools having an edge over public schools. But when the raw scores of students from the two types of schools were controlled for student characteristics like race, gender, parents' education, etc. the differences vanished. Similar results have been reported by some other comparative studies of school type and student modernity, including that of Duncan and Sandy (2007). Further, a couple of studies pertaining to India too have contested the common perception of superiority of private schools over public schools. For instance, Chudgar et al. found inconclusive evidence to accept that children in private schools perform better than those in public (government) schools. Instead, they found evidence to suggest that 'home background factors (income, education of parents to name a few) are quite crucial' (cited in Kurup, 2012). In much the same way, Rukmini Banerji, the head of ASER Centre, says, '... if you control for family background and parents education, the difference between private and government schools becomes smaller. A large part of child's performance at school depends on support at home' (ibid.).

Few will dispute the effects of family background and support on student performance. But that does not take away the contribution of school factors on it. In fact, school culture impacts student performance in a big way which is why school type matters. This is brought out in a revealing study titled 'Teaching Quality Matters: How Student Outcomes Relate to Quality of Teaching in Private and Public Schools in India' (cited in Singh, 2013). Based on a comparative study of the two types of schools (227 in all), it finds students of private schools performing better than those of government schools and attributes the same to better work put in by the teachers of the former. Eighty-two per cent of teachers in private schools were found to have regularly corrected almost every exercise given to children as against 40 per cent of teachers in public schools. This shows that what happens in school matters. It also explains the growing popularity of private schools even among the poor sections. The trend is not limited to urban areas. It is visible in rural areas too. According to a recent ASER estimate, as many as 40 million rural children are receiving education in private schools. Not much information is available about the quality of instructions in the rural private schools. It is likely to vary with the rank of the school depending on whether it is a low fee or a high fee charging school.

On the whole, high ranking private schools, including trust managed and missionary ones, have an edge over the government schools. That is understandable in view of the fact that the former generally outpace the latter on all the three measure of our quality criterion. They are known for better infrastructure and faculty, for greater rigour in teaching-learning processes, and for better outcomes. But most important of all, they are known for greater teacher involvement in improving and monitoring student performance.

By contrast, government schools are known to be severely deficient on all the three parameters. Take, for instance, quality assurance factors: many of them lack even such basic facilities as drinking water, a toilet, especially a girls' toilet or a blackboard. A survey (Basu, 2004) of 188 government schools revealed that 59 per cent of them lacked drinking water facilities and 89 per cent lacked toilets. Similarly, another survey (Singh, 2005) by National Institute of Educational Planning and Administration (NIEPA) showed that only 3.5 per cent schools in Bihar and Chhattisgarh and 12.16 per cent in Madhya Pradesh, Maharashtra, Andhra Pradesh, Gujarat, Rajasthan and Himachal Pradesh had girls' toilets. In the last few years, however, this situation seems to have changed for the better. According to the District Information System for Education (DSE) records, the percentage of schools with a toilet has increased from 42 per cent in 2003 to 72 per cent in 2012. Yet, the deficiencies persist with the result that the Supreme Court had to direct the government on October 3, 2012 to provide within six months 'toilet facilities for boys and girls, drinking water facilities, sufficient classrooms, appointment of teaching and non-teaching staff'. These directions are 'applicable to all the schools, whether state-opened or privately-owned, aided or unaided, minority or non-minority'. As for the shortage of teachers, it is massive: as many as 12.5 lakh positions of school teachers are lying vacant throughout the country, with large states like Uttar Pradesh, Bihar and West Bengal accounting for 50 per cent of them, as per the HRD Ministry's latest presentation before the Parliament's Consultative Committee (*Times News Network*, 2012). As for Punjab, as many as 7,000 out of 12,000 approved posts of teachers are lying vacant in the aided schools, according to a recent news report (*Dainik Jagran*, October 2, 2012). Add to it the rampant practice of teacher truancy. A study (Kremer et al., 2004) of a nationally representative sample of government primary schools found 25 per cent of teachers absent and only 50 per cent teaching during the unannounced visits. Similarly, a UNESCO study (2007) reported 25 per cent of government primary school teachers missing from classes and ranked India second, next only to Uganda, among the countries with high incidence of teacher absenteeism. In much the same way, public schools trail behind private schools on teaching-learning processes. The former relied on teaching by dictating notes and learning by cramming while the private schools encouraged interactive teaching and learning by observing, engaging and imagining. Consequently, government schools flounder on educational outcomes too. Little wonder that parents seek to opt for private schools over government schools. This is also reported by IDFC Foundation's India Infrastructure Report 2012 (cited in Dhawan, 2013). To be fair to government schools, not all of them deliver indifferent quality instructions. Some of them, especially Kendriya Vidyalayas, Navodaya Vidyalayas, Rajkiya Pratibha Vikas Vidyalayas and some select model schools enjoy credible repute for quality education. As with high ranking private schools so with reputed government schools, it is the performance of teacher factor that stands out as a decisive factor influencing quality education.

College Type: Insufficient Evidence

The situation is not quite the same at the level of higher education as at the school level. If any thing, it is the other way round. To begin with, there seems to exist no comparative study of the two types of institutions at the university/college level. We assiduously looked for one but could not find any. The National Assessment and Accreditation Council (NAAC), which has conducted quality assessment of hundreds of colleges and universities, both public and private, has also made no attempt in this direction. The NAAC would make a valuable contribution if it undertakes such a comparative analysis. It should involve no huge effort for the NAAC since it already has the necessary wealth of data available with it on this subject. The finding, nevertheless, would be highly valuable as it may yield at least some empirical clue on a subject on which there exists none.

In the absence of research-based evidence, what we have is mostly impressionistic judgement. The prevailing impression is that the quality of education delivered by the privately funded and managed higher education institutions is relatively poor compared to that of the government-run and aided colleges and public universities. This impression is validated by the widely held preference of students for government/aided institutions over the private ones. A major reason for it is the greater acceptability of the standards of public colleges and universities by the employers. Little wonder that students think of private institutions only when they fail to get admission in public institutions. There are only a few reputed private institutions which are able to command student preference over public institutions. That is so because a vast majority of private institutions are found lacking on quality standards. Many of them have shabby infrastructure, though some have pretty impressive outfits. In respect of faculty, they play tricks. For a few top positions they hire the services of reputed senior teachers, including ex-Vice Chancellors and heads, and pay them hefty sums. For the rest of the teaching positions they employ mediocres who in most cases are underpaid. One can well imagine the quality of teaching and learning, leave aside research, in such institutions. It is anything but inspiring. No wonder their graduates lack requisite competence and fail to find favour with the employers.

Worst of all, they allegedly indulge in corruption, shady deals and unethical pratices. Bhagat's (2011) observation tells it all: 'To ensure quality, government has put in place procedures like elaborate approval processes and regular inspections. However, these are abused and corruption is rife. Many private college owners have personally admitted to me that they had to pay bribes at every step of opening the college – from getting land and building approvals to approving the course plan and to set fee structures. Corruption in the private sector education is such a norm that nobody in the know even raises an eyebrow anymore.' To recover their money paid as bribes and to get returns on their investments they employ dubious methods despite the government's mandate of treatment education as a not-for-profit venture. What is more, a number of such institutions run courses without affiliation or recognition with the result that many students become unwitting victims of their designs.

For a proper understanding of the role of private sector in higher education, it is necessary to locate it in the context of education market in India and the government policy of allowing private sector in education as a no-profit zone. According to Gaurav Marya (2012), 'The dollar 80 billion Indian education market is the third largest education market globally, serving a market size of more than 500 million students.' Government's policy of education as a no profit service notwithstanding, the private sector has been quick to capture it as a lucrative business opportunity. Since there is an overflowing demand for technical and professional disciplines, including both conventional such as engineering, medicine, law, teacher education, etc. and emerging such as management, computer application, hospitality, media, architecture, pharmacy and dentistry, the private sector has patronized mainly these streams of higher education. While that is understandable, what has contaminated the participation of private sector in higher education is the significant presence of wily politicians, businessmen, real estate dealers, etc. among the owners of such institutions, besides the shady role of the regulatory agencies. The AICTE, for instance, has allegedly granted affiliation to so many substandard engineering colleges while it refused to recognize some of the leading management schools which are generally regarded as second only to IIMS or even on par with them. These include Indian School of Business (ISB) in Hyderabad, Indian Institute of Foreign Trade (IIFT) in Delhi and Institute of Management in Chennai. Some others are: The Indian Institute of Planning and Management, ICFAI, Amity Business School and IIM. The reason: AICTE's restrictive norms pertaining to infrastructure and curriculum. That explains the proliferation of corruption in private sector education as also why some credible corporates have abstained from the field of higher education. The net result is dilution of standards of technical and professional education.

While the above description of relative quality deficit of private education institutions fits a large majority of them, it will be unfair to generalize it for all. There are notable exceptions such as the institutions of Manipal Education Group, Narsee Monjee Institute of Management Studies, BITS Pilani, Symbiosis International University, Indian School of Business, Aptech, XLRI and NIIT, among others. They may not be at par with the public sector institutes like the IITs, IIMs, AIIMS but they are certainly known for their high standards.

These exceptions apart, overall private institutions of higher education carry a relatively lower status, vis-à-vis public institutions. This comes as a contrast to the school-level education where private institutions enjoy a relatively better image than public institutions. How to account for this image inconsistency of the private institutions at the two levels of education? A plausible explanation is that the private institutions at the school level have to compete with the well-established missionary, trust-managed and in many cases renowned private schools for which reason they have to care for standard quality. At the college level, on the other hand, they face no such competition, thanks to the great demand for technical and professional education which is what they capitalize on.

The relatively lower position of private institutions of higher education in India also represents a contrast to their counterparts in some other parts of the world. In countries like the US, UK, Japan, South Korea and Indonesia, private universities and colleges enjoy enviable distinction. In the US, for instance, a number of private universities such as Harvard, Berkeley and Stanford are private universities. Similarly, in the UK, Oxford and Cambridge, both world renowned universities, are private universities. Likewise, in South Korea, Japan and Indonesia, more of the private universities have made a grade to top class. We have no private university of international stature. It would be worthwhile to look into the reasons for this. One reason is that private universities in the US, UK and Japan have evolved over long time in competition with the state universities. In India, on the other hand, the private universities are still in a nascent stage and face no competition on account of easy availability of students. Another reason is that over there private universities are run and managed mostly by trusts, while here most of them are owned and managed by private players of doubtful credentials. A third reason is that there private universities view investment in quality education as an aid for their business interests, while here business interests take precedence over excellence. Our educational entrepreneurs will do well to set their priorities right and give excellence the pride of the place in raising their education institutions. That will also help their business interests. On its part, government needs to rethink its present policy of education as a not-for-profit zone for private sector and provide for a reasonable margin of profit on it so as to attract credible corporates to invest in the field of education. It should also provide an enabling regulatory framework in place of the present restrictive one.

Overall Quality Uninspiring

The relative quality deficit of private sector higher education institutions aside, a more critical problem is the decline in the quality of education in general. This is evident from all the available ratings. Blackwell (2004), for one, observes that India has failed to produce world-class universities both in the public and the private sector. Similarly, in the three latest world university rankings, i.e. Times Higher Education World University Rankings, Academic Ranking of World Universities and QS University Rankings, all released in 2012, none of our universities figures among the top-class universities. Even at home, Prime Minister Manmohan Singh, an educationist himself, has expressed lament at the substandard quality of our higher education. Delivering his address at the 150th Anniversary Function of the University of Mumbai (2007), he said, 'Our university system is, in many parts, in a state of despair ... in almost half the districts in the country, higher education enrolments are abysmally low, almost two-third of our universities and 90 per cent of our colleges are rated as below average on quality parameters.' This poor report card given by the Prime Minister is as valid for the present education scenario as for 2007. This is further confirmed by the NAAC Report (2012) which rates the quality of 68 per cent of our universities and 90 per cent of our colleges as either average or below average.

It is the same story at the school level too, despite the relative quality edge of the private schools over the government schools. The three successive reports released in 2012, namely, the Quality Education Survey

(QES), OECD's Programme for International Students Assessment (PISA) and Pratham's Annual Status of Education Report (ASER) provide ample evidence of it. While the first report found schools in metropolitan cities lacking on quality parameters, the second ranked higher secondary students from two of our educationally better performing states – Himachal Pradesh and Tamil Nadu – close to the bottom (second last) among 74 countries and the third found the students of the rural schools faltering on reading and mathematical abilities. Such is the rank shame suffered by India that she chose to back out of PISA survey for 2014.

Thus, overall quality scenario of education in the country is rather grim. It serves little purpose to blame it on the methodological flaws of the ranking systems, a stand taken by some scholars, including Gudavarthy and Mannathukkaren (2012). Whether or not we like it, the rankings mirror our ground reality. Given the acute shortage of faculty (with one-third or more of the sanctioned positions lying vacant at all levels); under-performance by teachers (with heavy reliance on notes dictation or boring monologue based on ill-digested ideas), shabby and bogus research (with little evidence of new discovery), it is hardly surprising that none of our institutions has featured among the top-class of the world.

The real question, therefore, is why things are the way they are. The reasons for it seem to lie in the domains of politicization and commercialization of education, populist policies, bureaucratic framework, declining intellectual integrity of academics and lackadaisical attitude of educational authorities. The political control over education operates in several ways such as the appointment of Vice Chancellors, the financial hold and influence pedaling in faculty and staff recruitments, among other things. All this severely undermines academic autonomy. Further, privatization of education has injected an element of commercialization which has resulted in dilution of standards. Similarly, university bureaucracy often tends to resist new ideas and experiments because of its 'rigid organizational structure and territorial mindset' (National Knowledge Commission, 2008). Then, there are populist policies and schemes such as reservations, merit promotions and rotation of headship down to the level of lecturer which take their toll over quality. No less important is the lack of intellectual integrity and commitment of academic professionals which is evident from their ritualistic approach to curriculum development, neglect of classes, under-utilized laboratories, dubious research and unenviable publications. Finally, we have compelling evidence of lackadaisical attitude of educational authorities towards quality which can be seen in their indifference to the huge backlog of unfilled faculty positions, as well as insufficient attention to quality research.

Needed Special Drive

The good thing to note is that those at the helms of affairs, including the President, the Prime Minister and the HRD Minister, have expressed their serious concern about the unacceptable quality of our education. However, it has made no positive difference to the situation except that some more central universities and IITs have been opened. Mere increasing the number of such institutions is not likely to help the cause of quality much. What we need are some radical measures. It is time to review the existing system of affiliating universities, separation of undergraduate and postgraduate programmes, liberal and professional streams, and teaching and research institutes. Similarly, the idea of placing too much reliance on elite specialized institutes merits a second thought. Instead, there is a need to promote the system of comprehensive universities with both undergraduate and postgraduate programmes, both liberal and professional streams, and both teaching and research, as suggested by some educationists (Pental, 2012).

Besides these academic reforms, there is also an urgent need for a policy rethink in respect of populist schemes. Better alternatives may be found to promote the cause of equity and democratization. It is equally important to initiate steps to depoliticize education, break free academic and research projects from bureaucratic control and evolve reasonable norms for private sector participation in education.

Nothing is as urgent as the need to focus on faculty recruitment and development. It gains an added significance in the light of our fundamental observation that quality of teaching and research holds the key to quality education. In view of this, there is an urgent need to fill all the vacant faculty positions. To ensure quality recruitment, it is also necessary to review and revise procedures of faculty recruitment from the prevailing quantitative to qualitative criteria. For promoting the goal of faculty development, it may be rewarding to send 10–15 per cent teachers every year to some of the best universities of the world. Such international exposure to quality institution will be a highly valuable input for teachers' personal and professional growth. Some other measures that may help the cause of faculty improvement are: to form quality circles of 10 to 20 promising teachers in every institution to interact among themselves as well as with motivated students and research scholars, to incentivise excellence by offering best teacher/best researcher awards in every institution and, above all, to adopt the best practices of the leading universities and institutes of the world.

For doing all this, there is a need to significantly enhance budget provision for education. Central government has already committed 6 per cent of GDP to education which is commendable but not adequate. There is a need for more. What is even more important is the actual spend. The combined spending on education by central and state governments was combined at 3.8 per cent of GDP in 2012 which notably is no higher than the level already reached in 1991–92. Ways and means, therefore, have also to be devised to ensure timely release and proper utilization of the budgeted allocation. If the above measures are put in place that will hopefully enhance the quality of our education in a significant way and make it globally competitive.

References

Aslam, M. 2003. 'The Determinants of Student Achievement in Government and Private Schools in Pakistan'. *The Pakistan Development Review*, Vol. 42, No. 4, pp. 841–76.

Basu, Kaushik. 2004. 'Combating India's Truant Teachers'. Retrieved from: http://news.bbc.co.uk.

Bhagat, Chetan. 2011. 'The Business of Teaching'. *The Times of India*, New Delhi, October 8.

Blackwell, Fritz. 2004. *India: A Global Studies Handbook*. United States of America: ABC-CLIO, Inc.

Dhawan, Himanshu. 2013. 'Government Schools Lag Behind Private Institutions'. *The Times of India*, New Delhi, February 7.

Duncan, K. and J. Sandy. 2007. 'Explaining the Performance Gap between Public and Private School Students'. *Eastern Economic Journal*, Vol. 33, No. 2, pp. 177–91.

E&Y. 2011. 'Private Sector Participation in Indian Higher Education'. FICCI Higher Education Summit.

Gudavarthy, Ajay and Nissim Mannathukkaren. 2012. 'Comparing Harvard Apples with JNU Oranges'. *The Hindu*, December 27, New Delhi.

International Commission on Education. 1996. *Learning: The Treasure Within*. Report to UNESCO of the International Commission on Education for the Twenty-first Century, Chairman: Jacques Delors, UNESCO.

Jhingan, Amitabh. 2011. 'Foreword: Private Sector Participation in Higher Education'. FICCI Higher Education Summit.

Jimenez, E., M. Lockheed and N. Wattanawaha. 1988. 'The Relative Efficiency of Public and Private Schools: The Case of Thailand'. *World Bank Economic Review*, Vol. 2, pp. 139–64.

Jimenez, E. and D. Cox. 1990. 'The Relative Effectiveness of Private and Public Schools: Evidence from Two Developing Countries'. *Journal of Development Economics*, Vol. 34, pp. 99–121.

Jimenez, E., M. Lockheed, E. Luna and V. Paqueo. 1991a. 'School Effects and Costs for Private and Public Schools in the Dominican Republic'. *International Journal of Educational Research*, Vol. 15, pp. 393–410.

Jimenez, E., M. Lockheed and V. Paqueo. 1991b. 'The Relative Efficiency of Private and Public Schools in Developing Countries'. *World Bank Research Observer*, Vol. 6, pp. 205–18.

Kingdon, Geetika Gandhi. 1996. 'Quality and Efficiency of Private and Government Schools: A Case Study of Urban Uttar Pradesh'. *Oxford Bulletin of Economics and Statistics*, Vol. 58, No. 1, pp. 57–81.

Kremer, M., K. Muralidharan, N. Chaudhury, J. Hammer, and F. Halsey Rogers. 2004. 'Teacher Absence in India: A Snapshot'. *Journal of the European Economic Association*, Vol. 3, Nos 2–3, pp. 658–67.

Kurup, Saira. 2012. 'Lessons in Learning'. *The Times of India*, New Delhi, November 25.

Marya, Gaurav. 2012. 'Enterprising Business of Education'. *The Times of India*, New Delhi, April 11.

Mathur, Meha. 2013. 'Quality of Higher Education Warrisome: Jamia V.C.'. *Millennium Post*, New Delhi, February 18.

Murthy, Radha Srinivas. 1977. 'Student Modernity: A Comparative Study of Convent and Government School Students'. M.Phil. Dissertation (Unpublished), Panjab University, Chandigarh.

National Knowledge Commission. 2008. *Second Annual Report*. Chairman: Sam Pitroda, Government of India, New Delhi.

Newhouse, D. and K. Beegle. 2005. 'The Effect of School Type on Student Achievement'. *The Journal of Human Resources*, Vol. 41, No. 3, pp. 529–52.

Pental, Deepak. 2012. 'A Rank Shame'. *The Times of India*, New Delhi, February 20.

Sharma, S.L. 1979. *Modernizing Effects of University Education*. New Delhi: Allied Publishers.

——. 2004. 'Rethinking Quality Parameters in Higher Education'. *University News*, Vol. 42, No. 3, January 19–25, pp. 1–5.

Singh, Renu. 2013. 'Equity Concerns in Enrolment'. *Education Times: The Times of India*, New Delhi, May 13.

Singh, Shivani. 2005. 'Education Cess: Are Government Schools Any Better Now?'. *The Times of India*, New Delhi, April 7.

Times News Network. 2012. 'Education System Faces Massive Faculty Crunch'. *The Times of India*, New Delhi, July 4.

UNESCO. 2007. 'Corrupt Schools, Corrupt Universities: What can be Done?'. Cited in *Times of Chandigarh*, June 25.

Varma, Subodh. 2012. 'The Slide: Dreams Die First'. *The Times of India*, New Delhi, October 18.

2

Privatization and Globalization of Higher Education in India

B.S. GHUMAN

Knowledge has emerged as a leading source of economic growth. The economies having good quality human resources and well-developed network of knowledge-driven institutions are thriving across the globe. India has all the potential to thrive on the basis of knowledge, the need is to steer the economy in a proper direction. In India, the First Five Year Plan postulated agriculture sector as an engine of growth. From the Second Five Year Plan onwards, industry emerged as a leading source of growth. In the Eleventh Five Year Plan (2007–12), a paradigm shift took place in which for the first time social sector, particularly education, has been acknowledged as a principal driver of growth.

According to Hon'ble Prime Minister, the Eleventh Five Year Plan is an 'Educational Plan'. The Eleventh Five Year Plan states, 'The role of education in facilitating social and economic progress is well recognized …. Improvements in education are not only expected to enhance efficiency but also augment the overall quality of life. The Eleventh Five Year Plan places the highest priority on education as a central instrument for achieving rapid and inclusive growth' (Planning Commission, 2007: 1). Further, within education, higher education for the first time is given prominent place.

The objective of this paper is to examine privatization and globalization of higher education in India. The paper is organized into five sections. Section I deals with the conceptual framework. Section II discusses the existing situation of higher education in India. Privatization and globalization of it is analysed in section III, while rationale for regulation is described in section IV. Section V contains the concluding observations.

I
Conceptual Framework

Conceptually and technically speaking, privatization means change of ownership of an enterprise from public (government) to private hands. Privatization, however, is in practice far wider than ownership dimensions and also includes introduction of market-based practice in the operations of even public sector organizations. Privatization, thus, covers the following possibilities:

(i) Transfer of ownership (i.e. de-nationalization);

(ii) Decontrolling/deregulation/de-licensing (i.e. reducing government regulation over private provision of goods and services);

(iii) De-reservation (i.e. opening the economic activities to the private sector which were hitherto reserved for the public sector), for example, permitting private sector to set up Universities and Deemed Universities and

(iv) Promotion of private sector like business culture/the discipline of market forces within public sector. For example in case of higher education, introduction of self-financing courses, steep hike in tuition fee, contractual appointments, etc. in publicly funded educational institutions amounts to privatization.

Privatization programme was initiated in the late seventies and early eighties, particularly in the United Kingdom. The initial results of the UK experience of privatization were so impressive that within a short span of time privatization has become a universal policy paradigm. Privatization has encompassed both economic and social sectors like education and health. However, different issues are involved in the privatization of economic and social sectors.

Education: Public or Merit Good?

Goods/services can be classified into three categories, namely, (a) Public Goods; (b) Private Goods and (c) Mixed/Merit Goods.

(a) Public Good

Public good is a good which fulfills the following principles:

(i) Principle of Non-Excludability

(ii) Principle of Non-Rivalness in Consumption

Under the principle of non-excludability, the producer is not in a position to exclude those consumers of goods who are not paying for it, i.e. free riders. The principle of non-rivalness in consumption implies that if more and more consumers start consuming the product, the consumption of the earlier consumers is not adversely affected. Defense, street light, light houses are classical example of public good.

(b) Private Good

The concept of private good is opposed to public good and is defined in economics as a good that exhibits the properties such as:

(i) *Excludable* – Under this, it is reasonably possible to exclude those consumers from consumption who are not paying for it.

(ii) *Rivalrous* – According to this, consumption of the earlier consumers is adversely affected if more and more consumers start consuming the product. Food, clothing, automobiles, refrigerators are amongst many private goods.

(c) Merit Good

Merit good is a good, which is important from the societal point of view. An individual, however, underestimates its significance and, hence, has a tendency to under-consume it. Merit good also has positive externalities. Health and education are the typical examples of merit good. From societal perspective, thus, the provision of merit good/services cannot be left to market forces alone. Effective regulatory regime is essential for ensuring universal coverage of merit good. In the light of classification of goods described above, it can be inferred that education is a merit good and, hence, either this good should be provided by the government or private sector effectively regulated by the government.

In the backdrop of this conceptual framework, the present paper is an endeavour to analyse issues, challenges, merit and demerits of privatization of higher education in India.

II
Existing Situation

The existing situation of education, particularly higher education, is not very impressive. Access to higher education is very low in India. According to an estimate, only 18 per cent of students reach institutions of higher learning in India against the world average of 27 per cent (Table 1). In Republic of Korea, Gross Enrolment Ratio (GER) in higher education is 103 per cent whereas in the US, it is around 95 per cent. In the case of Russia, Sweden, Argentine and Canada, GER in higher education is respectively, 76 per cent, 74 per cent, 75 per cent, and 62 per cent.

Table 1

Gross Enrolment Ratio (GER) in Higher Education in Select Countries

S. No.	*Country*	*Gross Enrolment Ratio (GER)*
1.	Republic of Korea	103
2.	USA	95
3.	Russia	76*
4.	Sweden	74
5.	Argentine	75
6.	Canada	62
7.	Brazil	34
8.	China	26
9.	India	18
10.	World Weighted Average	27

* Relates to year 2009.

Source: World Bank, 2010; UNESCO Institute of Statistics, 2010 and Ministry of Human Resource Development, 2013.

The low GER in India further varies across gender, location and socio-religious groups. For example, overall GER in urban areas is 30 per cent whereas in rural areas it is only 11.1 per cent. Further, in the rural areas GER in case of male is higher than that of female. Interestingly, in the urban areas, GER in case of female has an edge over their male counterpart (Table 2). Sharp variation exists across religious groups with Christian general having the highest GER (44.9%) followed by Hindu General (32.9%). Muslims have the lowest GER (9.6%). In case of social groups, OBC has the highest GER (14.8%) whereas Schedule Tribes have the lowest GER (7.7%).

Table 2

GER at Higher Education Level across Location, Gender and Socio-Religious Groups

(Figures are in percentages)

Location and Gender						*Socio-Religious Group*					
Rural			*Urban*			*Major Religious Groups*			*Social Groups*		
Male	Female	Total	Male	Female	Total	Christian General	Hindu General	Muslim	OBC	SC	ST
13.7	8.3	11.1	29.6	30.5	30	44.9	32.9	9.6	14.8	11.6	7.7

Source: Planning Commission, 2012.

III
Privatization and Globalization of Higher Education in India

As stated earlier, in the Eleventh Five Year Plan, India has identified education as a new engine of growth. For making this policy operational, Government of India has prepared an action plan. Under this plan, India aims to increase the GER to 23 per cent by the end of Twelfth Five Year Plan (2012–2017). In quantitative terms, the aim is to increase enrolment in tertiary education from 13 million at present to 40 million by 2020. At present, there are about 634 universities and 33,023 colleges. For achieving a three-fold increase in the enrolment, the government has set a target of opening 1,000 universities and 45,000 additional colleges by 2020.

For making India a hub of higher education institutions, huge amount of capital is required, which is beyond the capacity of government sector. The inability of government to invest heavily in education sector necessitates inviting private capital both domestic and international. Government has already opened higher education to domestic private sector in a big way. Private sector has made its presence felt over a span of short period in the field of higher education. Table 3 shows that out of 33,682 institutions in higher education, 20,121 are privately owned or managed, which constitutes 62.41 per cent of the total.

Table 3

Status of Educational Institutions by Ownership

Type of Institutions	*Ownership*	*Financing*	*Number of Institutions*
Central Government Institutions	Public	Public	152
State Government Institutions	Public	Public	316
Private Institutions	Private	Private	191
Sub Total			659
Central Government Colleges	Public	Public	69
State Government Colleges	Public	Public	13,024
Private Colleges	Private	Private	19,930
Sub Total			33,023
Total			**33,682**

Source: Planning Commission, 2012.

The breakup of student enrolment on the basis of ownership of the institutions also suggests the pre-dominance of private owned institutions of higher learning. For example, out of 218 lakh students, 58.9 per cent are enroled in private institutions. In government institutions only 41 per cent students are enroled. Within government institutions the major chunk of students (38.5%) are enroled in state government institutions and only

2.6 per cent students are with central government institutions. The growth profile reveals that private institutions are growing at a faster rate whereas central government institutions have registered marginal growth. As per enrolment, state government institutions show a declining trend (Table 4).

Table 4

Growth of Enrolment in the Eleventh Plan

(Figures are in Lakhs)

Ownership	*Year*		*Change Percentage Points*	*Growth Trends*
	2006–07	*2011–12*		
Central Government	**3.06** (2.2)	**5.67** (2.6)	+ 0.4	Growing
State Government	**60.60** (43.6)	**83.93** (38.5)	–5.1	Declining
Private	**75.34** (54.2)	**128.40** (58.9)	+4.7	Growing

Note: Figures in parentheses are percentages.

Source: Planning Commission, 2012.

Table 5

Top 10 Private Engineering Institutes and Private MBA Colleges/B-schools in India

S.No.	*Top 10 Private Engineering Institutes in India*	*Top 10 Private MBA Colleges/B-schools*
1.	BITS (Pilani)	XLRI (Jamshedpur)
2.	IIIT (Hyderabad)	S.P. Jain Institute (Mumbai)
3.	BIT Mesra (Ranchi)	IMT (Ghaziabad)
4.	PSG College of Technology (Coimbatore)	XIM (Bhubaneshwar)
5.	Manipal Institute of Technology (Manipal)	NMIMS (Mumbai)
6.	Thapar Inst. of Engineering & Technology (Patiala)	IMI (New Delhi)
7.	VJTI (Mumbai)	SCMHRD (Pune)
8.	RV College of Engineering (Bangalore)	KJ Somaiya Institute of Management (Mumbai)
9.	IT, Nirma University (Ahmedabad)	TAPMI (Manipal)
10.	PESIT (Bangalore)	Goa Institute of Management (Goa)

Source: Outlook, Private Engineering Institutes Survey, 2012 and *Outlook*, MBA Colleges/B. School Survey, 2012.

Private institutions have thrived mainly in the field of sunrise disciplines like engineering and technology, and management (Table 5). According to Grewal (2012), '... the private sector accounts for 91 per cent of seats in engineering, 64 per cent in management studies, 95 per cent in pharmaceutical studies, 92 per cent in physiotherapy, 50 per cent in medicine and 94 per cent in hotel management'.

Recent educational reforms initiated in the wake of the New Economic Policy of 1991 has given a further fillip to privatization specially globalization of higher education. In India, there are around 150 foreign educational institutions having 12,000 students. These institutions have collaboration with Indian institutions. For facilitating the entry of foreign universities in Indian education sector, the Foreign Educational Institutions (Regulation of Entry and Operation) Bill, 2010, is likely to be taken up soon in the Parliament. The purpose of this Bill is to regulate the entry and operation of all the foreign educational institutions for maintaining the standards of higher education within India as well as to protect the interests of students and public.

Salient Features of the Bill

(i) The foreign educational institution should have twenty years' standing under a law of the country in which such institution is established;

(ii) The foreign educational institution should be accredited by the accrediting agency of the country concerned;

(iii) The foreign educational institution has to meet the quality parameters of education laid down under the Indian Law from time to time being in force;

(iv) A foreign institution shall ensure that the standards of courses/programmes are in conformity with the standards maintained by the institution on its campus back home;

(v) The foreign institution will not be allowed to offer education through distance mode;

(vi) Foreign institution can offer educational programmes independently or in collaboration or partnership or in a twinning arrangement with an Indian institution;

(vii) An undertaking for maintaining a corpus not less than ₹ 50 crores or such sum as may be notified from time to time by the government;

(viii) Out of income received from the corpus fund, the foreign institution should not utilize more than 75 per cent for the purpose of development of its institutions in India and remaining un-utilized income should go to corpus fund; and

(ix) No part of the profit earned by such foreign education provider shall be invested for any purpose other than the growth and development of the educational institution established by it in India.

Strengths and Weaknesses of Privatization

Privatization and globalization of higher education has both strengths and weaknesses.

The Strengths

The strengths of privatization of higher education include (i) availability of capital; (ii) more choices in sunrise disciplines; (iii) infrastructure; (iv) quick decision-making process.

(i) Availability of Capital

As observed earlier, access to higher education in India is only 18 per cent, which is less than the world average (27%). By the end of Twelfth Five Year Plan, India aims to attain the objective of 23 per cent. For achieving this ambitious goal huge amount of capital ($150 billion) is required, which is beyond the capacity of government sector. India is at present spending only around 4 per cent of its GDP on education, which is lower than the 6 per cent target suggested by Kothari Commission way back in 1966 (Government of India, 1966). Further, within education sector, the spending on higher and technical education amounts to only 11 per cent of the total. Thus, for achieving the two-fold increase in the access to higher education, India needs the participation of private sector both in terms of financial and human resources. Private sector has come up in a big way in the form of its investment in higher education. Private sector constitutes around 50 per cent of the total investment in *education* sector which is likely to increase further in future.

(ii) More Choices in Sunrise Disciplines

Most of the newly set up private colleges, deemed and private universities have been offering courses in the sunrise areas like engineering, medicine, computer science, management, bio-technology, pharmaceutical sciences, law, etc. According to the Planning Commission, courses like engineering, law management, medicine, nursing and pharmacy have witnessed more growth vis-à-vis traditional disciplines like arts, social science and basic sciences (Planning Commission, 2012: 94). Thus, privatization of higher education provides more choices to the students in the emerging areas.

(iii) Infrastructure

A number of private institutions have created state-of-the art infrastructure and other facilities, which is generally regarded as one of the criteria for ranking top private institutions in the field of engineering (Table 6). Prominent among these engineering and technology institutes are BITS (Pilani), BIT Mesra (Ranchi), Thapar Institute of Engineering & Technology (Patiala) and PSG College of Technology (Coimbatore).

Similarly, management institutes like XLRI (Jamshedpur), S.P. Jain Institute (Mumbai) and IMT (Ghaziabad) have good quality infrastructure. Among health education institutes, Christian Medical College, Vellore, Dayanand Medical College & Hospital (DMCH), Ludhiana, ACPM Medical College, Dhule, and Manipal University are some of the private sector institutes which are known for their well developed infrastructure practices.

Table 6

Top 10 Private Engineering Colleges in Terms of Infrastructure

S. No.	*Colleges*
1.	BITS (Pilani)
2.	BIT Mesra (Ranchi)
3.	Thapar Inst. of Engineering & Technology (Patiala)
4.	PSG College of Technology (Coimbatore)
5.	IIIT (Hyderabad)
6.	Mepco Schlenk Engineering College (Sivakasi)
7.	Manipal Institute of Technology (Manipal)
8.	SSN College of Engineering (Chennai)
9.	Chaitanya Bharathi Institute of Technology (Hyderabad)
10.	PES College of Engineering (Mandya)

Source: Outlook, Engineering Institutes Survey, 2012.

(iv) Quick Decision Making Process

The state-funded colleges and universities are very slow in decision making relating to introduction of new courses, revising the existing curriculum, creating new infrastructure, hiring top class faculty, and signing MoUs for collaborating with other institutions. These institutes have many layers of decision-making bodies and follow very cumbersome and time consuming process. In a number of cases, by the time final approval is granted, the utility of the decision is no longer valid in the light of changed circumstances. By contrast, the management in the private educational institutions enjoys more autonomy to take quick decisions relating to the above-mentioned areas.

The Weaknesses

Weaknesses of privatization of higher education are (i) high fee structure, inequalities and exclusion, (ii) low quality of education, (iii) marginalization of social sciences and humanities, (iv) malpractices including corruption in granting affiliation to private institutions, (v) fragile service conditions.

(i) High Fee Structure, Inequalities and Exclusion

High fee structure, including capitation fee and auction-like situation in the case of management quota seats, is a normal trend in the case of majority of the private educational institutions. On an average, the ratio of fee structure between private and publically-funded university works out to be around 10:1. The high fee structure of the private institutions has accentuated the existing inequalities in higher education across caste, location, gender, class, religious group and region. Prior to privatization education was all inclusive. The high fee structure has made higher education inaccessible to poor strata of society in the private sector. In this way privatization in higher education has been excluding most of disadvantaged economic and social groups. This outcome of privatized higher education is contrary to most cherished objective of planning, namely making education all inclusive. Further, most of the private institutions of higher learning have been set up in Southern and Western States like Karnataka, Tamil Nadu, and Andhra Pradesh, Maharashtra and Gujarat and, thus, created regional imbalances in the access to higher education.

(ii) Low Quality of Education

Most of the private corporate houses have entered into the field of education to make money with little concern for the quality of education. According to Hon'ble HRD Minister, private technical institutions are sub-standard. MHRD received 130 proposals under second component of the Technical Education Improvement Programme of the World Bank. None of the institutions fulfilled the criteria laid down by the World Bank (*The Tribune*, 2011). No doubt there are quality norms laid down by the institution granting approval and affiliation to the newly set up institutions. The adherence to quality norms is evaluated from time to time by the National Assessment and Accreditation Council (NAAC), National Board of Accreditation (NBA), etc. In spite of these accreditating agencies, the cases of manipulating the norms in favour of private institutions are widely reported. For example, out of 125 deemed universities, only 38 are adhering to the norms, whereas, 43 deemed universities are defaulters for non-compliance of the norms. Remaining 44 are halfway in this regard (Government of India, 2009b). Accordingly, a senior official of the UGC observes: 'These institutions (i.e. private) make huge profits. This raises questions of affordability and equity. They do not even reserve seats for the marginalized groups with severe implications of equity. These institutions do not hesitate to admit students with poor academic credentials. They also attempt to be financially efficient by reducing costs on vital components which adversely affects the quality' (Prakash, 2007).

(iii) Marginalization of Social Sciences and Humanities

Privatization and globalization of higher education have been indifferent to social sciences. They have given boost to sunrise disciplines like engineering, information technology, management, pharmaceutical sciences, law, etc. and neglected social sciences. Consequently social sciences have suffered on account of (a) funds, (b) number of students as well as their quality (in a couple of cases seats of social science stream remain vacant as most of the students are opting for professional courses) and (c) introduction of new courses in social sciences. Marginalization of social sciences is mainly attributed to the application of business culture based approaches. For example, social science courses are evaluated by applying techniques like cost-benefit analysis which have been devised to evaluate corporate sector projects. Social sciences' mission and core concern is to cater to the societal needs and by no stretch of imagination social sciences can qualify the test of market forces, i.e. of earning profit. Leave aside earning profit, social sciences cannot even reach the stage of break-even point (i.e. cost and revenue being equal) of financial analysis. For the marginalization of social sciences and humanities, the society would pay a very high opportunity cost. The upsurge of many chronic ills in the society, like increase crime rate, specially against women, corruption, declining sex ratio, honour killing, drug addiction, intolerance, etc. clearly indicate the absence of developing and nurturing of social sensibilities in our educational institutions.

(iv) Malpractices Including Corruption in Granting Affiliation to Private Institutions

There are a number of bodies which approve and grant affiliation to institutions of higher learning. These include University Grants Commission (UGC), All-India Council for Technical Education (AICTE), Bar Council of India (BCI), Medical Council of India (MCI), Dental Council of India (DCI), and universities. Cases of malpractices, including corruption, have been reported while granting approval to the institutions of higher learning. As a result, the Government of India has been reviewing the 'Deemed University Status' awarded to over 125 institutions (Government of India, 2009b). All other pending requests for the 'deemed university status' have also been kept in abeyance. Many of the private educational institutions have been accused of (a) misleading students by opening off-campuses, off-shore campuses, new departments and study centres without approval of competent authority; (b) charging steep fee; and (c) poor academic and infrastructure standards. Both the National Knowledge Commission (NKC) and the Prof. Yashpal-led Higher Education Committee have taken cognizance of these allegations and have also strongly recommended the scrapping of the concept of deemed universities. Recently, the Central

Bureau of Investigation (CBI) has conducted raids across the country on the premises of some of the officials of All India Council for Technical Education (AICTE) and Medical Council of India (MCI) on the charges such as corruption and unethical conduct of business, while granting approval to professional colleges not meeting the necessary norms for affiliation and, subsequently, arrested several senior officials.

(v) Fragile Service Conditions

Barring top class educational institutions in the private sector, the other institutions are not following transparent and objective procedure to recruit faculty and pay according to the UGC grades. Thus, the faculty recruited is sometimes under-qualified and work on ad hoc basis for years together with the result that the students suffer in the long run. The service conditions are also not friendly to the employees of private institutions. In most of the cases, employees are under paid and work on contractual basis having no other social and economic benefits during and after service.

IV
Rationale for Independent Regulatory Mechanism

In view of the above problems, the Government of India has proposed to set up an Independent Regulatory Authority for Higher Education (IRAHE) to regulate educational institutions in the field of higher education. The proposed authority would protect the interest of students in matters of price/tuition fee, access to education, quality of education, etc. The National Knowledge Commission, in its 'Report to the Nation 2006–2009', while recommending setting up an Independent Regulatory Authority for Higher Education (IRAHE), has specified the following reasons: First, the IRAHE would minimize conflicts of interests as it would stay at an arm's length from stakeholders. Second, it would replace the present system, which is over-regulated but under-governed, through more appropriate forms of intervention. Third, it would rationalize the existing system where mandates are both confusing and overlapping. Fourth, it would dispense with the multiplicity of regulatory agencies, like UGC, AICTE, MCI, BCI, etc. by providing a single window clearance.

Functions of IRAHE

(i) The IRAHE would have to be established by an Act of Parliament, and would be responsible for setting the criteria and deciding on entry.
(ii) It would be the only agency that would be authorized to accord degree-granting power to higher education institutions.
(iii) It would be responsible for monitoring standards and settling disputes.

(iv) It would apply exactly the same norms to public and private institutions, just as it would apply the same norms to domestic and international institutions.

(v) It would be the authority for licensing accreditation agencies.

(vi) The role of the University Grants Commission (UGC) would be re-defined to focus on the disbursement of grants to, and maintenance of, public institutions in higher education. The entry regulatory functions of the All India Council for Technical Education (AICTE), the Medical Council of India (MCI) and the BCI would be performed by the IRAHE, so that their role would be limited to that of professional associations' (Government of India, 2009a).

The Government of India has re-named the IRAHE as the National Commission of Higher Education and Research (NCHER) in its proposed bill titled The Higher Education and Research Bill, 2011, which is pending in the Rajya Sabha.

V
Concluding Observations

Governments, both at centre and in states, face financial hardships and, hence, find it beyond their capacities to finance the expansion in higher education. The share of private capital (both domestic and international) in higher education has increased in India and it would increase further in backdrop of commercialization, privatization and globalization policies of government. The increasing role of private sector in higher education, however, is prone to serious problems. Private sector is driven by profit maximization dictum and has resulted into educational inequalities across economic strata, caste, location (urban-rural), religion and regions. Private sector invests only in sunrise disciplines which has good potential for profit and neglects basic sciences, social sciences and humanities. The marginalization of these foundational and socially relevant courses may prove costly for the nation. For making education as a powerful vehicle for growth, social, economic and regional equity, it is necessary to put in place a very effective regulatory machinery. The regulatory authority should be outside the purview of government. The regulatory commission should be a broad-based constitutional body having explicit role of state governments along with central government, educationists and civil society in its constitution.

References

Government of India. 1966. *Education and National Development: Report of the Education Commission 1964–66*. Ministry of Education, New Delhi.

——. 2009a. *Report to the Nation 2006–2009*. National Knowledge Commission, New Delhi, March.

——. 2009b. *Report of the Committee for Review of Existing Institutions Deemed to be Universities*. Department of Higher Education, Ministry of Human Resource Development, New Delhi, October 19.

——. 2009. *Report of the Committee to Advise on Renovation and Rejuvenation of Higher Education*. Department of Higher Education, Ministry of Human Resource Development, New Delhi, March 1.

Grewal, R.S. 2012. 'A Re-look at Private Institutions'. *The Tribune*, Tuesday, January 10.

Ministry of Human Resource Development. 2013. Rashtriya Ucchatar Shiksha Abhiyan. National Higher Education Mission, New Delhi.

Planning Commission. 2007. *Eleventh Five Year Plan 2007–12, Volume 2: Social Sectors*. New Delhi.

——. 2012. *Twelfth Five Year Plan 2012–17, Volume 3: Social Sectors*. New Delhi.

Prakash, Ved. 2007. 'Trends in Growth and Financing of Higher Education in India'. *Economic and Political Weekly*, Vol. 42, No. 31.

The Tribune. 2011. 'Private Technical Institutes Substandard'. Thursday, March 10.

Thorat, Sukhadeo. 2006. *Higher Education in India: Emerging Issues Related to Access, Inclusiveness and Quality*. Nehru Memorial Lecture, University of Mumbai, Mumbai.

World Bank. 2010. Retrieved from: http://data.worldbank.org/indicator/SE.TER.ENRR, last accessed online on 23 April 2013.

UNESCO Institute of Statistics. 2010. Retrieved from: http://stats.uis.unesco.org/unesco/TableViewer/document.aspx?ReportId=198, last accessed online on 23 April 2013.

3

Private Enterprise in Higher Education

Then and Now

S.S. MATHUR

The tradition of higher education is quite old in our country. So is the role of private enterprise in it. This is evident from the following observation of Rama Devi.

> The concept of higher education is not at all new to India, and neither is the sparkling attribution of private initiative in it. A rich tradition of higher learning in private or voluntary sector had already developed in ancient India. Leave vocational education through caste guilds apart, formal education was focussed mainly on imparting knowledge of various concepts of religious discourse to upper castes through the *guru-shisya* tradition. The Rig Vedic educational institutions consisted of small domestic schools run by teachers who admitted resident pupils in their *gurukuls*, which of course were private. The life of the student was regulated on the principle that he was to serve his teacher as a son, supplicant or a slave. His duties included such activities as collecting sacred fuel, grass, cow dung, earth and flower for sacrifice, and also to fetch water, gather fuel for cooking and begging alms.[1]

Higher education was given a concrete shape with the spread of Buddhism in this country. The Buddhist education was provided in the monasteries and the monks were the teachers. They established a number of university centres where the students were admitted on merit. In the jatakas there is a mention that students were admitted by their teacher on the payment in advance of their entire tuition fees. However, poor students were allowed to pay in the form of services to their teachers.

Sometimes the community also helped needy students to pay their fees. The fees paid by students was not the individual earning of any teacher but went to Vihar.[2]

Taxila, Nalanda, Vallabhi and Vikramshila were famous seats of higher learning in north India and attracted scholars from all parts of the world. These seats of learning were getting financial support from kings and rich persons in the society. But there was no interference in their administration by them. They had autonomy in planning and providing quality education. The universities were run democratically. There were various committees that looked after the affairs of administration. Eminent teachers controlled the quality of education provided in these universities.

In South India, the Brahmanical Ghatikas, the Buddhist Vihars and Jaina Pallis were centres of higher education. Financial help was provided to them by rich merchants and enlightened rulers. From all this it is evident that higher education in early India was controlled by private enterprise. The rulers and administrators provided their patronage but did not interfere in the administration and teaching.

It may be noted that during Muslim period the patronage of the kings, the landlords and army commanders continued in education up to the highest level. The Muslim institutions of higher learning known as madrsass were established in different parts of the country. 'Muhammad Ghori is reported to have established several madrsass at Ajmer, to be followed by a chain of madrsass at different places by successive rulers.'[3] The patrons of madrsass usually donated land and cash to build and maintain their structure. Land grants were given to the teachers and students as well.

The British brought to this country their own system of higher education. The first Europeanized institution of higher learning was established in 1817 as Hindu College in Calcutta. This was followed by a college at Serampore in 1818 and the Hoogly College in 1834. In 1857, on the model of London University, three universities were founded at Calcutta, Bombay and Madras. All the three were examining and affiliating bodies. The teaching was provided in the colleges only. Between 1855–1856 and 1921–22 the number of general colleges increased from 21 to 172 and pupils in them from 4,355 to 58,837. By 1947 there were 19 universities and 496 colleges with 2,37,546 pupils. The growth was mainly in the privately managed colleges.[4]

With the attainment of Independence in 1947, it was rightly thought that higher education is the key to achieve economic growth and an enlightened society in India. This realization resulted in the introduction of vital changes and improvement in higher education system in the country. The number of universities in India increased from 20 in 1948 to about 355 in 2006 – an eightfold increase. The number of colleges increased from 496 in 1948 to 18,064 in 2006. The number of university level teachers grew from 24,000 in 1951 to 4,88,000 in 2006. India now produces third largest number of graduates after US and China.[5] The professional education is also growing rapidly. It is covering all major disciplines. A very large, complex and modern system of higher and professional education has been established in this country.

One remarkable feature of the Indian education is the diversity within the system. Different types of institution were created to meet diverse needs. Institutions of higher and professional education comprise universities, institutes of national importance and colleges. The universities and the institutes of national importance are established by acts of Indian Parliament or State legislative assemblies. They are financed by the central or state governments. There are also institutes or colleges financed and managed by private enterprise. The private colleges fall in two categories – Aided (which receive grant-in-aid from the government) and Unaided (which manage all their expenditure from private sources through endowments or aids from religious or business establishments).

There are four types of universities, central, state universities, deemed universities (which can be either aided or unaided), and private universities. Central universities are established, maintained and funded by the national government and state universities are established, maintained and funded by the state governments. The universities are further categorized into three types as follows:

1. *Affiliating universities:* The main function of these universities is to hold examinations in the colleges affiliated to them. The teaching is mainly done in affiliated colleges. At present, most of the affiliating universities have undertaken some responsibility of teaching at postgraduate, doctorate or professional levels. Bombay University, Panjab University and many other universities that were formerly purely affiliating are now affiliating-cum-teaching universities.
2. *Unitary universities:* These universities exercise complete control over the colleges located on their campuses. Teaching is conducted either by university-appointed teachers or teachers working under the supervision of the universities. Many of the unitary universities are now given permission by the UGC and government to affiliate colleges existing within a narrow distance from the campus of the university.
3. *Federal universities:* These universities have colleges linked to them near the university that provide education under the guidance of the university.[6]

Dissatisfied with the British system of higher education, a series of national universities were founded by Gandhi during the first Non-cooperation Movement in 1920–21. They included Gujarat Vidyapeeth, Kashi Vidyapeeth, Bihar Vidyapeeth, Tilak Maharashtra

Vidyapeeth and Jamia Mililia Islamia. In 1921, Rabindranath Tagore established at Shantiniketan a university called Vishwa Bharti that was located in the natural surroundings and the education of fine arts, humanities, etc. was given in the lap of nature. Annie Besant started the Central Hindu College that, with the efforts of Pundit Madan Mohan Malviya, became the Banaras Hindu University. Besides these Christian missionaries established many Christian missionary colleges. In 1877, Sir Syed Ahmed Khan founded the Muhammedan Anglo Oriental College at Aligarh. It later took the shape of Aligarh Muslim University. The Arya Samajists founded the Dayanand Anglo Vedic College (DAV College) at Lahore in 1886. This was followed by many DAV colleges mostly in north India. The Sikhs established Khalsa Schools and Colleges after the Sikh Sabha Movement in 1873 and the establishment of Khalsa Diwan. In 1911, Jamshedji Tata founded the Tata Institute of Science at Bangalore. D.K. Karve started women's university called SNDT Women's University in 1918 in Poona.

All the above accounts clearly highlight that private enterprise has had a long history in the management of higher education in India. Throughout its existence it has performed the following five roles:

1. Providing access to higher education to large number of aspirants especially those who wanted to get education somewhat in a different mode than what was taught in the universities established by the government or aided by it.
2. Providing quality education by appointing qualified and dedicated teachers and paying them high salaries.
3. Making available education to those who are unable to get admission in government sponsored universities or colleges.
4. Providing additional finances for higher education than what the government was providing.
5. Involving business and industry in educational enterprise.

Private Enterprise in Education Today

Higher education in India has rapidly expanded in the last two decades. At present, the Indian system of education is the third largest in the world after US and China. However, as regards the number of institutions, India is largest higher education system in the world. At present, it has 17,625 colleges and 348 universities; 63 single deemed universities with enrolment of 60,000 students, and 7,650 unaided private colleges with enrolment of 31,50,000 students. This means that nearly one-third of the total students are studying in unaided private institutions. The unaided private institutions are growing rapidly. Hardly 8 or 9 per cent of the population in the age group 17–23 years is enrolled in the institutions of higher education.[7] But it has also led to lowering of standards of education. In the absence of a well thought-out policy by the government about the role of the private sector in higher education, the growth has been chaotic and unplanned. Today, we find a large number of colleges financed and managed by private enterprise that are ill-equipped, short of qualified staff, lack even the basic amenities for the staff and the students, have no library or reading room and function from old, depleted and rented buildings. These colleges provide education mostly in science. Science is taught in the laboratories whose equipment is often below the standard of a well-equipped public school. Among such colleges are also those that provide professional and technical education. A large number of private engineering colleges and colleges of education and nursing colleges have been established throughout the country without caring for the norms set by the universities or the government for equipment and building, faculty and management. These colleges also charge very high fees and fleece the needy students. The sponsors and managers of these institutions are usually powerful politicians or those who have right connections at the right places.

The deemed university provision in the UGC Act also help those who want to get their colleges raised to the status of the universities. All this is done through corrupt practices. The corruption cases against the Chair-person of the All India Council of Technical Education and the Chairman of All India Council of Medical Education bear testimony to it.

The experience over the last few decades shows that privatization has not led to any major improvements in the standards of higher and professional education. Generally better quality teaching and infra-structure is available in government colleges and universities. The private institutions of higher education in India capitalize on fashionable courses with minimum infrastructure.

The last decade has witnessed some significant changes in higher and professional education. Thousands of private colleges and institutes offering IT courses appeared all across the country by late 1990s and disappeared in less than a decade, with devastating consequences for the students and teachers who depended on them for their careers. Private institutions providing management education, bio technology courses, bioinformatics and many other emerging areas have been established throughout the country without any proper building, equipment, qualified teachers, classrooms, laboratories, libraries, etc. They pay very low salary to their teaching staff and charge high fees from the students. The government either through its Ministry of Human Resource Development or through its various statutory and advisory bodies appointed for the maintenance of standards has largely failed to exercise any control over them, mainly because they are established by powerful politicians, resourceful businessmen, bureaucrats or even mafia lords. All the regula-tions framed by the government and its statutory bodies have been softened to accommodate their commercial interests.

It may be pertinent at this point to illustrate the dubious role played by commercially oriented private enterprise in education. The following case studies tell it all.

Soon after the creation of a new state of Chhattisgarh, the government indiscriminately sanctioned the creation of 150 private universities and colleges. The scam got exposed by public interest litigation and the courts ordered the state government in 2004 to derecognize and close most of these universities or merge them with the recognized ones. This resulted in a large number of students losing valuable years of university education. They suffered irreparable damage to their careers, for no fault of theirs.

In a sting operation on the news channel IBN7, it was revealed that two private universities, one of them a deemed university and another private one, were enroling candidates for PhD degree in various subjects without any infra-structure or qualified teachers in those subjects. The students were assured of no attendance restriction classes or of meeting their supervisors. The only conditions laid down were the payment of fees for their enrolment which was more than ₹ 10,000 and the requirement of meeting their supervisors only two times before they submitted their thesis. The degree was ensured. Their supervisors would see to it that examiners approve their theses. The supervisors may also write the thesis on their behalf if they would be prepared to pay the money demanded by the supervisors. The exposure made by the channel shows how the highest academic degrees are sold by private universities.

Another case study is of one of the prestigious educational enterprises in Mumbai. The case has been reported in the weekly journal *The Week* of October 23, 2011. Under the title: 'Painful Business' Niranjan Takle writes in *The Week*:

In an age where education is one of the most lucrative businesses around, Sadashiv S. Pawar could not be faulted for thinking that he was making wise move when he partnered the D.Y. Patil group for investing in the sector. His bitter lessons cost him a few crores, and he is now accusing the Patils of fraud.[8]

The Patils run an education empire in Maharashtra. The patriarch, Dr D.Y. Patil, is the Governor of Tripura. In case no. 152/2011 filed at Wadgaon court, Pune on April 21, 2011, Pawer has accused the D.Y. Patil Educational Enterprises, Patil's wife and two sons of fraud, forgery and breach of trust. Patil's third son is the minister of state for home, Maharashtra. Pawar has accused him of trying to hush up the charges against his parents and siblings.

The Wadgaon court had ordered the police to lodge an FIR and investigate. But the Sessions court in Pune stayed it, before clearing it on September 12.

Pawar claims that he is cheated of land which is now worth ₹ 100 crore. From this it is evident that Pawar gave money to the educational enterprise to earn profit and the enterprise itself seems to be more interested in making money and exercising power rather than in any philanthropic activity. In this connection, another fact that *The Week* has revealed is that D.Y. Patil Educational Enterprises violated the Urban Land Ceiling Act while buying land in Charholi. The Educational Enterprises is registered as a private limited company and is not a charitable trust. As such it has to follow the laws enacted under the Urban Ceiling Act. But high placed members of the company in the government hierarchy are fighting vigorously to avoid paying any penalty.

Another instance of powerful politicians' interference in educational sphere is that of Sharad Pawar International School run by Patils getting water from a special 16-km pipeline from Pawana. Sharad Pawar's daughter, Superiya Sule, MP serves on the School's advisory board.

Besides the above examples of business interests of private enterprise in education, there are personal experiences of the author who was implicitly offered not only cash but even gold to grant affiliation to B.Ed. classes by National Council of Teacher Education by a number of private colleges. The author was appointed by NCTE to inspect these colleges for their capability in terms of equipment, building and staff for providing effective teacher training. The manager of one college requested me to grant affiliation to the college for B.Ed. course, while carrying a loaded pistol in his pocket. The threat seemed to be quite obvious in case I declined the grant of affiliation or made it conditional. Since money or threat was offered quite implicitly there was no direct proof with me of any corrupt practice.

All the above examples show that for private enterprise higher education has become a big business. But this business is conducted by adhering to corrupt practices. It is time to do something about it to contain the private players of dubious repute in the field of higher education.

Need for Involvement of Private Sector

The institutions of higher learning are much less in number than the requirements. The institutions run by the government or aided by it are totally inadequate in number for admitting all those young persons who are eligible to get higher education and aspire for it. Also most of the institutions of higher learning are established in urban or semi-urban areas. The rural youth has to travel long distances before he can find an institution of his choice. If he opts for living in a hostel he will hardly find accommodation in it because of limited number of hostels and high rate of fees and high living expenses. There are regional disparities also. The backward regions of the country do not take much interest in opening new colleges or in financing the already established institutions. The private enterprise avoids establishing new institutions in these regions because of financial constraints. The backward regions have more poor youths than the affluent regions so the opening of new college is considered as a bad investment that will not give any returns to the sponsors or founders in terms of purely a business enterprise.

At the Federation of Indian Chambers Commerce and Industry Higher-Education Summit at New Delhi, participants acknowledged that more work needs to be done to revitalize the country's beleaguered and somewhat antiquated higher education system. At this summit Sibal, the Human Resource Minister, Government of India, said, 'We need 800 more universities in 10 years, and no government in the world will have the resources or the know-how to build these. To achieve the lofty goal, the government needs to encourage the private sector to step up investment in higher education and foster partnerships between both Indian and International players.'[9]

Constitutional Perspective

Padmanabhan, in his article entitled 'Privatisation of Higher Education in India: Constitutional Perspectives and Challenges', highlights two issues concerning privatization of higher education from the point of view of provisions made in the Constitution of India. One issue is that of permissibility and the other of desirability.

The Preamble of the Constitution of India has given its citizens the fundamental rights of liberty, justice, equality and fraternity. Further the Preamble also proclaims adherence to socialist principles. There have been many court cases in which the questions were raised about the socialist principles being a hindrance in the privatization process of some key industries or institutions. The judgments were in favour of privatization if it leads to social and economic benefits to the society and country. Thus, the privatization of higher education is permissible from the constitutional point of view.

Its desirability is also upheld in view of the principle of equal right of every citizen to education. In the case of minority institutions, separate provisions are made in the constitution under Article 30 (1) that guarantees religious and linguistic minorities the right to establish and administer educational institutions of their choice. The constitution specifically recognises privatization in their case. In the perspective of fundamental rights it is well settled that private managements have the right to establish and manage institutions under Article 19 (1) (g) of the Indian Constitution. The right to establish and administer educational institutions under Articles 19 (1) or 30 (1) broadly comprises the right to admit students, to set up a reasonable fee structure, constitute a governing body, appoint well-qualified faculty, and take disciplinary action in cases of dereliction of duty.[10] The state can impose reasonable restrictions on the right guaranteed by Article 19 (1) (g) in the interests of general public under the provisions in 19 (6).

Recently the government of Bengal has scrapped the essentiality certificate of a private medical college run by an NGO associated with CPM leader Lakshman Seth in Haldia. The college has 88 students, each of whom paid capitation fees of ₹ 4.5 lakh on average. The state government found that it was not following the norms. It may be noted that Medical Council grants recognition on the basis of essentiality certificate of the state government.[11] This provision is considered essential for maintenance of standards and to provide adequate equipment, building and qualified faculty in the private institutions of professional and higher education. But this provision may as well be misused by the state governments to control the institutions established by the politicians of the parties in opposition to the government. The medical college in Bengal is being run by a Marxist politician while the ruling party is Trinamool Congress under the Chief Minister, Mamta Banerjee.

Financing of Higher Education and Role of Private Enterprise

We have already emphasized that there is a great need for establishing institutions of higher education and professional education. A large number of youth who aspire for higher education are not able to get admissions in the institutions of higher education or professional education or in the universities. Since India aspires to become a developed country with a high rate of economic growth, it has to think in terms of making higher and professional education accessible to all deserving youths. But opening of new institutions of higher learning and universities require huge funds that is not possible for the government alone to provide. There is, thus, a great need for the private enterprise in education that can provide required funds for setting up institutions and universities. Let us now examine the role played by the central and state governments in financing higher education.

The Indian Constitution assigns specific tax and expenditure responsibilities to the Centre and states. The revenue-raising responsibilities between the Government of India (GoI) and the states are determined in such a manner that the capability of the GoI is substantially higher than that of the states, although all subjects having a bearing on poverty eradication and well-being of the people, as well as requiring huge staff (teachers, doctors, etc.) are with the state governments. Even though education is now on concurrent list in the Indian Constitution, the major responsibilities of higher education are assigned to the state governments. Since the powers of the state governments for raising revenues are very limited, they are extremely shy of making commitments for the extension and expansion of higher education. Thus, the financial burden of quantitative and qualitative improvement in higher education falls upon the central government. The central government has already committed itself to introduce universalization of primary education, eradication of illiteracy and improving the quality of secondary education, but it is by and large not very enthusiastic in allotting required funds for higher education. It, thus, depends upon private enterprise for filling the gap between the needs and availability of finances for higher and professional education. Recently the central government has taken some initiative towards financing higher education and improving its quality. It is in this context that a news item in *Hindustan Times*, November 20, 2011 mentions two ambitious plans that are being worked out by the Planning Commission that might change the face of higher education in this country.

> The first proposes that tuition fees of the top 10 per cent performers passing out of school into under-graduate courses be paid for by the government. That means about eight lakh students will benefit, irrespective of caste, religion, economic status and discipline (arts, commerce, science).
>
> The annual benefit to a student would range from ₹ 2,000–5,000 for a conventional degree in a government college to ₹ 50,000 tuition fees as charged by the IITs. The selected students will be free to study whatever they want in any state-run institution of their choosing. According to estimates, more than 80 lakh students appear for 10+2 boards every year with about 8 lakh of them from CBSE.
>
> Fees or part of it in select, accredited private institutions could also be covered. The financial requirement for land-mark proposal taking the scholarship to an unprecedented level is to be worked out.
>
> A related plan proposes that financial aid for educating the disadvantaged – scheduled castes and tribes, minorities – be increased from ₹ 2,000 crore to ₹ 8,000 crore. Both the proposals have been worked out by the Planning Commission.
>
> The government has set for a target of increasing enrolment for higher education level from 15 per cent currently to 25 per cent of the eligible population, which will mean 4 crore additional students in universities and other institutions.[12]

The proposals for providing financial help to the deserving students who join the institutions of higher learning have the potential for increasing the quality of learning and the growth in the enrolment in higher learning. But there are some doubts in terms of the financial viability of the plan. It is doubtful if the government will be able to enforce its plan without imposing additional tax burden on the public. Rather than doing so it will be better to seek involvement of private sector to evolve out schemes of scholarships to all those who are enroled for higher education through a scientifically planned test.

Commenting on the question of scholarships, observes Suresh Babu, 'there has been a continuous elite domination on the one hand and perpetual marginalization on the other, over the accessibility of this scarce resource. Gradual departure of policies on education from the fundamental principle of social justice to privatization requires new theoretical explanations and their ideological positions as higher learning being treated as a private meritorious good than a public good.'[13]

The central government, nevertheless, considers that increased private participation in the higher education is a viable financial model. It has recommended raising fees in higher education institutions. The mid-year analysis for 2010–2011, tabled in Lok Sabha, suggests provision of financing grants for students belonging to the weaker sections. Such students can repay after they start earning so as to ensure sustainability of the system.[14] Planning Commission is also for proposing scholarships to all the deserving students irrespective of caste or religion whosoever gets admission after +2 in the institutions of higher learning.

The mid-year analysis appreciates the efforts of the Ministry of Human Resource Development for setting up a National Commission for Higher Education and Research (NCHER) as an overarching regulatory body for higher education. It also emphasizes that there is a dire need of efficient teachers for universities, colleges and professional institutions. It further says that many universities have to revamp the course structure and teaching methodology to meet the demands of the job market.

Quality Concerns

The UPA government has recently decided to shift its focus from quantity to quality in higher education. Its earlier efforts of establishing a large number of institutions and setting up of universities failed due to the paucity of qualified teachers for higher education and the reluctance of the state governments to provide adequate infrastructure and land for institutions of higher learning and professional colleges. The government has announced the setting up of 51 public-funded higher education institutions, including eight IITs and seven IIMs, during the Eleventh Five Year Plan period from 2007–2012. But these plans have had slow progress primarily because of delays in land acquisition and disputes between the Centre and the states on where they should be set up. The Twelfth Plan will go slow on adding more institutions. It will add four new IITs but no new IIMs. Fourteen innovation universities and 374 model colleges, that were already announced in the Eleventh Plan but could not be established, will also be included in the new plan.

'Ensuring quality in higher education to compete with the global best would be the objective in the Twelfth Plan and not opening a number of new institutes,' said an HRD ministry official.

Despite the Union Cabinet approving over ₹ 10,000 crore for setting up new IITs and IIMs in 2008, construction work for only four technology and five management institutes has started and about 40 per cent of faculty posts are lying vacant till the end of the year 2011. In the next few years, the Ministry plans huge investments to set up IITs and IIMs and 16 new central universities with international quality research facilities and faculties. 'IIT Bhubaneswar should have the same level of excellence as IIT Bombay or Delhi,' a Ministry official said.

Faculty shortages range from 30 per cent to 40 per cent in IITs and up to 30 per cent in IIMs. It is as high as 50 per cent of the teaching posts in the universities. 'Many new universities have started from temporary campuses with just a few courses because of faculty shortage and space,' a senior University Grants Commission official said.

The Twelfth Plan would also see a higher allocation of funds to support high quality research in educational institutions and incentives to have more PhD holders, whose number has been falling in recent years. The proposal accepted by the ministry will be submitted to Planning Commission for approval and for inclusion in the Twelfth Plan.[15]

We must recognize that knowledge, skills and productivity of our young and dynamic work force forms the backbone of our economy. It is urgently needed for the knowledge economy of India. According to Chakrabarty the progress from agrarian and/or industrial economy to that of knowledge economy is based on the ability to acquire ownership of knowledge and to use it to create goods or services. Workers in the knowledge economy differ from others insofar as they know what they are doing, how they are doing, and why they are doing the work. They also excel in their fields of knowledge and are often better at their jobs. Thus, we must strive assiduously to convert our young work force into potential power house of productivity and growth.

The private enterprise can contribute significantly in developing knowledge economy. Dedicated industrialists, social workers, affluent persons in the community can establish well-equipped professional and higher education institutions. They may appoint highly qualified faculty and pay them remuneration comparable to the best institutions in the world without depending on the government finances. In India the number of millionaires and billionaires are increasing year by year. If they can be motivated to contribute funds for higher education, the knowledge economy can get a big boost. Ultimately they will be the beneficiaries for knowledge economy is bound to increase cash flow in the country and make available more funds for business and industries as well as for paying higher emoluments to the captains of industries and executives.

Committees and their Recommendations

Several committees were appointed to explore the implications of privatization of higher education. Here is a brief account of the committees and their recommendations.

1. The Punnaya Committee 1992–93: This committee was set up by the UGC. It recommended that universities should generate 15 per cent of its annual maintenance expenditure through internally generated resources and this should go up to at least 25 per cent at the end of 10 years. The committee recommended that students who are getting benefits of higher education should also bear a reasonable proportion of the cost of higher education.
2. Dr Swaminathan Panel 1992: The Swaminathan Panel was set up by the All India Council for Technical Education. It suggested the mobilization of additional resources for technical education so that the necessary qualitative and quantitative growth of technical education is ensured. The Panel suggested that educational cess may be collected from industries and other organizations. The cess will provide additional finances for technical and professional education.
3. The Birla Ambani Report 2000: A committee headed by Mukesh Ambani and Kumarmangalam Birla was appointed by 'The Prime Minister's Council on Trade and Industry' to suggest reforms in the educational sector. The committee submitted its report in the year 2001. It highlighted the role of the State in the development of education. The following are some of the important suggestions presented by the committee.
   (i) The government should take responsibility for primary education and the higher education should be provided by the private sector.
   (ii) Private University Bill should be passed.
   (iii) Government must encourage business houses to establish educational institutions.
   (iv) Loans and scholarships must be liberally distributed to the economically and socially weaker sections of the society.
4. Committee on 'Financing of Technical and Higher Education of the Central Advisory Board of Education' recognized the limitation of non-government funding. It also emphasized the role of state financing of higher education in promoting growth. It recommended the allocation of 1 per cent of the National Income for higher education.[16]

Conclusion

To wrap up, it may be said that private sector has always been present in the field of education in India. Its role, however, has changed significantly in present times. Earlier, it played more of a benevolent role. Now it has developed business interests in education. That notwithstanding, the fact remains that the need for the involvement of private sector in higher education was never so great as today. What is, therefore, needed is to explore the ways and means to so manage its participation that it becomes a positive force to promote access, equity and excellence in higher education.

Notes

1. Rama Devi. The Address at X Convocation of Sri Krishnadevaraya University, Anantapur, 5 June 2000.
2. Ibid.
3. Ibid.
4. Ibid.
5. University Grants Commission. *Annual Report 2005–2006*, www.ugc.ac.in
6. S. Bhatnagar. *Education in India*, Meerut: International Publishing House, 2007.
7. 'Some Problems of Indian Education', Saagam Blog, 2 November 2011, http://saagam.com/blog/index.php/some-problems-of-Indian-higher-education/.
8. Niranjan Takle. 'Painful Business', *The Week*, 23 October 2011.
9. Shailaja Neeiakantan. 'India's Business Leaders Applaud Progress on Higher Education', Federation of Indian Chambers of Commerce and Industry Higher Education Summit, New Delhi, 11 November 2011.
10. TMA Pai Foundation v. State of Karnataka (2002) 8 SCC 481.
11. News item, yahoo.com, 19 November 2011.
12. Prasad Nichenametla. 'Government may Pay Fees for Top 10% Students', *Hindustan Times*, 20 November 2011.
13. Suresh Babu G.S. 'Privatization of Higher Education in India: Challenges of Social Equality', Global Conclave of Young Scholars of Indian Education, National University of Educational Planning and Administration (NUEPA), New Delhi, January 27–29, 2012.
14. 'Privatization of Higher Education Suggested by Government of India', Digital Learning, December 17, 2010.
15. News item, *Hindustan Times*, dated November 21, 2011.
16. C. Premsai. 'Higher Education in India: From Socialism to Capitalism', 20 October 2010, http://www.legalserviceindia,com/articles/he.htm

4

Whither Higher Education in India? Need for an Ennobling Mission

B.P. MATHUR

Education is fundamental to a civilized society. Proper education alone builds the character of an individual and awakens the consciousness in him to serve the society. Education should aim at producing young men and women of knowledge, character and cultural values so that they are prepared to face life and become responsible citizens. Education serves both public and private interests. It addresses public interests by preparing the young to assume adult roles that promote civic responsibility, embrace a common set of values and dedicate themselves to the service of community. Education serves private interests in promoting individual development, knowledge, intelligence and sensitivity so that he/she can lead a harmonious and fulfilling life.

Indian education today is characterized by poor standards and lack of emphasis on character building. The Constitution had envisaged free and compulsory education for every child and eradication of illiteracy within ten years of the Constitution coming into being. But six and half decades after Independence a large percentage of population is illiterate and even those considered literate in the official statistics books do not possess basic knowledge of 3 Rs and can hardly read, write and do simple arithmetical sums. The higher education continues to bear heavy imprint of colonial legacy, shaped as it was by Macaulay's[1] famous Minute on Education, 'We must do our best to form a class, who may be interpreters between us and the millions we govern, a class of persons, Indian in blood and colour, but English in taste, opinion and morals'. The whole focus of existing education system is for the individual to get a degree, earn some money and become a careerist. There is no emphasis on development of personality, creation of an ideal citizen and imbibing feeling of nationalism.

The leaders of Indian renaissance were fully conscious of the importance of education for nation building. Swami Vivekananda, who appeared in the national scene like a blitz in late nineteenth century, ignited the Indian mind and mesmerized the West, forcefully emphasized the importance of education. 'A nation is advanced in proportion as education and intelligence spread among the masses .... If we have to rise again we shall have to do it in the same way (Western countries), that is by spreading education among the masses ... . Education, education alone! Traveling through many cities of Europe and observing in them the comforts and the education of even the poor people, there was brought to my mind the state of our own people, and I used to shed tears. What made the difference? Education was the answer I got. Through education comes faith in one's own self.'[2] Elaborating further his views on education, Vivekananda asserted, 'The education which does not help the common mass of people to equip themselves for the struggle for life, which does not bring out strength of character, a spirit of philanthropy, and the courage of a lion – is it worth the name? Real education is that which enables one to stand on its own leg.'[3]

During freedom movement all the national leaders fought for the cause of education and spent their life for expansion of education and independence and autonomy of educational institutions. As early as March 1910, Gopal Krishna Gokhale moved a resolution at the Imperial Legislative Assembly for free and compulsory education in the country. Mahatma Gandhi completely rejected colonial education and came forward with an alternative model. His critique of Western, particularly English education, was part of his critique of Western civilization as a whole. Gandhi[4] developed his own model of basic education (*nai-talim*) which is best obtained through action. Education has to be through a craft, not merely through books and abstractions and should be self-supporting as far as possible and equip the pupil to better his own economic conditions. Gandhi was strong advocate of medium of instruction in the mother-tongue, not English and primary education to be free and compulsory for all children. Gandhi's education model was part of his social philosophy as it favoured the child belonging to the lowest stratum of society, and helped in social transformation. Gandhi's basic education was an embodiment of his perception of an ideal society, consisting of small, self-reliant communities.

Rabindranath Tagore envisioned an education that was deeply rooted in one's immediate surroundings but connected to the cultures of the wider world and individualized to the personality of the child. He felt that a curriculum should revolve organically around nature with classes held in the open air under the trees to provide for a spontaneous appreciation of the fluidity of the plant and animal kingdoms, and seasonal changes. He emphasized the importance of an empathetic sense of interconnectedness with the surrounding world. 'The highest education is that which does not merely give us information but makes our life in harmony with all existence. But we find that this education of sympathy is not only systematically ignored in schools, but it is severely repressed. From our very childhood, habits are formed and knowledge is imparted in such a manner that our life is weaned away from nature and our mind and the world are set in opposition from the beginning of our days. Thus, the greatest of education for which we came prepared is neglected, and we are made to lose our world to find a bagful of information instead.'[5] In Tagore's philosophy of education, the aesthetic development of the senses was as important as the intellectual, and music, literature, art, dance and drama were given great prominence in the daily life of the school. He gave practical shape of his vision by opening Visva Bharati University, whose underlying ideal was the spiritual unity of all races and an ideal of brotherhood where men of different countries and language can come together. Tagore wanted to root Indian education to its ancient richness without loosing sight of the benefits that opening up to West could provide.

The leaders of India's freedom movement were deeply conscious of the damage done by colonial education and felt that education should give respect to country's ancient wisdom and tradition. In ancient times India was a place of great learning and scholarship. Takshila in north-west India (now Pakistan-Afghanistan), founded a few hundred years before Christ, was renowned as a place of learning and drew students from all over the world. It was a storehouse of learned teachers which included Panini, the fourth century BC grammarian and Kautilya – the mentor and guide of Chandragupta Maurya who wrote the celebrated treatise *Arthshastra.* Another great centre of learning flourished at Nalanda (Bihar) during the Gupta era and continued during the time of Harsha in the seventh century, and much thereafter. A place of great Buddhist scholarship, it had on its rolls two thousand teachers and ten thousand students and drew students from all over the world and can be said to be the first international university. A key feature of ancient Indian education system was *guru-shishya parampara.* Strict discipline: *brahamcharya* on the part of student, who stayed in monastery and showed great reverence to the *guru,* whose sole mission in life was search for knowledge and igniting the minds of students.

Post-Independence Development

Despite noble vision of our leaders, in the post-Independence era, there was very little change in the education system that we inherited from the British. Most universities and affiliated colleges continued to provide education on the colonial pattern and turned out graduates who were out of tune with the realities of life, unemployable and unable to stand on their own feet. The only redeeming feature was setting up of IITs and IIMs which produced high-class professionals. Government set up several committees and commissions to look into the problems of education and they came forward with valuable suggestions for reform but most of them remained on paper only.

The University Education Commission, which was headed by eminent educationist S. Radhakrishnan (1948), visualized a wide conception of the duties and responsibilities of universities. They have to provide leadership in politics and administration, the professions, industry and commerce. They have to meet the increasing demand for every type of higher education, literary and scientific, technical and professional. They must enable the country to attain freedom from want, disease and ignorance, by the application and development of scientific and technical knowledge. They should create knowledge and train minds who would bring together material resources and human energies to raise the living standards of people. The Commission underlined the fact that the universities are the organs of civilization. If India is to confront the confusion of our time, she must turn for guidance, to her men of letters and men of science, to her poets and artists, to her discoverers and inventors. These intellectual pioneers of civilization are to be found and trained in the universities, which are the sanctuaries of the inner life of the nation.

The Education Commission headed by distinguished scientist D.S. Kothari (1964–66) observed that the most important and urgent reform needed in education is to relate it to the life, needs and aspirations of the people and, thereby, make it a powerful instrument of social, economic and cultural transformation necessary for realization of the national goal. It suggested fivefold programme: (a) Relating education to productivity; (b) Strengthening social and national integration through educational programmes; (c) Consolidation of democracy through education; (d) Development of social, moral and spiritual values and (e) Modernization of society through awakening of curiosity, development of attitudes and values and building up certain essential skills. In order to achieve its most important recommendation, viz. – relating education to productivity, it came forward with a number of suggestions such as the following: (i) Science education should be an integral part of school education and ultimately become a part of all courses at university stage; (ii) Work experience to become an integral part of all education; (iii) Orientation of work experience to technology and industrialization and the application of science to productive processes, including agriculture and (iv) Vocationalization of secondary education and agricultural and technical education.

Two national education policies were formulated, one each in 1968 and 1986. Their objectives were laudable - improving the quality of education, developing vocational skill in the students and relating education to the needs of society. The vision of education envisaged by Radhakrishnan and Kothari Commissions and in National Education Policies has remained a pipe dream, as policy makers have had no real commitment to the cause of education and learning. There has been haphazard expansion of education without much consideration for quality.

At the time of Independence, there were 20 universities and 500 colleges. Presently, there are 504 universities and university level institutions – which includes 243 state universities, 53 state private universities, 40 central universities, 130 deemed universities and 33 institutions of national importance (January 2010). There are 26,000 colleges, including over 2,500 women's colleges. Over 137 lakh students are enroled in higher education courses, out of which 120 lakh (88%) are in affiliated colleges and 17 lakh (12%), in university departments. The faculty strength is around 5.90 lakh, with 90,000 teachers in universities and 5 lakh in affiliated colleges. All over the world, higher education is in universities with big campuses with a critical mass of students and staff strength that can sustain large libraries, well-equipped laboratories and advanced centres of research. In India, higher education is fragmented, scattered and takes place in over 26,000 institutions called affiliated colleges, which are small sized with no infrastructure and poor quality and inadequate teachers. These institutions of higher learning perform only classroom teaching, preparing students for examinations like tutorial colleges.

Despite serious flaws in higher education system, it has resisted all attempts at reform. The universities have not been able to imbibe the values required for institutions of higher learning and create an atmosphere conducive to research and scholarship. They produce students who are simply interested in earning a degree and are totally out of tune with the needs of society in post-industrial information age. There is considerable politicization of education and lack of autonomy to universities. This has resulted in deterioration of education, even in the old established universities. My alma mater University of Allahabad which was once considered Oxford of the East is a case in point. There is blatant interference in the appointment of Vice Chancellors. The fact that Government (Chief Minister/Governor) has reserved for itself the power to appoint Vice Chancellor is indicative of the extent to which they are controlled. The universities are totally dependent on government for their financial needs. This power allows them to dictate policies which critically affects universities' academic performance. The universities have no freedom to recruit teachers and select students – they have to follow Government's guidelines such as reservation of seats for special categories. In such a situation, how can universities remain centres of excellence and nurseries of knowledge?

The National Knowledge Commission

The National Knowledge Commission[6] (NKC), headed by Sam Pitroda, has made wide-ranging recommendations regarding future of higher education (2005–08). It has proposed massive expansion of higher education, increasing the Gross Enrolment Ratio (GER) to 15 per cent by 2015 from existing level of 7 per cent. In order to achieve this, it has recommended opening of 1,500 universities by 2015, including 50 new national universities. This would involve massive public funding, besides private participation and industry linkages. In order to control quality of education, NKC has recommended setting up an Independent Regulatory Authority for Higher Education (IRAHE) which would be beyond the approach of all stakeholders and would accord degree granting power to universities. To ensure quality, NKC has called for reform of existing universities to ensure frequent curricula revisions, introduction of course credit system, enhancing reliance on internal assessment, encouraging research and reforming governance of institutions. It has suggested restructuring the system of affiliated undergraduate colleges, which no longer provide a viable model for quality higher education and has proposed models for community colleges that provide credit and non credit courses leading to two year associate degrees.

Indiscriminate Expansion

Some of NKC's key recommendations regarding expansion of higher education have been incorporated in the Eleventh Five Year Plan (2007–12). The Plan aims to achieve quantitative expansion in enrolment through expansion of existing institutions both government and private and creation of new government-funded universities. Thirty central universities will be set up, including 16 in states, which do not have a central university. In the field of technical education, the Plan envisages setting up of eight new IITs, seven IIMs, 10 NITs (National Institutes of Technology) and 20 IIITs (Indian Institutes of Information Technology). The main thrust of government policy is quantitative expansion and inclusive education.

In pursuance of NKCs recommendations and the policy laid down in the Eleventh Plan, government has opened 15 central universities through enactment of Central Universities Act of 2009. Twelve of these are new universities and three are cases of conversion of existing state universities. A university has been allocated to every state, which does not have a central university. Vice Chancellors have been appointed in these universities and they have been asked to start classes with non-existent infrastructure. Under the rules for establishment of these universities, the state governments are required to provide 500 acres of land, free of cost. The state governments have no interest in higher education and look at a fully-funded central project in terms of vote-bank politics. In Ranchi, Jharkhand, the state government is prevaricating the land allotment for last three years, and the hapless Vice Chancellor has to carry on undergraduate classes in make-shift arrangement. In Bihar, the university has managed to start classes in Patna by hiring temporary accommodation, but the Chief Minister wants it to be shifted to backward Motihari, to pander to his voters constituency, much against the wishes of the Ministry of Education and the Vice Chancellor. In J&K, a central university has been allocated, although Jammu has already a well-established state university, purely as a political move. There is no real autonomy to the newly created central universities. The Ministry of HRD and UGC nominees sit on the Executive Committee and other important bodies and dictate the policies to be followed. Even the appointment of a routine administrative post, such as Finance Officer may take up to one year as it has to undergo not only a tortuous selection process but also approval of the Ministry of HRD, and the Visitor, who happens to be the President of India. Can any worthwhile research and knowledge-creation take place when universities are set up as a political gimmickry, without proper infrastructure and teaching faculty, and do not have any autonomy?

IITs and IIMs are the only world-class professional institutes which India has. Presently, there are six well-established IITs (including Roorkee). A decade back, an additional IIT was opened at Guwahati, which is still struggling to find ground. As a result of mass expansion policy, government has opened eight new IITs at Hyderabad, Patna, Jodhpur, Gandhinagar, Bhubneswar, Ropar, Indore and Mandi. Same is the case with IIMs. There are four well-established IIMs – three more were set up some years back at Indore, Kozikode and Shillong and they are still struggling to come up to the standard of first class institutes. Six more IIMs have been opened and four of them have commenced classes at Raipur, Rohtak, Ranchi and Tiruchirapalli to be mentored by IIMs at Indore, Lucknow, Kolkata and Bangalore. There is no physical infrastructure and worthwhile teaching faculty in these new IITs and IIMs. One can imagine the standard of teaching they would impart. It takes years to build and nurture a high standard institution. Such indiscriminate expansion will only result in lowering the standard of existing premier institutions and bring them to the lowest common denominator.

There is a serious flaw in government policy relating to higher education. According to the Eleventh Plan, the objective of education is quantitative expansion and inclusive education. Inclusive education is proposed to be achieved by 'reduction of regional imbalances, support to institutions in hilly, remote and small towns, supporting institutions with larger population of SCs, STs, OBCs and minorities students'. Can any world class institution of higher learning be created with such lop-sided objectives, where excellence, creativity and scholarship is sacrificed at the altar of 'mass production'? Can regional imbalance be removed and socially deprived classes be uplifted simply by opening a university?

Not a single Indian university features amongst the first 300 universities ranked by Times World University Rankings – there is only one institute, IIT Mumbai, which finds place amongst 400 universities graded by it. Presently, not a single Indian university has the environment of research and scholarship for extending frontiers of knowledge and innovation, a pre-requisite for moving the society forward. All the four Indian Nobel prize winners, Hargobind Khorana, S. Chandrashekhar, Amratya Sen and Venkatraman Ramakrishna of the post-Independence era did all their scholastic work abroad. All over the world, higher education takes place in big clusters of learning which are built over long years of patience through hard and dedicated effort of teachers and students. They have big libraries, modern research labs, motivated students and highly qualified and dedicated teaching community with an atmosphere which encourages research, creativity and innovation. MIT has 3,000 faculty members and 30,000 students. It took several centuries of nurturing for Oxford and Cambridge to become the world's prime centres of knowledge-creation and scholastic excellence, inspiring scholars all over the world. To develop world class centres of learning we should have nurtured old and established universities which are presently languishing for want of funds and lack of autonomy. The existing IITs and IIMs should have been developed as centres of excellence of technical and management education, instead of converting them into factories for mass production of students, whose sole ambition is to look for a cushy, white collared, high-salaried corporate job.

Commercialization of Education

There seems to be a huge contradiction in the objective of education as professed by the Government and as practised by it on the ground. While every policy document recognizes that aim of education is quest for knowledge and production of good and enlightened citizens, recent developments indicate that educational policy is geared to produce huge manpower to meet the needs of the market. The Knowledge Commission, despite its high sounded rhetoric of ideals of education, perceives the production of manpower for the market as the main mandate of the education system. The policy of free entry of private players makes education a tradable and marketable commodity. In the process, an exploitive band of private players, mostly belonging to political or business class, with no background in education and commitment to serve the society, have entered in the domain of education. They exploit the new-found aspiration of the rising middle class, who consider a professional degree, howsoever earned, as a passport to success. Due to weakness and corruption in the regulatory bodies, they circumvent every control to maintain a basic minimum standard of education. In the process, a new education industry has emerged which is guided by the only objective of making profit.

Hundreds of capitation fee engineering, management and medical colleges have sprung up all over the country. They have poor infrastructure and lack qualified teaching faculty. They exploit the gullible parents who are prepared to put all their savings and take loans, in order to capitulate their progeny into the aspiring upwards mobile class to rise up the social ladder. The most alarming situation relates to admission in a medical college – where upwards of ₹ 50 lakh can buy you a seat. With no hospital infrastructure and a handful of semi-qualified medical professionals on the rolls to do the teaching, they produce half-baked doctors, who are in no position to treat patients, even for simple ailments, and can even pose serious health hazard to them. The regulatory agencies, such as MCI, AICTE and UGC, are riddled with corruption and many of their officers are facing CBI inquiry and unable to enforce even the minimum quality standards. As per market gossip and wide spread rumours, the then Minster for HRD in UPA I government took money to grant recognition to private institutes. An inquiry commission set up by the Ministry of HRD, UPA II government, found large number of private institutions sub-standard and took steps to derecognize them. The management of these institutions have managed to secure a stay order from the Supreme Court and they continue to run their teaching shops.

The privatization of higher education is serving the very opposite of the professed objective of inclusive education as it restricts the access of the deprived section to education. Only the rich and moneyed have finances to buy a seat in private colleges. Education has become a commodity available to the highest bidder. The overall story of private participation in higher education is sordid incompetence, corruption, nepotism and abysmally low standards. One can imagine the quality and competence of young boys and girls who come out from these colleges and on whose shoulder rests the future of the country.

Education for a Humane Society: Need to Correct the Misdirection

All the great minds of the world, in the East as well as in the West, regard education's main purpose as building character and civic virtues so that a humane and cultured society could be created. Abraham Lincoln[7] said, 'Education is not given for the purpose of earning a living; it is learning what to do with a living after you have earned it'. Will Durant[8] observed that 'education is transmission of civilization'. Education is not simply imparting knowledge, but to ignite a life-long search for knowledge with a view to enlarge mental horizon. Education is the training of the will, which enables man to make use of knowledge to benefit not only himself but the society. Unfortunately, the commercialization of education, with its emphasis on market forces, encourages baser human traits such as competition, greed and selfishness with money-making becoming the prime objective of life. Modern education with its emphasis on technical efficiency, devoid of value-orientation, may produce clever devils, devoid of social conscience and responsibility. Bertrand Russell[9] (*Impact of Science on Society*) had remarked, 'Unless men increase in wisdom as much as in knowledge, increase of knowledge will be increase in sorrow'. Historian Arnold Toynbee[10] (*Mankind and Mother Earth*), while reflecting on history of civilization, observes that while mankind has made phenomenal economic progress due to advances of technology which has vastly increased his wealth and power, 'the "morality gap" between Man's physical power of doing evil and his spiritual capacity for coping with this power has yawned wide open as the mythical jaws of Hell. During the last 5,000 years, the "widening gap" has caused mankind to inflict on itself grievous disaster.' Rabindranath Tagore underlined this dichotomy in following words of perennial wisdom (The Education Mission of Visva Bharati):

> Great civilization in the East as well as in the West have flourished in the past because they produced food for the spirit of man for all time; they tried to build their life upon the faith in ideals, the faith which is creative. These great civilizations were at last run to death by men of the type of our precocious schoolboys of modern times, smart superficially critical, worshippers of the self, shrewd bargainers in the market for profit and power, efficient in their handling of the ephemeral, who presume to buy human souls with their money and throw them into their dustbins when they have been sucked dry, and who, eventually, driven by suicidal forces of passion, set their neighbour's houses on fire and are themselves engulfed by the flame ... . It is some great ideals which create great societies of men, it is some blind passions which break them into pieces. They thrive so long as they produce food for life; they perish when they

> burn up life in insatiate gratification. We have been taught by our sages that it is truth, and not things which saves man from annihilation.[11]

It is time our policy makers and educationalists pause and reflect on the disastrous direction in which they are taking the country's education system. This trend should be reversed and the ennobling mission of education should be restored. Education should ignite the mind, develop a spirit of enquiry and create a consciousness to serve the society, to make the world a better place to live for everyone.

Notes

1. T.B. Macaulay's Minute on Education, 1834; quoted in B.N. Pandey, *A Book of India*, New Delhi: Harper Collins, 2000, p. 50.
2. Quoted by Swami Kamalananda, Swami Satyaproyananda, Br Mahan. *Education: Total Development of Personality*, Mysore: Ramakrishna Institute of Moral and Spiritual Education, 2003, pp. 5–6 (from *The Complete Works of Swami Vivekananda*, Vol. 4, Kolkata: Advaita Ashram, pp. 482–85).
3. Swami Budhananda. *Vivekananda: His Call to the Nation*, Calcutta: Advaita Ashram, 1969, pp. 50–51 (from *The Complete Works of Swami Vivekananda*, Vol. 4, Kolkata: Advaita Ashram, p. 483).
4. Cited by Henry Fagg. *A Study of Gandhi's Basic Education*, New Delhi: National Book Trust, 2002.
5. Rabindranath Tagore. 'My School', in Rabindranath Tagore, *Personality*, London: Macmillan, 1965, p. 116.
6. Government of India. *Compilation of Recommendations Regarding Education*, National Knowledge Commission, October 2008.
7. Cited by Swami Kamalananda et al., op. cit., p. 72.
8. Quoted by Swami Kamalananda et al., op. cit.
9. Ibid., p. 8.
10. Arnold Toynbee. *Mankind and Mother Earth*, London: Book Club Associates, 1976, pp. 591–92.
11. Rabindranath Tagore. 'The Education Mission of Visva-Bharati', in Rakesh Batabyal, *The Penguin Book of Modern Indian Speeches*, New Delhi: Penguin Books, 2007, pp. 742–43.

5

Regulation of Higher Education in India

B.S. GHUMAN, RANJEET SINGH
AND SOHAIL MOHAMMAD

Knowledge has emerged as a very powerful source of growth. Government of India has also recognized the kinetic power of knowledge in the development process. For thriving on the basis of knowledge, the Government of India in 2005 set up National Knowledge Commission (NKC). The Commission submitted its final report in 2009. The basic premise of the Commission is that for building knowledge society educational institutions, including higher educational institutions, play pivotal role. Higher educational institutions are fountainheads of the generation, dissemination and application of knowledge.

The Indian higher education system is very large as about 33,682 higher education institutes are in place in India which caters to the 21.8 million students enroled in them and it is also experiencing a continuous expansion (Planning Commission, 2012). Higher education sector requires an investment of ₹ 360,640 crores ($76 bn) by 2020 to create the additional capacity (Anandakrishnan, 2007). Keeping in mind the enormity of higher education sector and for tapping full potential of institutions of higher learning towards building knowledge economy, it is essential for the government to steer and regulate these institutions in the right direction. It is in this backdrop that the present paper has been conceived.

The objective of the paper is to examine the working of existing regulatory bodies in higher education and suggest remedial measures to improve the efficacy of regulatory mechanisms. The paper is divided into four parts. Part I deals with the rationale of regulation in higher education. Part II focuses on regulatory bodies covering composition and functions. Performance appraisal of select regulatory bodies is discussed in Part III, and Part IV contains concluding observations.

I
Rationale of Regulation in Higher Education

Higher education is a merit good. Therefore, it is the responsibility of the State to make provision for higher education to its citizens. There is also need for regulation of higher education in order to promote autonomy and accountability of its institutions. The task of regulation has assumed added dimension in the light of opening of higher education to private sector on a large scale. The phenomenal growth of educational institutions in the recent past has thrown up issues like corrupt practices at the time of recognition and affiliation, charging exorbitant fee including capitation fee, less qualified faculty, fragile service conditions, lack of quality infrastructure, low employability, etc. The irregularities reported relating to deemed universities and spurious recognition of engineering, management and medical institutions clearly suggest the need for effective regulation.

The contours of higher educational institutions would also change with entry of foreign players in the field of education. The government is in the process of opening of higher education to foreign educational institutions. In this regard, a bill titled, 'Foreign Educational Institutions (Regulation of Entry and Operations) Bill, 2010' is pending with the Parliament. The fast changing scenario of higher education necessitates steering the educational institutions in right direction so as to make education all inclusive and reliable engine of economic and social development.

II
Regulatory Bodies Covering Composition and Functions

In India, initially higher education was treated as a homogenous good and hence only one regulatory body, namely, the University Grants Commission was set up in 1956. Gradually higher education segmented on the basis of specialization and technical considerations. Segmentation of higher education led to the setting up of various statutory regulatory councils along with the UGC. The prominent regulatory bodies include the University Grants Commission (UGC), the All India Council of Technical Education (AICTE), Bar Council of India (BCI), Council of Architecture (COA), Indian Nursing Council (INC), Medical Council of India (MCI), National Council on Teacher Education (NCTE), Pharmacy Council of India (PCI), Distance Education Council (DEC), etc.

There is now a move for setting up of a single independent regulatory body for higher education. The path covered by higher education from single regulatory body to multiple regulatory bodies needs to be surveyed for learning lessons from the past experience and designing a sustainable regulatory body. Hence, this comprehensive analysis of selected regulatory bodies in the field of higher education is undertaken.

University Grants Commission

University Grants Commission is the first regulatory body set up for development and regulation of higher education. It is patterned on the University Grants Commission of the United Kingdom. The UGC was formally set up in November 1956 as a statutory body of the Government of India through an Act of Parliament (The UGC Act, 1956).

The mandate of the UGC is disbursing grants to the universities and colleges for the promotion of higher education across the country. It is also to coordinate, determine and maintain standards of university education in India. Other objectives of the UGC are to monitor developments in the field of collegiate and university education.

Composition and Organization

The University Grant Commission consists of 12 members, including a Chairman and Vice Chairman. The other 10 members are selected from different fields such as two officers of the central government; four serving teachers of the universities and the remaining members are drawn from the academic fields of agriculture, commerce, forestry or industry; members of the engineering, legal, medical or any other learned profession; or the Vice Chancellors of the universities.

The headquarters of UGC are located at New Delhi. It has Regional Offices, Inter University Centres and National Facilities Centres. Presently, the Commission has seven regional offices, namely, Southern Eastern Regional Office (SERO) located at Hyderabad; Western Regional Office (WRO) at Pune; Central Regional Office (CRO) at Bhopal; Northern Regional College Bureau (NRCB) at Delhi; North-Eastern Regional Office (NERO) at Guwahati; Eastern Regional Office (ERO) at Kolkata and South-Western Regional Office (SWRO) at Bangalore. The UGC has set up seven autonomous centres, with a view to provide common facilities for research and for other various services and programmes to the universities. These centres are Inter University Accelerator Centre (IUAC); Inter University centre for Astronomy and Astro-Physics (IUCAA); UGC-DAE Consortium for Scientific Research; Consortium for Education Communication (CEC); Information and Library Network (INFLIBNET); Inter University Centre for International Studies (IUC-IS) and National Assessment and Accreditation Council (NAAC).

The UGC has established four National Facilities Centres in the selected universities such as Western Regional Instrumentation Centre, Mumbai, Mumbai University; M.S.T. Radar Facilities, Sri Venkateshwar

University, Tirupati; Inter University Centre for Humanities and Social Sciences IUCHSS, Indian Institute of Advanced Study, Shimla and Crystal Growth Centre, Anna University, Chennai.

The Commission has Academic Staff Colleges (ASC) through which it organizes various courses for the teaching community in order to help them to be familiar with the latest developments in their disciplines. All over India, 45 academic staff colleges were created by the UGC offering special short-term courses for serving teachers from institutions of higher education.

Major Powers and Functions

The major function of the UGC at the time of its constitution was the allocation of grants-in-aids to the universities from the public funds. The UGC is also entrusted with the responsibility for the promotion and co-ordination of university education by determining and maintaining the standards of teaching, examination and research in universities. For this purpose, the UGC looks into the financial needs of universities, allocates and disburses funds and grants to universities and advises universities for improving the standard of education. It also advises the central and state governments on issues related to higher education and the allocation of grants to universities out of the consolidated fund of India or the consolidated fund of the state.

The other functions include regulation of fee structure through consultation with the concerned university and carrying out the inspection of the universities in regard to funding. It has the power to reject any grant to a university after its inspection.[1] Accreditation and assessment of the universities and colleges is another function of the UGC. This has been entrusted to National Accreditation and Assessment Council.

All India Council for Technical Education (AICTE)

Technical education has always been significant in the course of development of a nation. To regulate technical education, AICTE was set-up in November 1945 as a national level Apex Advisory Body. In 1987 AICTE got statutory status pursuant to the recommendations of the National Working Group constituted by Ministry of Human Resource Development, as the All India Council for Technical Education Act, 1987 was enacted and came into force w.e.f. March 28, 1988. Thus, the Statutory All India Council for Technical Education was established on May 12, 1988 and is headquartered at New Delhi.

Composition and Organization

The AICTE as an organization gives representation to every area, every Board, Council and other organizations related to or working in the field of technical education. The AICTE Act provides for the detailed composition of the Council with a total of 51 members; 34 of whom are appointed by the central government, 15 are ex-officio and two are elected members.

The appointed members by the central government include Chairman, Vice Chairman, one member to represent the Ministry of Finance, one member to represent the Ministry of Science and Technology, four members to represent the Ministries and Departments of the central government, other than Ministry of Finance and Ministry of Science and Technology, eight members to represent the states and UTs on the recommendations of the states and UTs concerned, four members to represent the organization in the field of Industry and Commerce, seven members to represent the Central Advisory Board of Education, the Association of Indian Universities, the Indian Society for Technical Education, the Council of Indian Institutes of Technology, the Pharmacy Council of India, the National Productivity Council and Council of Architecture, four member to represent the professional bodies in the field of technical education and not more than two members to represent such interests as one not covered by the foregoing clauses, as the central government may deem fit.

The ex-officio members are: the Secretary of the Union Ministry concerned with education; the Education Advisor (General) to the Government of India; the Chairman of four Regional committees and the Chairman of the Boards such as the All India Board of Vocational Education, the All India Board of Technical Education, the All India Board of Under graduate studies in Engineering and Technology, the All India Board of Post Graduate Education and Research in Engineering and Technology and the All India Board of Management and studies. The other ex-officio members are the Chairman, University Grants Commission, the Director, Institute of Applied Manpower Research, the Director-General, Indian Council of Agricultural Research and the Director-General, Council of Scientific and Industrial Research.

Two elected members are Member of Parliament, one each elected from Lok Sabha and Rajya Sabha. The Act provides the term of three years for elected and nominated members.

The Council has an Executive Committee, ten Boards of Studies, eight Regional Committees, National Board of Accreditation, eight Bureaus and eight regional offices.

The AICTE provides for the establishment of five Boards of Studies to advise the Executive Committee on academic matters relating to norms, standards, model curricula, model facilities, structure of courses, etc. The Boards of Studies are: All India Board of Vocational Education, All India Board of Technical Education, All India Board of Under-Graduate Studies in Engineering and Technology, All India Board of Post-Graduate Studies in Engineering and Technology, All India Board of Management Studies, All India Board of Hotel Management and Catering Technology, All India Board of Information Technology Education, All India Board of

Pharmaceutical Education, All India Board of Town and Country Planning and All India Board of Architecture.

The Council has eight Regional Committees covering different geographical regions, namely, Central Region, Western Region, South-Western Region, Eastern Region, North-Western Region, Northern Region, Southern Region, and Southern Central Region.

The National Board of Accreditation was set up under clause 10 (u) of the AICTE Act to periodically conduct evaluation of technical institutions on the basis of guidelines, norms and standards specified by it for quality assessment.

The AICTE comprises eight bureaus, namely, Engineering & Technology (E&T) Bureau, Management & Technology (M&T) Bureau, Quality Assurance (QA) Bureau, Planning and Coordination (PC) Bureau, Research and Institutional Development (RID) Bureau, Academic Bureau, Administration Bureau and Finance Bureau. Each bureau is headed by an Adviser/Director who is assisted by technical and other staff.

Besides this, the Council has eight Regional Offices situated in Bhopal, Bangalore, Chandigarh, Chennai, Kanpur, Kolkata, Hyderabad and Mumbai, for the efficient discharge of the Council's functions within their respective regions.

Major Powers and Functions

The Council has been entrusted with functions for ensuring coordinated and integrated development of technical and management education and maintenance of standards. The Council undertakes surveys and collects data for growth and development of technical education in the country. It allocates and disburses funds and grants to technical institutions and universities imparting technical education. Promotion of innovation, research and development in technology for over-all improvement of educational process and formulation of schemes for promoting technical education for women, handicapped and other weaker sections of the society also come within the jurisdiction of the Council's functions. The Council maintains suitable performance appraisal systems for technical institutions and universities imparting technical education, enforces accountability and build effective links between technical education systems and industry, development organizations and community. It grants approval for starting new technical institutions and for introduction of new courses or programmes in consultation with the agencies concerned. The Council carries out inspection of technical institutions and universities imparting technical education and ensures compliance of high standards.

The Council lays down norms for granting autonomy to technical education institutions and prevents commercialization of technical education. It also certifies the fitness of technical institutions at various levels to receive grants for offering courses. It advises the UGC for declaring any institution imparting technical education as a deemed university.[2]

Medical Council of India

Medical education has expanded in a big way. The number of medical colleges has increased steadily after Independence. Keeping in view the emerging needs of medical education in 1956, the old Act, i.e. Indian Medical Council Act, 1933, was repealed and the Indian Medical Council Act, 1956, was enacted, thereby establishing Medical Council of India (MCI). Its headquarters are at New Delhi.

Composition and Organization

The MCI has a total of 15 members, including eight nominated and seven elected members besides three members to represent each state; one nominated by the central government in consultation with the state government, two elected members, one to be elected from amongst the members of the medical faculty of the universities and the other one is elected from amongst themselves by persons enroled in State Medical Register. The elected members are from amongst the persons enroled on any of the State Medical Registers. The nominated members are nominated by the central government.

The President and Vice President of the Council are elected by the members of the Council from amongst themselves.

The Council works through two main committees: Executive Committee and the Postgraduate Medical Education Committee. In addition to the above mentioned committees of the Council, there are certain sub-committees to facilitate smooth functioning of the related activities within the framework of various regulations and policy decisions of the Council. The sub-committees include Migration Sub-Committee, Teacher's Eligibility Qualification Sub-Committee, Finance Sub-Committee, Ethics Sub-Committee and Continuing Medical Education Advisory Committee.

Board of Governors is the recent development in the organization of the council.

Major Powers and Functions

The main functions of the Medical Council of India include the establishment and maintenance of uniform standards for undergraduate medical education and regulation of postgraduate medical education in medical colleges accredited by it. It also recognizes medical qualifications granted by medical institutions in India and also approves recognition of foreign medical qualifications in India. The Council gives accreditation to the medical colleges and maintains directory of all registered doctors (called the Indian Medical Register) with recognized medical qualifications.[3]

National Council for Teacher Education (NCTE)

Based on the recommendation of the National Policy on Education (NPE), 1986, the National Council for Teacher Education was constituted as a statutory body under the National Council for Teacher Education Act, on August 17, 1995. The main objective of the NCTE is to achieve planned and coordinated development of the teacher education system throughout the country. The head office of NCTE is located at New Delhi.

Composition and Organization

The Council consists of a total of 28 members, 16 of whom are appointed by the central government, three are nominated members and nine are Ex-officio members. The Council has a Chairperson, a Vice Chairperson, and a Member-Secretary to be appointed by the central government. The other appointed members include 13 persons possessing experience and knowledge in the field of education or teaching, nine members to represent the states and union territory administrations, three members from amongst the teachers of primary and secondary education and teachers of recognized institutions.

The nominated members include one nominated by the Chairman of the Rajya Sabha and two by the Speaker of the Lok Sabha.

The Ex-officio members include the Secretary of the Union Ministry concerned with education, the Chairman, University Grants Commission, the Director, National Council of Educational Research and Training, the Director, National Institute of Educational Planning and Administration, the Adviser (Education), Planning Commission, the Chairman, Central Board of Secondary Education, the Financial Adviser to the Government of India in the Department dealing with Education, the Member-Secretary, All-India Council for Technical Education and the chairpersons of all Regional committees.

The organizational structure of the NCTE consists of the committees, namely Executive Committee and Regional Committees. The Executive Committee of the Council comprises Chairperson, the Vice Chairperson, the Member-Secretary and other members drawn from the Council.

The NCTE has four Regional committees namely; the Eastern Regional Committee at Bhubaneswar, the Western Regional Committee at Bhopal, the Northern Regional Committee at Jaipur and the Southern Regional Committee at Bangalore. Each Regional committee is headed by a Regional Director.

Major Powers and Functions

The NCTE is mainly concerned with the regulation and proper maintenance of norms and standards in the teacher education system. It undertakes surveys relating to various facets of teacher education and publishes the result. It makes recommendations to the central and state government, universities, University Grants Commission and recognized institutions for preparation of suitable plans and programmes in the field of teacher education. The Council has the responsibility of coordinating and monitoring teacher education and its development in the country by laying down guidelines on minimum qualification for a person to be employed as teacher. It also lays down guidelines for compliance by recognized institutions, for starting new courses, for providing physical and instructional facilities, staffing pattern and staff qualification.

The Council regulates the standards for courses of teacher education qualifications and other aspects such as criteria for admission, method of selection of candidates, duration of courses, course content, tuition fees and other fees, etc. It promotes innovation and research in teacher education system. It examines and reviews periodically the implementation of the norms, guidelines and standards laid down by it and suitably advises the recognized institutions. The Council maintains suitable performance appraisal system, norms and mechanism for enforcing accountability on recognized institutions and prevents commercialization of teacher education.[4]

Pharmacy Council of India (PCI)

The regulatory mechanism in the field of pharmacy was introduced with the passage of the Pharmacy Act, 1948 by the Parliament. The PCI was constituted on August 9, 1949 under the Pharmacy Act, 1948 as a statutory body to regulate the pharmacy education and profession in India up to graduation level. Its headquarters are at New Delhi.

Composition and Organization

The Council consists of the representatives of various organizations and teaching staff related to the field of pharmacy education. The Council has a total of 17 members, 15 of whom are elected and nominated, and two are ex-officio members. Six members elected by the UGC from amongst the teachers of the colleges imparting pharmacy education, one each from the subjects of pharmaceutical chemistry, pharmacy, pharmacology and pharmacognosy. Six members are nominated by the central government from among the persons possessing a degree or diploma in, and practicing pharmacy or pharmaceutical chemistry. Three members are from the MCI, UGC and AICTE. Another two members to represent each state, one elected by the State Council and one nominated by the state government

Besides this, the Council has two ex-officio members, i.e. the Director General of Health Services and the Director of the Central Drug

Laboratory. The Act provides for the term of five years for the nominated and elected member of the Council.

The Council consists of the Executive and other committees. The Executive Committee consists of the President of the Council, who is also the President of this Committee, and Vice President as an ex-officio member and five other members elected by the Central Council from amongst its members.

The present Council has other Committees, namely, Law Committee, Education Regulation Committee, Finance Committee, Professional Pharmacy and Public Relation Committee, PCI Committee on curbing the menace of ragging.

Major Powers and Functions

The PCI regulates various aspects of pharmacy such as prescribing minimum standard of education required for qualifying as a pharmacist, making regulation for the new institutions seeking approval for imparting pharmacy education, ensuring uniformity in implementation of educational standards in the field of pharmacy education throughout the country. One of the major functions of the Council is to carry out the inspection activities in institutes imparting pharmacy education in order to maintain the standards of pharmacy education and also punish those institutes which do not conform with the prescribed rules and regulations and standards. Another major function of the Council is to grant approval to foreign qualification.[5]

Distance Education Council (DEC)

The regulatory mechanism in the field of distance education was introduced with the passing out of the Indira Gandhi National Open University Act (IGNOU), 1985. The regulatory body was named as Distance Education Council. It was formed in order to maintain, coordinate and determine the standards of distance education in India. Its head office is at New Delhi.

Composition and Organization

The Council has a total of 16 members including the elected and nominated members. It includes the Chairman, who is the Vice Chancellor of IGNOU, and the Secretary who is the in-charge of the Education Department of MHRD. The Council has three members from UGC, i.e. a nominated member, the secretary and the Director of NAAC. The Board of Management nominates some of the Council's members; two members from amongst themselves, two heads of the institutes of distance education from other than open universities, one teacher from the distance education or from any open university. The Chairman of the Council also nominates some of the members; two Vice Chancellors of state open universities, three persons who possess expertise in Vocational/technical education, mass media/mass communication.

Major Powers and Functions

The Council maintains, determines the standards of distance education in India. The Council has the responsibility to promote excellence in distance education and also to be responsive to the major developments taking place in the field of distance education. It is also expected to facilitate the expansion of distance education through the network of open universities and distance education institutes. The Council suggests the procedure to the Board of Management for granting the financial assistance to the open universities or the distance education institutes. Another major function of the Council is the evaluation or inspection of the concerned institutes in order to ensure their conformity to standards of distance education. It also defines the procedure for admissions, fees and courses to be provided.[6]

Indian Nursing Council (INC)

Indian Nursing Council was constituted under the Indian Nursing Council Act, 1947, of the Parliament. It works as an autonomous body under the Ministry of Health and Family Welfare. The objective of the INC is to establish uniform standards of training for nurses, midwives and health visitors. Its headquarters are at New Delhi.

Composition and Organization

The Council has a total of 24 members comprising 11 elected members, four nominated and seven ex-officio members. The composition includes President and Vice President elected from among the members. The elected members are one each from bodies such as Medical Council of India, Central Council of the Indian Medical Association and the Council of the Trained Nurses Association of India. Two members are elected by the heads of the institutes imparting training in nursing and one member from the institutes in which health visitors are trained. It also includes one nurse from among the nurses registered under the State Council and one midwife or auxiliary nurse-midwife enroled in a State register (elected by each of the State Councils in the four groups of the states devised by INC, each group of States being taken in rotation). Three members are elected by the Parliament, two by the House of the People and the other by the Council of States from amongst their members.

The nominated members are nominated by the central government at least two from amongst the nurses, midwives and nurses enroled in State register another one being an experienced educationalist.

The ex-officio members include; the Director General of Health Services; the Chief Principal Matron, Medical Directorate, General

Headquarters; the Chief Nursing Superintendent, office of the Director-General of Health Services; the Director of Maternity and Child Welfare, Indian Red Cross Society; the Chief Administrative Medical Officer of each State other than a Union territory; the Superintendent of Nursing Services (from each of the States in the two groups described by the Council, each group of States being taken in rotation).

The Act provides for the term of Five Years for the nominated and elected members of the Council.

The Act also provides for the constitution of Executive Committee formed from among the members of INC. There are such other committees as the Nursing Education Committee and Equivalence Committee specifically formed for regulating the issues concerned mainly with nursing education and the issues of recognition of foreign qualifications.

Major Powers and Functions

The Council recognizes the qualifications for the purpose of employment in India and abroad in the field of nursing. It gives approval for registration of Indian and Foreign Nurses possessing foreign qualification. The Council is also responsible for prescribing the syllabus and for regulation of the nursing programmes. The Council is authorized to disapprove those institutes which fail to maintain the prescribed standards of nursing education. It also advises the State Nursing Councils, Examining Boards, State Governments and central government on various issues of importance concerning Nursing Education in the Country.[7]

Council of Architecture (CoA)

The COA is a body corporate established under the Architects Act, 1972, of Government of India, which came into force on September 1, 1972. The COA is responsible to regulate the education and profession of architecture throughout India. The CoA operates from New Delhi.

Composition and Organization

The Council consists of total 21 members, including President, Vice President, 10 elected members, six nominated and three ex-officio members, besides one member nominated by each state government in order to represent each state. The elected members include five architects possessing recognized qualification elected by the Indian Institute of Architecture from among its members and five persons elected from among themselves by heads of architectural institutions in India imparting full time instructions for architectural qualification. The nominated members include two persons nominated by AICTE, one nominated by central government, two nominated from the members of the Institute of Engineers and one nominated from among the members of the Institute of

Surveyors of India. The ex-officio members are the Chief Architect in Central Government's Ministries of Defence and Railways and head of the architectural organization in the Central Public Works Department.

The President and the Vice President are selected from among the members of the Council. All the nominated and elected members hold office for the term of three years.

The Council has the provision of the Executive Committee to discharge such functions as prescribed by the Council. The President and the Vice President of the Council are the ex-officio members of the Committee and other five members are selected from amongst the members of the Council. The Council has also three sub-committees namely, Admission Committee, Board of Undergraduate Education and Board of Postgraduate Education.

Major Powers and Functions

The Council advises the central government on recognition of architectural qualifications granted by any authority in India. The Council carries out the inspection of the institutes imparting architectural education, through the Executive Committee as also the inspectors appointed by the Executive Committee, for recommending to the central government to recognize the architectural qualifications granted by a college or an institution. It reviews whether the courses of study, examination, proficiency required from the candidates, staff, equipment, accommodation, training and other facilities provided by the institutes conform to the prescribed standards. The council also prescribes minimum standards of architectural education required for granting recognized qualification by the institutes in India and it also prescribes standards of professional conduct and etiquette and code of ethics for architects. The Council maintains the register of architects in India.[8]

Bar Council of India (BCI)

The Bar Council of India is a statutory body constituted under the Advocate Act, 1961, in order to regulate and represent the Indian Bar. The objective of the BCI is to regulate the standards of legal education in India and it also recognizes universities which provide degree in legal education. The BCI is headquartered at New Delhi.

Composition and Organization

The Advocate Act provides for the composition of the Council. The Council has a Chairman and a Vice Chairman. To represent each state, every State Council elects one member from amongst themselves for the BCI. The Council has the Attorney-General of India and Solicitor-General of India as ex-officio members.

The Advocate Act provides for the committees such as Legal Education Committee, Executive Committee and Disciplinary Committee. The Act also authorizes the Council to form such committees as may help in carrying out its functions. The members of these committees are elected from among the members of the BCI. The Council is authorized to delegate the necessary powers, duties and functions to these committees. The present Council has committees such as Executive Committee, Legal Education Committee, Disciplinary Committee, Advocate Welfare Committee, Legal Aid Committee, Building Committee and Rules Committee.

Major Powers and Functions

Functions of the BCI are: to lay down the standards of professional conduct for advocates, to safeguard the rights, privileges and interests of advocates, to promote and support law reforms. The BCI exercises control over State Bar Councils and also disposes matters which are referred to it by the State Bar Councils.

The BCI promotes legal education and lays down standards of legal education in consultation with the universities imparting legal education in India. It provides recognition to universities whose degree in law is acceptable for enrolment as an advocate under the Indian Bar. It also visits and inspects the universities or directs the SBCs to do so.

In order to promote legal education, BCI conducts seminars and organizes talks by eminent jurists and publishes journals and papers of legal interest. It also provides recognition to foreign qualifications in law for the purpose of admission as an advocate. The other functions include organizing legal aid to the poor, managing and investing the funds and conducting the election of its members.[9]

III
Performance Appraisal of Select Regulatory Bodies

The detailed account of the composition, organization and functions of the regulatory bodies in higher education provides a basis for assessment of the working of these regulatory bodies. As discussed earlier, regulation is necessary in higher education to (i) maintain standards of education, (ii) ensure quality of teaching and research, (iii) regulate fee and aspects of higher education. Regulation becomes all the more necessary in the light of commercialization, privatization and globalization of higher education. Sector specific regulatory bodies are conceived with an idea of providing focused attention on general and specialized areas of disciplines. Here we discuss the assessment of some of the regulatory bodies in the field of higher education.

University Grants Commission

The UGC is the first regulatory body set up for development and regulation of higher education. Its performance appraisal is as under:

Recognition to New Universities and Colleges

The UGC accords recognition to the newly set up universities and colleges. At the time of Independence there were 20 universities and 500 colleges recognized by the UGC in India. After Independence, the UGC accorded recognition to 639 universities/other degree awarding institutions and 32,523 colleges with a total strength of 21.59 million students.

Disbursement of Grants

One of the major functions of the UGC is allocation of grants to the universities. During year 2010–11, the UGC granted ₹ 4391.77crores as plan grants, out of which 44.96 per cent was allocated to central universities, 18.95 per cent to state universities and 7.30 per cent to colleges of state universities and 2.27 per cent to deemed universities. In the same year, non-plan grant to the tune of ₹ 3896.80 crores was released by the UGC, out of which 67.10 per cent was allocated to central universities, 24.46 per cent to colleges of Delhi and Banaras Hindu University and 5.24 per cent to deemed universities. During year 2010–11, there were 42 central universities out of which 38 universities were provided plan and non-plan grant. Out of 345 state and state private universities, only 137 state universities, excluding agricultural and medical universities, received Plan (Development) Grants. In the same year, a sum of ₹ 29.75 crores was paid to 12 state universities which were not covered by the UGC development grant earlier due to lack of infrastructure and other facilities so as to make them eligible to receive regular development grants from the UGC. The UGC also provided development grant to 24 deemed universities. Development and maintenance grant was given to 10 deemed universities. There are 33,023 colleges in India out of which only 7,802 colleges were recognized till march 2011. The UGC released grants for 6,417 eligible colleges out of 7,802 recognized colleges received grants under College Development Scheme of XI Plan.

Promotion of Standards of Teaching

For promoting standards of teaching, the UGC has been regulating the qualifications for recruitment, promotion, pay scales and service conditions of teachers in universities and colleges. The latest UGC regulation on Minimum Qualifications for Appointment of Teachers and Other Academic Staff in Universities and Colleges and Measures for the Maintenance of Standards in Higher Education was notified on September 16, 2010. This notification was based upon the recommendations of Prof. G.K. Chadha Pay Review Committee in the Backdrop of Sixth Pay Commission of India.

For ensuring minimum standards for entrants in the field of teaching as career, National Eligibility Test (NET) is conducted twice in a year by the

UGC and on its basis, it awards scholarship for pursuing research. Similarly, the UGC has granted accreditation to states for conducting State Eligibility Test for minimum eligibility of candidates to apply for the post of lecturer/Assistant Professor in universities/colleges of respective states.

There are 66 Academic Staff Colleges offering orientation programmes, refresher courses and short-term courses. In year 2010–11, around 320 orientation programmes, 710 refresher courses and 260 short-term courses had been conducted by the UGC, thereby benefitting 40,000 teachers.

The UGC also prepares model curricula for the adaptation of various universities and colleges. The UGC has prepared model curricula for 38 disciplines.

The UGC also appoints it observers for selection process and promotion to the post of professor from reader/associate professor under Career Advancement Scheme (CAS) in all recognized universities. During 2010–11, the UGC has appointed 158 observers for the said purpose. In the revised guidelines, the institution of observers have been abolished.

The UGC is actively engaged in bilateral exchange programme in higher education with 44 countries.

Promotion of Standards of Research

For the promotion of standards in research, the UGC has adopted various approaches such as granting status of 'University with Potential for Excellence', 'Innovative Universities', 'Centres with Potential for Excellence', 'College with Potential for Excellence'. Special assistance Programme (SAP) is another tool for achieving excellence in research in university departments by financially supporting them. For promotion of research, the UGC has scheme of research projects for teachers.

Table 1

Promotion of Standards in Research

S. No.	*Scheme*	*Year*	*Number*	*Funds Allocated (₹)*
1.	University with Potential for Excellence	2007–12	6 Universities	50 crore to each
2.	Centres with Potential for Excellence	2007–12	12 Centres	Not Available
3.	College with Potential for Excellence	2007–12	302	28.47 crore
4.	Innovative Universities	2012–17	Proposals are being processed	
5.	Special Assistance Programme (SAP)	2007–12	745 Departments	49.20 crore
6.	Research Projects for Teachers	2010–11	5,937 Projects	Not Available

Source: University Grants Commission (UGC), Annual Report 2010–11.

For status of 'University with Potential for Excellence', each university is provided ₹ 30 crore in a plan. During the Ninth Five Year Plan five universities were granted this status and in Tenth Plan, four more such universities and in Eleventh Plan six more universities were granted this status with a grant of ₹ 50 crore each. During Eleventh Plan, the UGC approved 12 centres for status of 'Centres with Potential for Excellence' in various universities with an objective to facilitate the chosen departments to work cohesively and to launch new innovative research programmes. Proposal for granting this status to 25 more centres is in the pipeline. Under 'College with Potential for Excellence', till March 2011, 302 colleges were conferred this status and a grant of ₹ 28.47 crores have been released to the said colleges. Also, 371 colleges spread over 69 universities of 19 states were granted with status of autonomous college and the UGC regional offices released grants to the tune of ₹ 17.19 crores to 139 autonomous colleges during 2010–11.

Special Assistance Programme (SAP) is another tool for achieving excellence in research in university departments of Science, Engineering and Technology, Humanities and Social Science by financially supporting them. In March 2011, there were 745 SAP supported departments and these were provided financial assistance to the tune of ₹ 49.20 crores. The UGC provides assistance to approved departments to promote innovative and specialized courses in inter-disciplinary and emerging areas. Till March 2011, there are 53 departments identified for said purpose and a grant of ₹ 11.64 crores was released to 23 such departments.

For promoting excellence, UGC has scheme or research projects for teachers. In year 2010–11, 1,636 new major projects and 4,301 minor research projects were approved by the UGC and its regional offices, respectively. For promoting quality research at M.Phil and PhD levels, Enhancing Faculty Resources of Universities (ENCORE) scheme helps in gaining the support of professionals and experts outside the university. There are 706 positions for adjunct faculty and 512 scholars in residence. During 2010–11, a sum of ₹ 37.80 lakh was released for payment to faculty and scholars in various approved universities. The UGC also conducts accreditation exercise through National Assessment and Accreditation Council (NAAC). Till March 2011, 161 universities and 4,371 colleges had been accreditated by NAAC.

Governance Deficiencies

The entry process of new institutions is very cumbersome, prone to manipulations and, thus, has adversely affected standards of teaching, research and examination. Also, the process of setting up new universities through parliamentary legislation makes universities bulky structures. Universities keep on expanding by taking new colleges, whereas need is to set up a new university to administer the colleges in its vicinity (Mitra and Singh, 2008).

There had been mushrooming of deemed and private universities in the recent past. From 1956 to 1990, there were only 29 institutions which were granted deemed university status, whereas in last 15 years, 63 institutes were granted deemed university status (Government of India, 2008). Similarly, the number of private universities has grown phenomenally. This expansion is not coupled with standards of quality in higher education (*The Tribune*, 2012a, 2012b). Tandon Committee Report highlighted that out of 126 deemed universities, 44 had poor infrastructural facilities and their status should be withdrawn. Amongst these 44 institutes, 41 were private owned and three were government owned institutes (Government of India, 2009b). Regulators here were unable to inhibit the profit maximization tendencies of private institutes and to force quality norms so that interests of students could have been protected and accountability ensured by delivering quality education.

Comptroller and Auditor General of India (CAGI) also highlighted that four institutes, namely, Institute of Chartered Financial Analysts of India (ICFAI) in Hyderabad, Manav Rachana International University (MRIU) in Faridabad, Nehru Gram Bharati Vishwavidyalaya (NGBV) in Allahabad and Modi Institute of Education and Research (MIER) in Rajasthan were conferred 'confirmed deemed university' status against the recommendation of 'provisional deemed university' status by expert committees. AICTE informed to the UGC that ICFAI was imparting technical education without its approval (*The Tribune*, 2010). This case highlights the overlapping role of two regulatory bodies, namely UGC and AICTE as well as weak coordination between the regulatory bodies. In UGC, the decision-making process is time consuming particularly relating to the process and approval of various flagship programmes like University with Potential for Excellence, College with Potential for Excellence, Special Assistance Programme, etc. The process of release of funds is also lengthier and most of funds are released at the fag end of financial year. In case of Five-Year Plans also funds are released initially on ad-hoc basis and finally after the visits of committees almost in the middle of the Five Year Plan. Some of the funds are released almost at the end of Five-Year Plan.

Further, the funding pattern is skewed. Major share of the funds is allocated to central universities. The disbursement of funds is unfavourable to state and private universities and colleges. As observed earlier during the year 2011, out of total grant of ₹ 4391.77crores, 44.96 per cent was allocated to central universities, 18.95 per cent to state universities and 7.30 per cent to colleges of state universities and 2.27 per cent to deemed universities. Out of 345 universities, only 137 were funded by the UGC in year 2011 and out of 130 deemed universities, only 24 were funded by the UGC. Out of 7802 recognized colleges, 6,417 colleges were released funds. Also, the UGC had identified six new centres to promote inter-disciplinary research in 2010–11 and grants were released to only two centres. The UGC had identified 53 departments for promoting innovative and specialized courses in emerging areas in 2010–11, whereas it had released funds for 23 such identified departments. Notwithstanding a couple of governance deficiencies, the UGC on the whole has made a commendable contribution towards the promotion of higher education in India. Yashpal Committee has succinctly captured the role of the UGC by opining, 'Only a few organizations such as the UGC took major initiatives in fostering educational innovations such as setting up of inter-university centres to facilitate national synergy in research efforts among universities and to optimize the investments in sophisticated research infrastructure. The creation of country-wide educational communication facility through multiple platforms and creating large-scale contents; the setting up of national network of libraries, including e-journals, for convenient access to higher educational institutions across the country; special incentives to advanced centres of research; and additional resources to institutions with potential for excellence were some of the other initiatives of the UGC in the recent past. However, the initiatives occurred randomly with no sustainable goals for further multiplication' (Government of India, 2008).

All India Council for Technical Education

The AICTE regulates technical education. The performance appraisal of the AICTE is as under:

Recognition to Institutes of Technical Education

It has been effective in providing approval to new institutes by inspecting them. In 2011–12, the Council approved 642 new institutes of technical education; out which 154 institutes were at postgraduate level, 365 were at undergraduate level and 123 were at diploma level (Table 2).

Table 2

New Institutions Accorded Sanction in 2011–2012

S.No.	*Programme*	*Post Graduate Level*	*Undergraduate Level*	*Diploma Level*
1.	Engineering/Technology	—	331	120
2.	Management	124	—	—
3.	Master in Computer Application	30	—	—
4.	Pharmacy	—	23	3
5.	Hotel Management and Catering Technology (HMCT)	—	03	—
6.	Architecture and Town Planning	—	08	—
7.	Applied Arts and Crafts	—	—	—
8.	Total	154	365	123

Source: All India Council for Technical Education (AICTE), *Annual Report 2011–12*.

Till March 2012, the AICTE has approved total 4,592 technical institutions with sanctioned intake capacity to the tune of 16,03,012 students (Table 3).

Table 3

Total Number of Institutions and Intake Capacity

Discipline	*Programme/Institutions*	*Intake Capacity*
Engineering/Technology	3,346	14,73,727
HMCT	84	6,731
Pharmacy	1,065	1,15,437
Architecture	85	6,269
Applied Arts and Crafts	12	848
Total	4,592	16,03,012

Source: All India Council for Technical Education (AICTE), *Annual Report 2011–12.*

Disbursement of Funds

The AICTE receives grants-in-aid from the Ministry of Human Resource Development. The AICTE in 2011–12 received ₹ 230 crores for its various schemes under Plan Grant. Under Non Plan grant AICTE received nil amount, as there was ₹ 31862.95 lakh as unspent balance of the previous Financial Year (2010–11).

In 2010–11, the funding pattern as provided in the annual report of the Council shows that the AICTE spent ₹ 267.78 crore as its Plan Grant on career awards, emeritus fellowship, Entrepreneurship and Management Programme, Modernization and Removal of Obsolescence (MODROB), visiting professorship, PG course and research work, Research Promotional Scheme (RPS), Staff Development Programme (SDP) and seminar grant.

Under Non Plan Grant in 2010–11, the AICTE spent ₹ 61.91 crores for National Tech. Manpower Info System (NTMIS), Quality Improvement Programme (QIP), AICTE Headquarters and Regional Committee.

Promotion of Standards of Teaching

The AICTE undertakes various activities and schemes under its Faculty Development Programme in order to enhance the quality of teaching in technical education. In year 2010–11, the AICTE undertook 875 schemes for Faculty Development Programme (Table 4).

Table 4

Schemes under Faculty Development Programme (2010–11)

S.No.	*Scheme*	*Numbers*
1.	Quality Improvement Programme (QIP)	327
2.	Career Award for Young Teachers	12
3.	Emeritus Fellowship	14
4.	AICTE [Indian National Academy of Engineering (INAE)]	NIL
5.	Seminar Grant	206
6.	Travel Grant	78
7.	Staff Development Programme	238
8.	Total	875

Source: All India Council for Technical Education (AICTE), *Annual Report 2011–12*.

Promotion of Standards of Research

For promoting innovations in research and development, the Council operates three schemes, namely, Modernization and Removal of Obsolescence (MODROBS), Research Promotion Scheme (RPS) and Nationally Coordinated Projects (NCP). The details of funds spent on these three schemes by the Council in the year 2010–11 are provided in Table 5.

Table 5

Schemes of AICTE to Support Research and Development

S.No.	*Scheme*	*No. of Proposals Received in 2011–12*	*No. of Proposals Sanctioned in 2011–12*	*Amount (in Crores)*
1.	Modernization and Removal of Obsolescence (MODROBS)	3,962	536	49.65
2.	Research Promotion Scheme (RPS)	2,797	394	41.80
3.	Research Promotion Scheme (RPS)	38	5	Funding limit is 5–30 lakh for each proposal

Source: All India Council for Technical Education (AICTE), *Annual Report 2011–12*.

The AICTE has been effective in checking corruption and other malpractices by institutes for maintaining academic standards by withdrawing their recognition. In 2012, it cancelled recognition of five engineering colleges affiliated to Rajasthan Technical University (*The Times of India*, 2012a).

On the other hand, the Comptroller Auditor General of India (CAGI) reported that 171 institutes audited by it failed on one or other pre-requisites of the AICTE. The CAGI further reported that more than 50 per cent of these institutes had no proper library facilities and other deficiencies being inadequate classroom size and absence of basic facilities (*The Economic Times*, 2003).

It is interesting to note that the AICTE has approved institutions with doubtful antecedents and, on the other hand, it has not recognized some of the premier institutes such as Indian School of Business (ISB), Hyderabad (*The Economic Times*, 2008).

Medical Council of India

The MCI is a regulatory body, which looks after the maintenance of standards of medical education and inspects the medical educational institutes. In 2009–10, MCI conducted 423 inspections for approval of starting various postgraduate medical qualifications, 338 inspections for increase of seats in various courses and 81 inspections for compliance verification for recognition. The MCI regularly updates Indian Medical Register on annual basis by compiling data from various State Medical Councils.

The Council for maintaining ethical standards has constituted the Ethics Committee. In 2011, the Council received 769 matters related to unethical conduct out of which 254 have been referred to the concerned State Councils/authorities for necessary action, 21 complaints have been sent for comments and 494 complaints have been disposed.

The MCI is under scan on account of relaxing norms in favour of private colleges (*The Times of India*, 2012b). Also, the Council members were involved in corrupt practices. The MCI was dissolved by the President of India on May 15, 2010 following the arrest of MCI's President by the CBI. The MCI's President, in collusion with a middleman and two doctors, accepted bribe to permit a medical college to recruit a fresh batch of students without having adequate infrastructure (*The Times of India*, 2010).

In brief, in India presence of numerous regulatory institutions has made higher education 'over regulated and under governed'. Multiplicity of regulatory bodies often leads to over lapping of functions amongst them and sometimes these bodies are at loggerheads with each other fighting legal battles (Government of India, 2008).

A highly over-regulated system consists of interference by multiple agencies which hamper innovation and creativity, increase inefficiency and breed corruption. On the other hand, under-regulated system encourages exploitation and jeopardizes public interest. Therefore, it is important to design a balanced and all encompassing regulatory mechanism that is overarching, transparent and ensures accountability.

There is wide consensus emerging for setting up an umbrella regulator namely, National Commission for Higher Education and Research (NCHER) for higher education encompassing the powers vested currently in multiple agencies for regulating higher education (Government of India, 2008, 2009.

Rationale for National Commission for Higher Education and Research

The National Knowledge Commission's reports and that of Yashpal Committee have, on the one hand, criticized the existing system of regulation and on the other hand provided convincing and strong arguments for setting up of one National Commission for Higher Education and Research. The NKC has termed it as Independent Regulatory Authority for Higher Education (IRAHE). The pendulum of regulatory mechanism in higher education in India has swung back and forth, from being single regulator, namely, UGC, then to area specific regulators such as AICTE, UGC, NCTE, etc. and back to single or umbrella regulator in the form of IRAHE. In order to bring the aforesaid reforms, the Government of India has tabled a bill titled the Higher Education and Research Bill, 2011, in Rajya Sabha for setting apex regulatory body on the lines of IRAHE and renamed it as National Commission for Higher Education and Research.

National Commission for Higher Education and Research (NCHER)

The proposed Bill, i.e. Higher Education and Research Bill, 2011, provides for the Composition, Organization and Functions of the National Commission for Higher Education and Research as follows:

Composition of NCHER

The Commission shall consists of a Chairperson; three full-time members; three part-time members and one ex-officio member, who is a member of the National Commission for Human Resource for Health under the Ministry of Health and Family Welfare.

The members of the Commission shall be appointed by the President on the recommendation of Selection Committee, which shall comprise the Prime Minister as a Chairperson of the Committee. The other members are the Speaker of Lok Sabha, and the Leader of Opposition in Lok Sabha, the Minister in-charge of Higher Education and also that of Medical Education in the Government of India.

The Bill provides for the term of five years for all the members except ex-officio member or till they attain the age of 70 years, whichever is earlier.

Organization of NCHER

The Commission shall consist of General Council and Collegium of Scholars. The General Council shall consist of all the members of NCHER and the Chairperson of the Commission shall chair its meetings. Other members shall be the Chairperson or Vice Chairperson of State Education Councils to represent each state, members from the different academic organization, institutes and fields in order to represent the interest of all the concerned fields in the higher education system. The General Council will work as an advisory body and suggest the Commission on important issues related to the field of higher education namely access, equity, research and educational reforms.

The Collegium of Scholars shall consist of 30 fellows who possess integrity and eminence in the field of higher education and research. It will recommend and advise the Commission on important issues related to major developments in the field of higher education, in the selection of Chairperson and members of the Commission and also assess the performance of the commission.

Functions and Powers of the NCHER

The Commission shall perform functions to promote higher education and research. The Commission shall promote the autonomy of higher education institutes and also the accountability of regulatory mechanism. The Commission shall look after to develop curriculum in complementarity with new fields of knowledge and to provide conducive environment for flexible academic framework for self-development, entrepreneurship and skill acquisition of students. The Commission shall also strive for synergic relationship of research in higher educational institutions and other agencies and laboratories. To develop coordination between institutions of higher learning and industry for their mutual benefit and also of the society shall also be one of the areas of Commission's regulation.

The Commission shall prescribe norm and standards of academic quality for accreditation of higher educational institutes, affiliation of colleges by universities, warding any degree and enroling students in any course by institutes of higher learning. It will also regulate the entry and operation of foreign educational institutions and prescribes the mechanism through which the transparency, efficiency and accountability can be ensured in the governing system of universities. The Commission shall facilitate mobility of students from vocational education courses to general higher education. It shall also specify mechanisms for social audit of its process and also gather public feedback regarding its performance and achievements so as to promote accountability. It shall specify and coordinate standards for the leadership positions of higher education institutes such as the appointment of V Cs. It shall also be the duty of the Commission to specify the norms for the allocation of grants to the institutions of higher education for the maintenance, development and research.

The Commission shall render its advice to governments concerned and professional bodies on policies relating to the field of higher education and research. It shall, with the approval of Central government, establish inter-university centres to boost research in emerging areas of knowledge. It shall assess future knowledge manpower requirement in the various fields of higher education for meeting the needs of economy.

The Commission shall maintain the directory of academics for the leadership positions in the higher education institutes for the purpose of fulfilling the leadership positions. Finally, the Commission shall prepare the annual report on the status of higher education and research in India and provide the details of the activities of the Commission to be submitted to the President with recommendations (Rajya Sabha, 2012).

IV
Concluding Observations

The multiplicity of the regulatory bodies has been one of the reasons because of which the higher education sector is over regulated and undergoverned. The multiple regulatory bodies are also becoming a deterrent to the growth of quality higher education. The breeding corruption in the regulatory bodies, the misuse of the affiliation and recognition powers in approving substandard institutes, misuse of the deemed university status and their failure in maintaining the academic standards of higher education institutes are among the other reasons which provide a genuine reason to rethink the regulatory mechanism of higher education in India. Keeping in mind the contingent needs of higher education sector, an umbrella regulator namely National Council of Higher Education and Research (NCHER) is proposed. The passage of NCHER Bill in the Indian Parliament will help in rejuvenation of higher education and improving its quality.

Notes

1. Retrieved from: http://www.ugc.ac.in/orgn/commission, last accessed on July 12, 2012.
2. Retrieved from: http://www.aicte-india.org.in., last accessed on July 12, 2012.

3. Retrieved from: http://www.mciindia.org.in., last accessed on July 12, 2012.
4. Retrieved from: www.ncte.India.org.in., last accessed on July 15, 2012.
5. Retrieved from: www.pci.nic.in., last accessed on July 13, 2012.
6. Retrieved from: www.dec.ac.in., last accessed on July 13, 2012.
7. Retrieved from: http://www.indiannursingcouncil.org.in., last accessed on July 13, 2012.
8. Retrieved from: www.coa.gov.in., last accessed on July 15, 2012.
9. Retrieved from: www.barcounciloflndia.org.in., last accessed on July 15, 2012.

References

Abbott, Malcolm. 2005. 'An Economic Analysis of the Formal Regulation of Higher Education'. Occasional Paper No. 6, School of International Studies AIS St Helens, New Zealand.

All India Council for Technical Education. 2012. *Annual Report 2011–12*. New Delhi, retrieved from: http://www.aicteindia.org/downloads/annual_report_11_12.pdf#toolbar=0, accessed on 15 April 2013.

Anandakrishnan, M. 2007. 'A New Approach to Regulation of Higher Education'. Global Conference on Innovation for Quality and Relevance, FICCI, New Delhi.

Government of India. 2008. *Report of the Committee to Advise on Renovation and Rejuvenation of Higher Education*. Department of Higher Education, Ministry of Human Resource Development, New Delhi, March 1.

——. 2009a. *Report to the Nation 2006–2009*. National Knowledge Commission, New Delhi, March.

——. 2009b. *Report of the Committee for Review of Existing Institutions Deemed to be Universities*. Department of Higher Education, Ministry of Human Resource Development, New Delhi, October 19.

——. 2011. *Report of the Working Group on Higher Education for the Twelfth Five Year Plan*. Department of Higher Education, Ministry of Human Resource Development, New Delhi.

Mitra, Siddhartha and Vijay Vir Singh. 2008. 'Regulation of Higher Education in India'. Discussion Papers No. 1, CUTS Centre for Competition, Investment and Economic Regulation, Jaipur.

Planning Commission. 2012. *Twelfth Five Year Plan 2012–17, Volume 3: Social Sectors*. New Delhi.

Rajya Sabha. 2012. 'The Higher Education and Research Bill, 2011'. Bill No. LX of 2011, Ministry of Human Resource Development, Government of India.

The Economic Times. 2003. 'New Engineering Colleges Fail to Meet NICTE Norms'. New Delhi, May 25.

——. 2008. 'AICTE Comes Under Government Scrutiny'. New Delhi, January 31.

The Tribune. 2010. 'UGC Gets CAG Rap for Doling Out Deemed Tags: Recommendations of Expert Panel, State Government Ignored in Many Cases'. New Delhi, May 8.

——. 2012a. 'UGC has Failed to Deliver'. Letter to the Editor, December 21.

——. 2012b. 'Varsities Unfair Means: Private Set-ups Need Strict Regulation'. Editorial, December 15.

The Times of India. 2007. 'Panel for Closure of Teacher's Body'. New Delhi, May 27.

——. 2010. 'President Pratibha Patil Dissolves Medical Council of India'. New Delhi, May 15.

——. 2012a. 'AICTE Cancels Nod to 5 Engineering Colleges'. New Delhi, April 21.

——. 2012b. 'Medical Council of India Not Very Strict in Holding the Recognition Inspection'. New Delhi, June 14.

University Grants Commission. 2011. *Annual Report 2010–11*. New Delhi, retrieved from: http://www.ugc.ac.in/oldpdf/pub/annualreport/annualreport_0910.pdf, accessed on 15 April 2013.

Part II

Technical and Professional Education

6

Quality of India's Workforce

Education Holds the Key

G.K. CHADHA

Recent Growth Profile

In recent years, the Indian economy has put up a remarkable growth performance for which it has become the centre of global attention. Table 1 gives sector-wise distribution and growth profile of India's GDP since 1950–51. Many important developments need to be underlined. First, the over-dependence on the primary sector has witnessed a steep decline; no more than 16–17 per cent of India's GDP now originates in the primary sector. The share of the secondary and the tertiary sectors in GDP has been steadily increasing over time. India is no more an agrarian economy. Second, the rate of growth of GDP has been rising consistently, and impressively, from about 3.5 per cent during the fifties, the sixties and the seventies to 5.5 per cent during the eighties, and now, to a high of 8.5–9 per cent. It is this high growth rate that has put India in the league of the fastest growing economies of the world. Third, the steadily rising GDP growth rate has been contributed by similar growth performance of the tertiary and the secondary sectors. The low and highly fluctuating growth rate in the primary sector is still a matter of concern, and points, *inter alia*, towards weaknesses in rural infrastructure, most ostensibly, the sluggish pace of irrigation expansion, on the one hand, and the state of utter disrepair of rural roads, and lack of rural connectivity, on the other.

Fourth, the steep decline in the primary sector's share in GDP has not been accompanied by a commensurate decline in the primary sector's share in workforce. This suggests that the steadily improving growth regimes have been exasperating inter-sector income inequalities. This does not, however, detract from the fact that, even in the midst of the rising income inequalities, every segment of the society has witnessed, in absolute terms, some improvement in its economic standing. That a change in the consumption basket, most discernibly a varying degree of shift from food to non-food items in general, and from cereals to non-cereals within the group of food items in particular, has been occurring steadily during the past four decades, for all categories of households, lends adequate support to our point (Chadha, 2007, pp. 11–12; Government of India, 2005, pp. 66–69).

Fifth, the steadily improving rate of growth of per capita income has been yet another strong point of India's growth experience. The substantial mark-up since 1980–81, more spectacularly during the 2000s, compared with the earlier decades, is an outstanding achievement which has very few historical parallels, including India's own growth performance during the past one hundred years or so.[1] It is this fast rate of growth of real per capita income that provides convincing explanation for the fast expanding domestic market, heavily supported by the expanding size of the middle and upper-middle classes in the Indian society, irrespective of the growing income inequalities across sectors and persons. The implications for infrastructure expansion and upgradation need hardly to be emphasized.

Sixth, its steadily improving growth profile has brought India to the centre stage of international investment. India is becoming a popular destination for foreign investment. Multinational companies are flocking in; so are foreign technology, management practices and marketing acumen. Again, India is becoming a big work site for global workforce in whose reckoning, time and speed command the highest premium. Also, Indian capitalism is 'maturing' and expanding its investment vision to foreign destinations; the list of 'Indian multinationals' is expanding every day. We have already become world-class players in many branches of manufacturing and services; automobiles and parts, textiles, pharmaceuticals, steel, etc. besides our world-wide lead in the ICT sector and a fairly high standing in other scientific explorations and technological advances, are the well-known examples. Hardly surprising, therefore, the international community has started regarding India (and China) as a leading player in the future world economic order. The world community and development institutions strongly believe that, backed by a highly creditable growth record, a strong science and technology base, and capability of throwing up innovative solutions to problems of sustainable development, trade and finance for development, India has already cultivated for itself a fairly high economic standing among the developing economies. For nursing this standing to further heights, substantial quantitative and qualitative improvements would be inevitable on the infrastructure front, including human infrastructure. We cannot have 'tasty chips' without 'healthy potatoes'.

India in Global Reckoning

Because of the remarkable growth performance put up by the Indian economy in recent years, and the potential that the world at large foresees for further ascendency of India's economy on the global stage, it has already become a part of global development debate (Chadha, 2010, pp. 6–7; Mittal, 2011, p. 11). It is now acknowledged, world-wide, that India's national income and per capita income have been growing very fast; India is now in the league of the fastest growing economies of the world.[2] The structure of the Indian economy has been undergoing a sweeping transformation; it is no more an agrarian economy. The annual rates of savings and investment have scaled unprecedented heights; India is fast catching up with China. India is now an open economy with free inward and outward movement of goods and services; export of services is now a very strong part of India's external trade. India's share of world trade in merchandise is rising steadily; of services, it is rising much faster. It is becoming an attractive destination for foreign direct investment; the FDI inflows and technological hook-ups have increased manifold in recent years. India has demonstrated a fairly creditable, and domestically highly manageable, track record of foreign debt management; external debt to GDP ratio, or debt services to current receipts ratio, or short-term external debt to foreign currency assets ratio, have all been declining steadily in recent years (Government of India, 2008, pp. 135–38). Indian capitalism is 'maturing' and expanding its investment vision to foreign destinations; the list of 'Indian multinationals' is expanding every day. That the Indian economy is fast developing indigenous shock-absorbing capabilities, in league with China and some other countries, was apparent when, during the recent 2008 and 2009 financial crises encompassing a large part of the world economy, GDP growth rate came tumbling down, rather precipitously, in country after country, but in India it suffered just a marginal setback (Table 1).

Going by outside perceptions, we have already become world-class players in many branches of manufacturing and services; automobiles and parts, textiles, pharmaceuticals, steel, etc. besides our world-wide lead in the ICT sector and a fairly high standing in other scientific explorations and technological advances, are the well-known examples. Hardly surprising, therefore, the international community has started regarding India (and China) as a leading player in the future world economic order.[3] India's presence in diverse international economic fora, a respectful standing in regional economic groups, apart from other numerous bilateral trade agreements and partnerships, especially in South Asia, bear adequate testimony to such contentions (Chadha, 2007, pp. 2–8).

Table 1

Distribution and Growth of Real GDP (at 1999–2000 Prices) 1950 51/2008–09

Year	% Share of GDP					Per Capita
	Primary	Secondary	Manufac-turing	Tertiary	Total GDP	NNP (₹)
1	2	3	4	5	6	7
1950–51	56.5	13.6	9.0	29.9	100	5,708
1960–61	52.3	17.0	10.9	30.7	100	7,121
1970–71	45.9	20.4	12.6	33.7	100	8,091
1980–81	39.9	22.0	13.8	38.1	100	8,594
1990–91	34	23.2	16.6	42.8	100	11,535
1995–96	29.9	24.3	16.2	45.8	100	13,402
2000–01	26.2	23.5	15.3	50.3	100	16,172
2004–05	22.4	24.0	15.1	53.6	100	19,331
2005–06	21.7	24.3	15.1	54.0	100	20,868
2006–07	20.5	24.6	15.4	54.9	100	22,580
2007–08	19.7	24.7	15.4	55.6	100	24,295
2008–09	18.0	23.8	14.6	56.2	100	25,563
2009–10	16.9	25.8	16.0	57.3	100	27,148
2010–11*	16.5	25.7	16.0	57.8	100	—
Growth Rate						
50–51/60–61**	2.8	6.2	6.1	4.3	3.8	1.9
60–61/70–71**	2.0	5.4	5.2	4.6	3.5	1.2
70–71/80–81**	1.8	4.5	4.0	4.6	3.4	0.7
80–81/90–91**	3.1	6.9	7.6	6.9	5.5	3.1
90–91/02–03**	2.7	6.0	10.4	7.9	6.0	4.1
2000–01/2001–02	5.9	2.8	2.5	7.2	5.8	3.7
2001–02/2002–03	-5.9	6.9	6.8	7.5	3.8	2.0
2002–03/2003–04	9.3	7.8	7.1	8.5	8.5	7.1
2003–04/2004–05	0.7	10.5	8.1	9.1	7.5	5.5
2004–05/2005–06	5.2	9.3	9.6	11.1	9.5	7.8
2005–06/2006–07	3.7	12.7	14.9	10.2	9.7	8.1
2006–07/2007–08	4.7	9.7	10.3	10.5	9.2	7.7
2007–08/2008–09	1.6	4.4	4.2	10.1	6.7	5.2
2008–09/2009–10	0.2	8.0	8.8	10.1	8.0	6.2
2009–10/2010–11	6.6	8.1	8.8	9.6	8.6	7.1

Note: 1. The percentage figures up to 1990–91 are at 1993–94 prices and those for 2000–01 and beyond are at 1999–2000 prices.
2.* Figures for 2010–11 are advanced estimates.
3.** Growth rates are estimated by fitting semi-log curve.

Source: Government of India, 2010, A4–A5, 2010b, p. 6; 2011, pp. 5–6; Reserve Bank of India, 2009, pp. 10–13; EPW, 2011, p. 129.

Outside perceptions and interpretations notwithstanding, the pace and pattern of economic growth are affecting the Indian society in many different ways. Apart from freer and more frequent movement of people, capital, technology and ideas, the speed and intensity of movement of goods is also rising steadily. This is happening in the form of a fast expanding, and technology-intensive basket of inputs for sustaining an accelerated and more inter-connected pace of output growth, and in the form of a vastly multiplying variety of finished consumer goods and intermediate inputs. Thanks to the increasing volume, complexity and sophistication of production, practically in each sector of the economy, not only that more of goods have to move around but these have to move faster; the uninterrupted supply-chains are a must. The emerging technology-institutional-human interfaces are likely to defy the frontiers of ordinary movement of goods, especially to meet the exacting time schedules on production as well as marketing fronts. To be sure, a typical Indian manufacturing unit of tomorrow has to be markedly different from its predecessor of yesterday, in terms of the speed and the form in which it receives the production wherewithal and dispatches its finished products to consuming destinations.

Table 2

World Share of GDP for Select Countries in Terms of Purchasing Power Parity

Economy	*Decade Back*		*Current*		*Projected (2002 prices)*					
	1998		*2008 Unipolar*		*2015 Bipolar*		*2025*		*2035*	
							Tripolar			
	Share (%)	*Rank*	*Share (%)*	*Rank*	*Share (%)*	*Rank*	*Share (%)*	*Rank*	*Share (%)*	*Rank*
1	*2*	*3*	*4*	*5*	*6*	*7*	*8*	*9*	*10*	*11*
China	11.1	2	11.6	2	19.5	1.5	25.2	1	30.0	1
USA	21.8	1	21.4	1	19.5	1.5	17.8	2	16.0	2
India	5.5	4	4.91	4	8.2	3	11.2	3	14.3	3
Japan	7.7	3	6.4	3	6.2	4	5.5	4	4.8	4
Germany	4.8	5	4.3	5	3.5	5	3.0	5	2.6	5
France	3.3	6	3.1	8	2.7	6	2.4	7	2.1	8
UK	3.2	7	3.2	7	2.7	7	2.3	8	2.0	9
Russia	2.7	10	3.3	6	2.6	8	2.6	6	2.5	6
Italy	3.1	8	2.7	10	2.5	9	2.0	9	1.6	11
Brazil	2.9	9	2.9	9	2.2	10	1.9	12	1.6	12

Source: For 1998, UNDP, 2001, pp. 178–80; For 2008, UNDP, 2010, pp. 206–8; For 2015, 2025 and 2035 Projections, Virmani, 2004.

Table 2 sketches out, *albeit* conjecturally, the future standing of the major economic players of the world. Admittedly, the projections, based as they are on a mix of assumptions, may not dish out the precise magnitude of India's or the world's GDP, especially for the more distant future, yet the changing ranks may be taken to broadly, and roughly, reflect the forth-coming realities. A few trends clearly seem to be in the offing.

First, very soon, the US may cease to be the loco-motive of the world economy so that the world economy will no more be uni-polar. In less than a decade, around 2015, China, cashing on the cumulative effect of high growth rate for nearly three decades, and having been fiercely competitive world-class economic player for more than two decades, would register further ascendency, to stand side by side with the US. Clearly, it would then be a bi-polar economic landscape. Around 2035, it would be a tri-polar world when India too would stand on a high pedestal, in terms of the sheer size of its GDP while China would surge far ahead of the US, again, on the strength of its formidable share of world GDP. In plain terms, the future puts India on a fairly high pedestal among the major economies of the world, if only it continues with its onward march of high and sustained growth rate. And for that to happen, India's infrastructure, especially human infrastructure surrogated, *inter alia*, by high quality of its workforce, must show sizeable improvement, both in form and content. The future has to set completely different standards, and for that, we have to act now.

Second, and more creditable, is the increasing gap between India's share of world GDP and of those countries which are currently behind it, as we move into the next three decades. For example, while India's share of the world GDP is estimated to be 5 per cent in 2008, it is projected to go up to 8.2 per cent in 2015, 11.2 per cent in 2025 and 14.3 per cent in 2035, Japan's share is expected to be 6.4 per cent, 6.2 per cent, 5.5 per cent, and 4.8 per cent, during these years, respectively. Likewise, Germany's share may languish behind at 4.3 per cent, 3.5 per cent, 3 per cent and 2.6 per cent, and so on. Imagine, in 2035, Indian economy may be just about 11 per cent smaller than the US economy, while it would be three times as big as that of Japan, six times those of Germany and Russia, seven times those of France and United Kingdom, and nine times as big as that of Italy and Brazil.

We may not be swayed by absolute figures; the sheer size of the Chinese and the Indian economies needs to be seen and interpreted, in terms of the size of their population. In terms of per capita income (in ppp terms), these economies have miles to go to reach the present levels of most of the other countries given in Table 2. The moot point, in today's and tomorrow's context, is that big countries, such as India (and China) would have tremendous advantages in global economic arena if they command big and expanding domestic markets, for which their production frontiers have to improve continuously, and for that, their economic and soft infrastructures have, in turn, to continue improving, on an enduring basis.

High Growth, Low Export Mileage

It is now widely accepted that the recent high growth rate of the Indian economy owed itself, *inter alia*, to the introduction of sweeping economic reforms in the early 1990s. The spate of economic reforms, encompassing all major sectors and sub-sectors of the Indian economy, various policy areas and operational strategies, most ostensibly the increasing space granted to the 'maturing private sector', freer trade movement, the expanding presence of foreign capital, etc. did make a sizeable cumulative impact on domestic growth regime. The external sector too registered a substantial progress; India was clearly getting steadily linked with the world economy, and the earlier economic philosophy of 'domestic self-sufficiency' or 'import substitution' witnessed a substantial squeeze. For example, the total of exports and imports, as a proportion of India's GDP, rose steadily, from a low of 22–23 per cent at the beginning of the 1990s to a high of 52–53 per cent towards the close of 2000s. The composition of exports also steadily tilted away from agricultural and allied products, in favour of manufactured goods. For example, the share of manufactured goods in India's total exports was around 45 per cent in 1960–61 and it rose to about 70 in 2009–10; on the other hand, the share of agricultural and allied products declined sharply from about 44 per cent in 1960–61 to a low of 10 per cent in 2009–10 (Government of India, 2010, A86–A88).

The cheering performance on the external trade front needs, however, to be qualified. Exports did grow impressively, on year-to-year basis. The composition, value and the directions/destinations of exports also changed sizably during the 1990s and the 2000s. In total terms, there is sufficient ground to pat ourselves, yet the ground reality is that export earnings were not as much as these could have been, most ostensibly because the technology intensity of our exports which, in a broad sense, imply earning potential of the export-basket, registered very slow improvement. Table 3 is a grim reminder of our slow ascendency on the technology ladder of exports, compared with many other developing economies, contemporaneously plunging into global arena and struggling to enhance their net export earnings. Undoubtedly, India's group-I exports (traditional technology-based primary commodities such as food, non-ferrous metals, other primary commodities, etc.), in the total basket of its exports, declined sizably from 41 per cent in 1980 to 10.3 per cent in 2000, and the share of its group-II exports (labour-intensive and natural resource-based low technology products such as textiles, clothing, footwear, leather, wood and wood products, paper and paper products, non-metallic mineral products, etc.) did increase from 39 per cent in 1980 to 53 per cent in 2000. But then, there was practically no improvement for higher technology-based group-III and group-IV types of exports. The meek improvement in high technology-based group-V exports (industrial chemicals, pharmaceuticals, computers and office equipment, communication equipment and semi-conductors, aircraft, scientific instruments, etc.), from 9 per cent in 1990 to 12 per cent in 2000, does not negate the fact of India's sluggish ascendency on the technology ladder. The relatively far better performance of many other economies, most notably Taiwan, Malaysia, Korea, Brazil, China, etc. especially towards the upper-end of the technology-intensity of exports, clearly signals towards India's technological weaknesses on the export front. Apart from numerous other elements, strategic policy deficiencies, infrastructural and other operational infirmities, etc. that may be eluded to India's export market incapability, the absence of educated, skilled and trained high quality workforce, on a nationwide scale, may look to be a strong and convincing explanation for the limited export mileage that India could draw out of its high growth experience in recent years. That the limited availability of high quality workforce is a formidable drag for the economy as a whole, most certainly for sustaining a high growth profile in the coming decades, needs hardly to be emphasized. However, much is yet to be done for upgrading quality of India's workforce.

Table 3

Technology Intensity of Exports in Select Countries: 1980–2000

	Percentage of Total Non-oil Exports)					
Country	*Year*	*Group I*	*Group II*	*Group III*	*Group IV*	*Group V*
1	*2*	*3*	*4*	*5*	*6*	*7*
Argentina	1980	76.0	8.7	3.1	5.4	6.7
	1990	68.2	10.0	8.1	5.4	8.2
	2000	59.9	8.8+	4.9	14.9	11.1
Brazil	1980	60.3	9.4	6.4	15.0	8.3
	1990	46.3	12.7	13.5	15.6	11.0
	2000	39.8	12.9	8.6	19.3	18.8
China	1980	NA	NA	NA	NA	NA
	1990	20.4	38.9	5.9	13.7	14.8
	2000	8.7	33.2	8.4	15.7	26.2
Egypt	1980	69.6	26.5	1.9	0.1	1.7
	1990	39.8	44.8	6.7	1.2	7.0
	2000	36.3	36.9	5.3	5.5	13.1

Cont'd...

...Cont'd

Korea	1980	9.9	42.5	19.1	8.2	16.8
	1990	5.5	33.3	14.7	13.3	27.9
	2000	4.0	14.8	11.5	21.5	46.3
India	1980	40.9	38.5	5.7	7.0	5.1
	1990	26.6	51.1	4.8	6.6	9.3
	2000	18.9	52.6	6.6	6.6	11.7
Malaysia	1980	74.9	6.7	0.7	3.0	14.3
	1990	33.7	12.3	3.2	8.5	39.0
	2000	10.3	9.3	1.9	10.9	66.1
Mexico	1980	40.6	8.7	2.2	19.4	24.9
	1990	30.3	7.8	7.5	35.8	16.5
	2000	7.5	12.8	4.5	43.6	29.3
Taiwan	1980	10.7	40.6	8.6	12.3	18.6
	1990	6.7	28.3	10.3	18.7	27.5
	2000	3.6	14.1	10.5	19.5	48.2
Turkey	1980	70.6	22.2	1.4	3.0	2.4
	1990	30.6	42.0	13.6	4.9	8.0
	2000	16.9	44.2	9.9	16.4	10.3

NA: Not Available.

Note: Group I (primary commodities): food, non-ferrous metals, other primary commodities; Group II (manufactures based on labour and natural resources): textiles, clothing, footwear, leather, wood and paper and their products, non-metallic mineral products; Group III (manufactures characterized by low technology intensity): iron and steel, fabricated metal products, simple transport equipment, ships and boats; Group IV (medium technology intensity): rubber and plastic products, machinery, electrical machinery (excl. semiconductors), motor vehicles; Group V (high technology intensity): industrial chemicals, pharmaceuticals, computers and office equipment, communication equipment and semiconductors, aircraft and scientific instruments.

Source: Reserve Bank of India, 2004, p. 92.

Workforce Quality

Quality of workforce is a composite concept that encompasses educational attainment (e.g. formal and informal education including technical and professional education), health status (e.g. strong physique, disease-free body and mental fitness), work experience, including on-the-job training and learning-by-doing, variety of jobs handled, commitment to job, general alertness and knowledge-base of workers, etc. yet, in the literature, education has reigned supreme as its most reliable surrogate (Gemmell, 1997, p. 12; Birdsall et al., 1997: 313; Chadha, 2003: 3). Following the usual international convention, we take secondary or higher secondary level of schooling and other higher qualifications as the dividing line between educated and uneducated workers. For analytical convenience, those with primary and/or middle level schooling are categorized as semi-educated workers. Going by this classification, the illiterate workers are synonymous with low quality workers semi-educated workers represent medium quality workers and educated workers, as defined above, are proxies for high quality workers.

Admittedly, by using education alone as a proxy for workforce quality, we are consciously keeping aside definitional complexities and methodological niceties in the measurement of quality, most ostensibly, because, we are pretty much sure that even with this simple definition, the central message of our writing is directly and adequately conveyed to policy makers in India. It is embarrassing, yet true, that even in terms of this plain and unsophisticated measure, the Indian labour market does not reflect a flattering profile of quality improvement of its workforce. And, if we were to work with a composite, and more complex, index of workforce quality that goes beyond education alone, the clumsy side of the labour market would look clumsier. It is better to save ourselves of this embarrassment, at least at this stage.

No Flattering Step-up

Table 4 sketches out a two-decade-long profile of quality improvement of our workforce, most simplistically proxied by level of workers' educational accomplishments. By no objective yardstick, it is a trivial improvement but, by the same token, it cannot be characterized as flattering. Let us have a close look at the changes. First, there is no doubt that, between 1987–88 and 2007–08, the share of illiterate workers has declined, in varying proportion, both in rural and urban economies. In general, the decline was more marked in rural areas, from 60.5 per cent in 1987–88 to 41 per cent in 2007–08, against 26.5 per cent and 16.5 per cent in urban areas. Again, the post-1993 decline was far more sharper than its counterpart during the pre-1993 years, both in the rural and urban areas. It is at once clear that education-intensive demand for labour ensued soon after the Indian economy opened up its frontiers in 1992, and increased sizably for about a decade or so, after which it got fairly stabilized (Chadha, 2003: 55). The stalemate since 2004–05 is too conspicuous to be brushed aside.

Second, on the contrary, the proportion of educated (secondary level schooling and above) workers has witnessed a steady increase since mid-eighties, from 7 per cent in 1987–88 to 15.7 per cent in 2007–08 in rural areas, from 30.5 per cent to 45.4 per cent in urban areas, and from 9.3 per cent to 22.6 per cent in the economy as a whole. The markedly lower, *albeit* improving, proportion of educated workers in rural, compared with urban India, at every point of time during the past two decades, throws bare the continuing infirmity of rural production base. Agriculture being the main stay of rural areas, just as non-agriculture is that of the urban areas, the big and continuing rural-urban differentials in the proportion of educated workers, boldly testify to the farm-nonfarm, or agriculture-industry, or rural-urban productivity differentials that have been persisting all these years.

Table 4

Distribution of India's Usual Status Workers (15 Years and above) by Level of Educational Accomplishments: 1987–88/2007–08

Locale	*Year*	*Level of Educational Accomplishment (% of Workers)*					
		Illiterate	*Primary Schooling*	*Middle Schooling*	*Secondary Schooling and Above*		
					Total	*Male*	*Female*
1	*2*	*3*	*4*	*5*	*6*	*7*	*8*
RURAL	1987–88	60.5	24.2	8.3	7.0	9.4	1.8
	1993–94	54.5	24.9	10.6	10.0	12.8	2.6
	2004–05	44.3	26.2	15.0	14.5	18.2	6.1
	2007–08	41.0	27.1	16.2	15.7	20.1	6.8
URBAN	1987–88	26.5	28.9	14.1	30.5	32.7	21.3
	1993–94	23.7	24.7	15.6	36.0	38.2	25.8
	2004–05	17.7	22.3	17.7	42.3	44.5	31.9
	2007–08	16.5	19.9	18.2	45.4	48.1	33.9
RURAL + URBAN	1987–88	57.5	24.3	8.9	9.3	—	—
	1993–94	48.5	24.9	11.4	15.1	—	—
	2004–05	38.1	25.3	15.6	21.0	25.1	10.1
	2007–08	35.3	25.4	16.7	22.6	27.6	10.7

Source: Government of India, 1990, S194–S199; for 1993–94, 1997, A121–A126; 2006, A124–A132; 2010a, p. 37.

Third, irrespective of the improving educational background of the Indian work-force, a sizeable proportion of them cannot yet be classified as educated workers, let alone the technically and professionally qualified among them, even by the most elementary yardsticks. For example, as late as 2007–08, in the whole economy, only 22.6 per cent of workers (27.6% of males, and 10.7% of females) had secondary level schooling and/or higher levels of education. That this situation is not at all reflective of a high quality of India's workforce needs hardly to be emphasized. The most despairing situation, as Table 5 below shows, prevails, for example, in agriculture and construction where 10.3 per cent and 12.2 per cent of total workers, and 14.6 per cent and 13.3 per cent of male, and 4.3 per cent and 2.6 per cent of female workers could respectively be classified, in 2004–05, as 'educated workers'. Whatever way we look at the past developments, it is absolutely clear that India has yet to go a long way in fulfilling the very basic requirement of nurturing and expanding its educated and skilled workforce, before lodging its claim of being a knowledge economy, or firming up its standing as a world economic player. That this cleavage still remains far more unrealized for female needs to be underlined in particular.

Finally, as late as 2007–08, only a mid-level educational background (primary + middle level schooling) was discernible for no fewer than two-fifth of workers. The concentration of middle-level educated workers, prevailing nearly equally acutely in rural as well as urban areas, against a continuously declining proportion of illiterate workers, signals some, *albeit* meek, upward movement of quality, on the one hand, and the long way that the Indian economy has yet to traverse to convert its uneducated and lowly-educated workers into educated and trained workers, on the other.

Hump Not Yet Crossed

Table 4 showed improvements and weaknesses in the quality of Indian workforce, at the aggregate level, based exclusively on educational accomplishments of the workers. The position undergoes a substantial change when we peep into the educational status of workers in different sectors of the economy. Table 5 exposes the Achilles' heel of the Indian labour market, in a more telling manner. The distribution of educated (high-quality) workers varies markedly among individual sectors, between rural and urban areas, and between male and female workers. Many facts need to be underlined.

First, even as late as 2004–05, not more than 10 per cent of workers engaged in agriculture and allied activities can be classified as educated workers. This fact alone is a highly distressing aspect of our endeavour to become a global economic player, most ostensibly, because nearly 60 per cent of our national workforce is still engaged in agriculture. The fact that only about 4 per cent of female workers, engaged in agriculture, are educated hugely magnifies the distress, especially because no fewer than 80 per cent of rural female workers are engaged in this sector alone. Is it realistic to dream of nurturing a competitive agricultural production and marketing system when farm workers are still hugely dominated by semi-educated or uneducated hands?

Table 5

Distribution of Usual Status Educated Workers by Rural-Urban and Male-Female Breakup: 2004–05

Worker Description	*Percentage of Educated Workers*							
	Agriculture	*Manufacturing*	*Construction*	*Trade, Hotelling etc.*	*Transport, Storage, Communication, etc.*	*Finance, Insurance, etc.*	*Services*	*Total*
1	*2*	*3*	*4*	*5*	*6*	*7*	*8*	*9*
Rural	10.0	15.2	9.0	25.6	24.8	69.4	51.1	14.5 (15.6)
Urban	17.4	32.8	18.9	42.4	39.6	80.8	60.1	42.3 (45.4)
Male	14.6	28.8	13.3	37.3	31.5	77.3	60.3	25.2 (27.6)
Female	4.3	11.8	2.6	15.8	52.9	83.5	47.7	9.7 (10.7)
Total	10.3	23.4	12.2	34.5	32.2	78.0	55.9	21.0 (22.5)

Notes: 1. Following the usual international convention, a worker with secondary level of schooling and above is defined as an educated worker.
2. Figures in parentheses in Col. 9 are for 2007–08.

Source: Computed from unit level NSS data on employment and unemployment, 2004–5; Government of India, 2010a, p. 37.

Second, construction sector also poses equally serious problem of low or medium-quality workforce. In 2004–05, just about 12 per cent of workers engaged in all varieties of construction activities were educated; the male-female differentials are equally, if not more, glaring in this sector as well. We firmly believe that the technical sophistication, scientific precision, engineering skills, etc. are to go up in the future cob-web of construction activities, especially in the urban and more sensitive environmental-responsive and human-friendly buildings and other outfits. In that case, the quality of workforce presently discernible in the construction sector would hardly fit into the future requirements.

Third, even the future hope of the Indian economy, namely, manufacturing activities, are overshadowed by illiterate and semi-educated workers; in 2004–05, only around 23 per cent of them engaged in manufacturing were educated (or so-called high-quality) workers. Again, the male-female differences in the proportion of educated workers engaged in this sector, pose serious doubts about any sizeable improvement in the quality of female workers entering into this sector in the coming years. It is logical to foresee that the Indian manufacturing sector would continue to be run, at the bottom of the skill- and knowledge-intensive manufacturing activities, by a big bunch of uneducated (or low-quality) workers, while a small, but hopefully expanding, percentage of workers would continue to man the highly knowledge, capital- and technology-intensive, at the top. This does not promise any competitive edge to the Indian manufacturing sector as a whole, in as much as the future production regimes, even in respect of the smallest of the small enterprises, would be increasingly driven by more sophisticated technological processes and unforeseen intricacies, that would increase un-employability of the uneducated workers by every passing day.

Fourth, the only two sectors that reflect a pleasing scenario are finance-insurance-real estate, and services, where, in 2004–05, 78 per cent and 56 per cent of workers were educated, respectively. Still more happily, unlike in most other sectors, the male-female differentials do not tilt against the female workers. In fact, the proportion of educated female workers was as high as 84 per cent against 77 per cent for their male counterparts in the former, and 48 per cent against 60 per cent, in the latter. But then, these two sectors are not big employers, especially in the rural areas. In other words, the pleasing picture of these two sectors does not substantially alter the overall picture of the Indian economy. Only 21 per cent of the Indian workforce could be taken as educated (so-called high-quality) workers in 2004–05, the proportion increasing marginally to 22.5 per cent in 2007–08. The proportion of such workers among males was only 25 per cent in 2004–05 and 27.6 per cent in 2007–08, and was 10 per cent and 11 per cent among females, respectively.

Fifth, the workforce quality gaps between the rural and the urban areas continue to be quite substantial, practically in each sector of the Indian economy. The gaps in the manufacturing sector need to be underlined in particular since manufacturing is touted, by the Indian policy makers and other public analysts, to be the 'future sector of the Indian economy'. The rural India will remain hugely constrained in terms of the quality of the available workforce unless some formidable changes in rural education and training network come about in the very near future.

In sum, it is abundantly clear that in spite of a steady increase, since the mid-eighties, in the proportion of educated workers, or a steady decline in the proportion of illiterate workers, both in rural and urban areas, till as late as 2007–08, not more than 22.5 per cent of the total workforce (45.4% in urban and only 15.6% in rural areas, or 27.6% among male and only 10.7% among females workers) could be classified as educated workers. The most depressing scenario in agriculture and construction sectors, and a little less so in manufacturing, transport-storage-communication and trade-hotels-restaurants, need to be underlined in particular. Even if we take educated workers as synonymous with high quality workers, by our simple, *albeit* questionable, yardsticks, it is abundantly clear that the Indian economy is still characterized by the presence of a very high proportion of low (illiterate) and medium (up to middle-level of schooling) quality workers. The extremely low proportion of educated hands among our workforce is plainly because the secondary level of schooling (the usual yardstick for defining a worker as an 'educated' worker), much less college and university-level educational facilities, are not available to a vast majority of our population, most markedly to our rural population, and still more markedly, to rural females. The hump of quantitative gaps, let alone the qualitative deficiencies, in our educational system, must first be crossed if our dream of becoming a knowledge economy in general, and a global economic player in particular, is to come true.

Regional Unevenness in Workforce Quality

Table 6 throws bare the quality deficiencies of the Indian workforce for each of the 29 states, in respect of each major sector of the state economies. Here again, following the usual international convention, workers with secondary schooling and higher level of education are treated as 'educated workers'. By any objective reckoning, the table shows a mingle of 'a few good', 'many poor' and 'some embarrassing' states which, in total terms, throws up a fairly depressing scenario, for a big majority of states, and for most of the sectors. Let us delve a bit into inter-state variations, for major sectors.

First, the most depressing scenario is discernible in respect of agriculture. In 2004–05, in no fewer than eight of the 29 states, the proportion of educated workers engaged in agriculture and allied activities (fishing, forestry-logging, animal husbandry, etc.) was less than 6 per cent; in another 10 states, it varied between 7 and 10 per cent. It is only in seven states that the proportion of such workers exceeded 15 per cent and out of these, only in the two original green revolution states of Punjab and Haryana that the proportion of workers in this major sector was more than 20 per cent. It is, thus, abundantly clear that the future 'green revolutions' would lie beyond intellectual comprehension of most of the present generation of agricultural workers in a preponderant majority of states. As outlined in Section III, the future burden of technology-intensive farm operations, and the associated management and marketing skills, would hardly be absorbed by an overwhelming majority of these workers unless the rural education scenario undergoes a rapid improvement in the coming few years, and a sizeable number of the new entrants into the sector are 'educated'.

Table 6

Proportion of Educated (UPS) Workers (Level of General Education: Secondary Schooling and above) by Broad Sectors in Indian States: 2004–05

State	*Agriculture*	*Manufacturing*	*Construction*	*Trade, Hotel, Restaurants*	*Transport, Storage and Communication*	*Other Services*	*All Sectors*
1	*2*	*3*	*4*	*5*	*6*	*7*	*8*
Andhra Pradesh	6.52	18.27	9.75	25.19	30.35	48.55	15.07
Assam	9.18	15.14	9.89	22.22	18.11	44.32	15.61
Bihar	15.07	10.01	6.88	29.85	18.92	53.00	18.20
Chhattisgarh	5.52	21.19	20.55	32.21	26.11	56.87	11.78
Gujarat	10.19	37.48	21.34	38.28	35.71	59.07	23.51
Haryana	21.32	42.96	13.29	44.33	33.16	57.56	32.40
Himachal Pradesh	17.84	39.58	17.64	56.15	49.65	69.59	28.17
Jammu & Kashmir	10.15	11.82	11.63	37.85	23.34	64.34	22.64
Jharkhand	8.13	18.94	6.63	30.32	27.01	64.60	15.53
Karnataka	8.02	28.16	17.44	36.29	35.30	62.41	19.15
Kerala	17.88	25.17	21.17	32.27	33.31	63.89	30.03
Madhya Pradesh	6.06	15.67	9.20	37.05	28.94	60.07	14.42
Maharashtra	11.87	37.24	17.03	39.51	47.19	61.73	25.92
Orissa	5.62	11.46	7.06	26.13	26.72	57.65	13.03
Punjab	20.05	37.58	15.60	50.24	31.87	65.84	34.79
Rajasthan	6.09	15.19	4.42	28.96	17.98	52.44	13.32
Tamil Nadu	7.85	22.91	13.41	33.27	43.01	60.33	21.87
Uttar Pradesh	13.19	15.55	6.74	27.64	22.65	55.75	18.47
Uttaranchal	15.38	26.63	16.68	44.79	35.93	62.36	25.29
West Bengal	7.93	16.14	7.06	29.12	18.04	53.61	18.37
Arunachal Pradesh	5.81	27.25	20.66	36.13	17.02	54.16	14.94
Goa	6.39	74.87	37.28	47.70	47.55	69.98	44.85
Manipur	14.66	35.66	28.09	29.47	26.23	83.22	29.38
Meghalaya	2.46	7.68	12.84	14.84	35.63	66.70	11.39
Mizoram	10.79	28.47	15.42	26.66	34.91	65.69	21.51
Nagaland	10.48	33.40	61.24	41.30	31.03	76.13	29.34
Puducherry	16.35	39.55	13.80	37.00	27.43	59.97	31.64
Sikkim	3.57	5.85	4.72	23.15	22.12	59.80	16.68
Tripura	7.24	3.79	3.40	22.67	9.35	29.00	15.07
India	10.30	23.37	12.20	34.50	32.20	56.00	21.00

Source: Computed from unit level NSS data on employment and unemployment, 2004–05.

Second, the situation is only a shade better in the construction sector. In 2004–05, it is only among three major states (Gujarat, Kerala and Chhattisgarh) that the proportion of educated workers exceeded 20 per cent; among the smaller states, such a scenario was discernible for four states (Arunachal Pradesh, Goa, Manipur and Nagaland). On the other hand, the situation is hugely depressing in Bihar, Jharkhand, Orissa, Rajasthan, Uttar Pradesh, West Bengal, Sikkim and Tripura, and a little less so in Andhra Pradesh, Assam, Jammu-Kashmir, Madhya Pradesh, Meghalaya and Pondicherry. Here again, the present generation of construction workers cannot be relied upon for carrying out the intricacies, scientific temper and environmental pre-requisites of future construction activities, especially when the non-farm sector grows fast, and the nature, shape, texture and serviceability of new roads, bridges and buildings look vastly different and beyond the comprehension of the semi-educated or low-educated army of construction workers.

Third, the manufacturing sector, touted as the 'future sector of the Indian economy, in policy and academic circles, throws up more jitters, especially on grounds of technological advances and price and quality competitiveness in international markets. In 2004–05, it was only in five major and three smaller states (Gujarat, Haryana, Himachal Pradesh, Maharashtra, and Punjab in the former, and Manipur, Nagaland, and Pondicherry in the latter group) that the proportion of educated workers exceeded 35 per cent. That is hardly comforting for ensuring future industrial efficiency and labour productivity standards. That it is all the more disconcerting for Andhra Pradesh, Assam, Bihar, Jammu-Kashmir, Jharkhand, Madhya Pradesh, Orissa, Rajasthan, Uttar Pradesh and West Bengal among the major, and Sikkim and Tripura among the smaller states, where the proportion of educated workers engaged in manufacturing varied, in 2004–05, from as low as 3.8 per cent in Tripura and did not go beyond 18.3 per cent in Andhra Pradesh. The prospects for India to stage a head-on march over the industrialized world of today, and more likely of tomorrow, seem pretty bleak if the quality of the present army of manufacturing workforce is to be reckoned with. Undoubtedly, much needs to be done

Fourth, serious inter-state disparities are similarly discernible for other sectors as well. The position is not, however, as alarming as in the case of agriculture and construction sectors, and to a lesser extent, manufacturing sector. As is expected for the services sector, especially for the finance-insurance-banking sub-sector, the proportion of educated workers (i.e. those with secondary schooling and higher level of education) is far higher than in other sectors. For India as a whole, in 2004–05, nearly 56 per cent of workers engaged in services could be categorized, as per our criterion, as 'educated workers'. Except for Assam and Tripura, in the remaining 27 states, the proportion of educated workers engaged in these activities is 50 per cent and above; for as many as ten major states (Himachal Pradesh, Jammu-Kashmir, Jharkhand, Karnataka, Kerala, Madhya Pradesh, Maharashtra, Punjab, Tamil Nadu, and Uttaranchal) and seven smaller states (Goa, Manipur, Meghalaya, Mizoram, Nagaland, Pondicherry and Sikkim), no fewer than 60 per cent of workers could be taken as 'educated workers'. It may not be wrong to conclude that human capital endowment of the services sector is not too bad for putting up an impressive domestic growth profile, on the one hand, and to catapult its export capability to further heights, on the other.

Grasping Future Technology Challenges

In recent years, India has undoubtedly learnt a lot of lessons from its own internal development dynamics as also through the fiercely competitive compulsions that have been coming in exogenously. Technology up-gradation has been occurring in differing degree in various sectors and sub-sectors. The quality of workforce has also been improving but its pace was extremely sluggish, on the one hand, and its spread was hugely uneven across regions, economic sectors, between rural and urban areas, and between male and female workers, on the other. The quality of workforce is, thus, a continuing cause of concern. It is high time that the policy makers align their thinking with the challenges that are inextricably linked with global production and distribution outfits. To say the least, the proverbial Indian mindset of 'business as usual', already under erosion, needs to be completely abandoned.

By now, it should be pretty clear that the constellation of changing international circumstances would dictate that expanding frontiers of knowledge *alias* increasing stock of human capital *alias* expanding presence of educated workforce, would be an inescapable input for the future of the developing economies (Mahmud, 2010: 2–6). This is especially true of India since the lop-sided employment structure that has steadily evolved itself over the preceding decades leaves no options but to effect a substantial shift of workers from agriculture to non-agricultural activities, in the years to come. To remind ourselves, against its 16–17 per cent share in gross domestic product, Indian agriculture is still employing around 60 per cent of the total, and nearly 72 per cent of the rural workforce. Lack, or low level, of education has, *inter alia*, kept many a rural resident tied to agriculture, and the access of non-farm employment has often been confined to more and better educated job aspirants. But then, we must also reiterate that, in the days ahead, the quality of workforce has to improve in agriculture as well; the new agriculture too cannot 'survive' with the army of illiterate or uneducated workers.

That education and knowledge-endowment have to improve not only for all categories of economic functionaries but also for the general run of Indian citizens, needs hardly to be emphasized. Education would have a definite role in facilitating the day-to-day living of our people, more markedly for the rural citizens. To keep oneself informed about what is going around in the world at large, in particular, how our daily life is linked to the happenings in far-off economic locales, political epicentres and cultural hubs, education and knowledge are inescapable. A computer and the computer-generated information would have to be a constant companion, to people of all ages, to workers in all sectors and to rural inhabitants no less than their urban counterparts. Knowledge about laws of the land, people's institutions and rights, decentralized government machineries, etc. coming up through more and better education is bound to throw up more enlightened and responsible citizenry, than otherwise.

For sure, over the preceding decades, we have reached significant milestones in improving the quality of our workforce, yet, going by what many other developing economies have done, and what more we could have done, the quality gaps in our labour market would still look to be astounding. The gaps are, indeed, extraordinarily astounding for some sectors, most markedly agriculture, construction and mining-quarrying, which have somehow been sustaining themselves largely with an army of illiterate or low-educated workforce. As a part of global economy, Indian economy too has to keep pace with the fast and vastly changing technologies, new products and product varieties, expanding and complicated information systems, well-educated and trained workforce, besides developing new market strategies, new services and so on. To be sure, a typical Indian worker of tomorrow has to be markedly different from his predecessor of yesterday just as production and marketing tomorrow would demand a vastly different orientation and commercial alertness than what the Indian economy could do with, say, 30 years back. He has now to operate in a totally different, and diffused, economic regime; he is not only to keep his eye on what is happening in the domestic product and service markets, but has also to read, assimilate and interpret the commercial happenings abroad. Tomorrow's worker will have to wear a global outfit. The role of knowledge and skill is paramount; education holds the key to all these emerging pre-requisites.

Education for New Agriculture

The new agriculture is, and is likely to become a more involved, cob-web of *bio-tech* and *genetic complexities. Numerous soil-related and environmental issues, that have direct bearing on sustainability of agriculture and occupational safety of the agriculturist, have to be resolved at the level of the farm household itself.* Again, under the new dispensations, rigorous *farm production* and *time management schedules* are a must. In some branches of production, especially those catering to the export market, IT-based production or *precision farming* might become the normal practice which, according to some analysts, may 'save more than 60 per cent on fertilizers, weedicide, water and electricity' (Prabhu, 2010: 16). Yet again, an extremely important ingredient of efficient agriculture would be *quality of water*; salinization and contamination of ground and surface waters by pesticides, nitrates and selenium needs to be warded off. The composition, quantity and frequency of fertilizer- and pesticide-use are bound to become critical parameters of productivity levels, agricultural growth and sustainability. Uninformed and unscientific use of such inputs in the past have done tremendous damage to agriculture in many parts of India which needs to be halted, and gradually liquidated, through wide-spread dissemination of farm skills and techniques and given the increasing trend towards public-private partnership in extension education, farmers' own education, knowledge and comprehension would be inescapable inputs.

Numerous problems and challenges, having significant bearing on agricultural growth and its sustainability over time, are emerging at the local, national and international levels. Vulnerability of agriculture and allied sectors (e.g. forests and fisheries) to climate change exemplified by rise in temperature, de-glacialization, de-forestation, rising sea level, frequency and intensity of floods, land inundation, soil degradation and collapse of eco-system, environmental pollution and increase health risks, changing calendar and quantum of rainfall, shorter crop-growing seasons, etc. is already posing formidable challenges not only to the national and international community of scientists but also to individual farmers, in terms of injecting flexible crop production cycles, newer crop-noncrop combinations, water management and other farm practices, etc. The knowledge-base of the farming community, especially in areas of fast depleting ground water resources, land degradations, erratic and unseasonal weather events, etc. has to witness huge improvement, if agriculture is to survive.

Some analysts strongly believe that the next Green Revolution will happen outside the farm. 'For the next Green Revolution to succeed, three things are critical: favourable legislation, investments in modern post-harvesting infrastructure and post-harvest management' (Jain, 2010: 11). Keeping aside the wider societal or country-level implications of these newer developments, suffice this to say that a farmer's own understanding of the diverse issues involved, his stake and role in each area of policy, his interpretation of market behaviour and price vicissitudes, etc. would put considerable premium on his educational background and his knowledge and alertness in pre- and post-harvest matters. An educated farmer would obviously be a better market player, a more informed post-harvest investor and an alert political strategist.

Finally, every farmer will have to be not only an efficient producer but also a well-informed market strategist. In particular, if the production is linked to external market, SPS considerations, product quality and price competitiveness, will have to reign supreme, in his economic calculus. In this new incarnation, an Indian farmer has to be vigilant of numerous new issues which probably never touched his predecessor. His vision and business acumen is constantly under test and he alone has to bear the burden of wrong decisions. An educated, and well-informed, farmer alone would be able to absorb all these obligations more purposefully, at his own level.

Education for Industry

Human capital, *alias* educated and skilled workforce, would be hugely crucial for survival, and growth, of a very large segment of the industrial sector. The significance of this fact cannot be lost to an analyst who knows that a preponderant majority of industrial enterprises in India, are tiny and small units, which cannot withstand the whirlwind of increasing competition from bigger production units at home and highly technology-savvy production systems abroad. Technological changes are occurring by the day; not only that new machines or new raw materials are coming in but also new products or new designs of the existing products and products with much higher performance capabilities, are flooding the market for industrial goods. Moreover, from consumers' point of view, newer and more exacting standards are being set, practically in all branches of manufacturing. For example, in food processing, hygienic and health-safety standards, in agro-processing, especially for the products directed to foreign markets, fashioning and patterning product designs to ensure product smoothness, quality standardization, charming designs, tempting colour-combinations, high quality finish with adequate aesthetic appeal, in other industries, especially the technology-intensive branches of manufacturing, scientific precision, mathematical accuracy and an exceptionally high level of product standardization are a must for ensuring a steadily expanding demand for these industries. Educated workforce is bound to make a substantial impact on product standardization, quality enhancement and productivity improvement even among the group of traditional village industries, handicrafts, handloom, etc.

Newer organizational outfits are also emerging, and are likely to multiply themselves both in numbers and functioning styles. Sub-contracting and ancilliarization may grow in the days ahead, and with that, the chain of vending may grow longer and deeper. In that case, the technology of the tiny and small sub-contracting industrial enterprises would essentially be a part of the technology of the large industry. Technical sophistications, product designing, finishing standards, safety norms, mathematical precision, etc. would all demand a high level of understanding, alertness of mind, scientific approach to industrial production and an awareness of the emerging market trends, on the part of the workers engaged in the ancillary or sub-contracting units. Uneducated job aspirants would naturally engage low consideration of the prospective employers. As a matter of fact, a minimum educational accomplishment is already being insisted upon by industrial employers in general, and sub-contracting units, in particular. That the doors of multinational corporate enterprises functioning in India, or of those working with foreign collaboration and technology-sharing, would be completely shut to uneducated or lowly-educated Indian job aspirants needs hardly to be emphasized. That the number of such foreign-linked enterprises would increase steadily in future needs to be underlined as well.

Technological upgradation and refinement are inextricably woven into the future cob-web of construction activities as well. For example, the future buildings, especially in big and expanding cities, would have to conform to more exacting and human-friend norms, be highly land-intensive, more often multi-storeyed, of newer and integrated designs, heat- and cold-resistant as well fire-proof, using new, and newer combinations of, building materials, newer construction methods, watchful of toxic chemicals in the interiors, paints and colour configurations, and so on. The future concept and pattern of building roads and bridges would entail newer and complicated designs, more exacting tests on the strength of materials used, weather-friendliness, and considerations of traffic intensity and composition, and so on. The illiterate and semi-educated workers, even at the lowest levels of the workers' hierarchy, would not do the job in tandem with the changing needs.

Education for Services

Educational endowment of workers would hold its sway, equally crucially, in the services sector. The types of newer developments and expectations already occurring in hotel and restaurant activities under trade, communication network under transport-storage-communications, banking transactions under finance-insurance-real estate, sanitary services, community services, recreational and cultural services, and personal services under community-social-personal services, should convince us of the great premium that educated workers would command over their uneducated, or low-educated, counterparts. For example, trade, especially the wholesale trade, in a wide variety of products, has already started going into the hands of the educated persons, first because the product variety is getting astonishingly large, second because the imported component of the stocks is steadily increasing, especially in the urban areas, and third because the consumers' queries and level of psychological satisfaction can be more readily answered by them. Hotel management too is already attracting many educated young men and women, mostly from urban India. Again, computer and related activities are likely to expand fairly substantially in the very near future, undoubtedly because computer application is now becoming common, practically to all branches of economic activities; many of the small and tiny industrial and service enterprises, including those located in the rural areas, are using computer for accounting, product development and designing, market exploration, information gathering, and so on. And, this is an area that can absorb many of the upcoming educated job seekers; here, the needed levels of education, technical training and skills vary markedly from a minimum of the secondary level of schooling, at the bottom, to computer engineering and application expertise, at the top.

In sum, there is an increasing emphasis on quality of service which is, in fact, tending to sustain a dual, perhaps a multi-layered, consumer price system. The educated workers are likely to wrest larger pecuniary benefit in such a market scenario. Undoubtedly, the pressure on the quality of service would rise steeply in the days ahead when more service sectors open themselves to international competition. And with that, the possibility for the uneducated workers to survive in the vastly changing labour market would decline. This development may not occur immediately but the medium-term fall-out of globalization along the anticipated lines is a reality that cannot be brushed aside.

A Parting Word

We have laboured hard to emphasize the crucial significance of education and educated workforce in sustaining the high growth profile that the Indian economy has put up during the recent past. India cannot afford to buy any laxity, whatsoever, in terms of assuring to itself 'an educated and skilled workforce that continuously upgrades and adapts skills to efficiently create and use knowledge', in the coming decades (Chen and Suh, 2007: 4). The quality of workforce must improve, and education being the most fundamental pre-requisite and best surrogate of workforce quality, the nation has to lend urgent and high priority to development of education, especially higher education. Further, for effecting the much-needed structural economic transformation, most crucially, the shift of workforce from low-productivity agriculture to high-productivity non-agricultural activities, education, *inter alia*, has a crucial role to play. Again, for meeting the challenges of their increasing integration with the world economic system, especially in areas of expanding exports, India has no choice but to produce more competitively, price-wise, quality-wise and delivery-wise. In the opinion of many a public analyst and development thinker, the right time has arrived for the knowledge-economy to take firm roots in India, both because the operational pre-requisites have been gathered steadily over the preceding development decades, and because the future growth momentum critically hinges upon its knowledge- or technology-base. How is India responding to such calls? What is happening in the education sector, in general, and higher education in particular? It seems, the issue has gained considerable eminence in recent years and the present team of policy makers seem to be pretty clear about India's existing educational deficiencies, especially the glaring accessibility gaps. Many initiatives are already afoot to bridge the accessibility gaps among the states, between rural and urban areas, and between males and females. To say the least, the central government's commitment seems to be complete and hugely forward-looking, most markedly on the funding side. The states are also agog with new visions. The private sector too is jumping in, in a big way. We cannot visit the whole range of the recent policy initiatives, and the associated on-going controversies. Our parting word is that the issue should suffer no laxity.

Notes

1. The pace and pattern of India's recent economic growth looks far more authentic if we measure it in relation to the pre-Independence growth scenarios. For example, during 1900–47, the average annual growth rate of real per capita was negligible, 0.04 per cent (Maddison, 1985). According to another set of estimates, it was 1.07 per cent during 1885–1910 and -0.20 per cent during 1911–1950 (ibid.). Decade-wise, 1911–20, 1931–40 and 1941–50 were the most depressing phases, when per capita real income grew negatively.
2. Undoubtedly, guided by their own perception of the impact of the recent process of global slow-down on India's economy, some academic and policy circles in India and abroad, were pessimist about India's capability to stay on, for long, on the high growth trajectory. Some slow-down in India's growth rate did occur during 2008–09 but it was, at best, a short-lived episode. The fast recovery and soon, thereafter, India jumping back to the high growth profile of the past few years leaves no doubt that during the coming few decades, the growth rate of the Indian economy would remain one of the highest in the world, most unmistakably far too higher than its own growth rate during the 1950s, 1960s and 1970s.
3. Whether a slow-down in its economic growth rate occurs in the next decade or so, it is pretty sure that even on the basis of its most cautious anticipated growth profile, India would steadily improve its share in the

world GDP, and would, at some time-point, be an economic force to reckon with. The tri-polar configuration of the world economy may be delayed a bit, but, who knows, it may come off a bit earlier. In the ultimate analysis, much depends on India's own re-shuffling of development policies, to meet the on-going contingencies as also to capitalize on the growth opportunities that may come her way in years ahead.

References

Birdsall, Nancy et al. 1997. 'Inequality and Growth Reconsidered: Lessons from East Asia', in Frank Ackerman et al. (eds), *Human Well-Being and Economic Goals*, Washington, DC: Island Press.

Chadha, G.K. 2003. 'Rural Employment in India: Current Situation, Challenges and Potential for Expansion'. Discussion Paper 7, ILO-UN, Geneva.

——. 2007. 'Domestic Demand for Agricultural Commodities: Recent Trends and Expected Future Patterns'. Presidential Address at the 20th National Conference on Agricultural Marketing, Nagpur, February 22–24.

——. 2009. 'India's March Towards a Knowledge Economy: Crucial Milestones Yet to Accomplish'. *The Indian Economic Journal*, Vol. 57, No. 1, April–June.

——. 2010. 'Envisioning India as a Knowledge Economy: Critical Hump Not Yet Crossed'. *Contributions to Indian Social Science*, Vol. 29, Nos 3–4, July–December.

Chen, Derek H.C. and Joonghae Suh. 2007. 'Introduction', in Derek H.C. Chen and Joonghae Suh (eds), *Korea as a Knowledge Economy: Evolutionary Process and Lessons Learned*, Korea: Korea Development Institute.

EPW. 2011. 'India's Quarterly GDP Estimates from 2007–08 to 2010–11'. *Economic and Political Weekly*, 2004–05 Series, June 13–17.

Gemmell, Norman. 1997. 'Evaluating the Impacts of Human Capital Stocks and Accumulation on Economic Growth: Some New Evidence'. *Oxford Bulletin of Economics and Statistics*, Special Issue on Human Capital in Economic Development, Vol. 58, No. 1, February.

Government of India. 1990. 'Results of the Fourth Quinquennial Survey on Employment and Unemployment, All-India, NSS 43rd Round (July 1987–June 1988)'. *Sarvekshana*, Special Number, NSSO, New Delhi, September.

——. 1997. 'Employment and Unemployment in India, 1993–94'. Fifth Quinquennial Survey, NSS 50th Round (July 1993–June 1994), NSSO Report No. 409, March.

——. 2005. 'Level and Pattern of Consumer Expenditure in India, 2004–05'. NSS 61st Round (July 2004–June 2005), NSSO, August.

——. 2006. 'Employment and Unemployment Situation in India: 2004–05 (Part-I)'. NSS 61st Round (July 2004–June 2005), NSS Report No. 515, NSSO, September.

——. 2008. Economic Survey 2007–08. Ministry of Finance, February.

——. 2010. Economic Survey of India 2009–10. Ministry of Finance, February.

——. 2010a. 'Employment and Unemployment Situation in India, 2007–08'. NSS 64th Round (July 2007–June 2008), NSS Report No. 531, NSSO, May.

——. 2010b. Economic Outlook for 2010–11. Economic Advisory Council to the Prime Minister, July.

——. 2011. Press Note on Advanced Estimates of National Income, 2010–11. CSO, May 31.

Jain, Raj. 2010. 'Next Green Revolution will Happen Outside Farm'. *The Economic Times*, February 15.

Maddison, A. 1985. 'Alternative Estimates of the Real Product of India: 1900–46'. *Indian Economic and Social History Review*, Vol. 22, No. 2, April–June.

Mahmud, Wahiduddin. 2010. 'Beyond Education for All: Meeting the Human Resource Needs in Less Developed Countries'. Paper for the UN Committee for Development Policy, March.

Mittal, Sunil Bharti. 2011. 'India's High Growth is Set for Long Haul'. *The Economic Times*, January 17.

OECD. 2011. Economic Surveys of India. Overview, June.

Prabhu, M.J. 2010. 'Precision Farming Makes Floriculture Profitable'. *The Hindu*, February 18.

Reserve Bank of India. 2004. *Report on Currency and Finance, 2002–03*. January.

——. 2009. *Handbook of Statistics on the Indian Economy 2008–09*. Mumbai, September 15.

UNDP. 2001. *Human Development Report 2001: Making New Technologies Work for Human Development*.

——. 2010. *Human Development Report 2010: The Real Wealth of Nations: Pathways to Human Development*. 20th Anniversary edition.

Virmani, A. 2004. 'Economic Performance, Power Potential and Global Governance: Towards a New International Order'. ICRIER Working Paper 150, December.

7

Technical Education in India

S.C. BEDI

Technical education plays a crucial role in the growth of human resources by generating skilled manpower, enhancing industrial productivity and the quality of life. Technical education offers courses and programmes in engineering, technology, management, architecture, town planning, pharmacy, applied arts, hotel management and catering technology. Technical education in India is coordinated by the All India Council for Technical Education (AICTE), which is the statutory body for proper planning and development of the technical education system. Over the years, India has registered a substantial advance in technical education, which is being further accelerated by the policy of economic reforms and liberalization. Indian policy makers have recognized the importance of technical education for nation building and have provided full policy support and public funding to create one of the world's largest technical education systems. Accordingly, measures are being taken to improve the quality of technical education by greater use of technology in the teaching-learning processes.

Engineering and technical education has been a driving force for human development in the wider sense and has an impact on technological development and competitiveness. However, most technical institutions/universities have not been able to maintain high standards of engineering education and are unable to keep pace with international developments. The lag is attributed to the limited financial support from the government and a slew of controls. Therefore, the National Knowledge Commission has suggested for 'a new paradigm in regulation, accreditation, governance and faculty development' across the engineering education spectrum. In this paper, an attempt is made to gauge the current status of Indian technical education, to understand critical issues in technical manpower development and to identify strategies to reform the system.

Technical education in India has seen phenomenal growth over the past decade or so, both in number of students and number of colleges and has come to dominate the education scenario. However, the average quality of the colleges and their graduates is an area of concern. The question of quality technical education in the context of globalization of economy and emergence of knowledge society cannot be over emphasized. A survey of human resource professionals at multinational corporations in India revealed that only one quarter of technical graduates with a suitable degree could be employed irrespective of great demand. Another survey of employers shows that only a handful of the existing technical colleges in India are recognized as providing world class education with graduates worthy of consideration for employment. The current situation, with an abundance of low quality technical education, is projected to stifle growth of the Indian economy. It is intended here to investigate the factors that lead to the current state of technical education in India and to suggest ways that would rectify the situation.

Technology is an important engine of development as it plays a vital role in enhancing in productivity with reduced costs and response time. In the era of globalizing of the economy, the developing countries have to compete with the technologically advanced countries that have the advantage in using technology to enhance their productivity, thereby getting a competitive advantage. The quality of technical education, research and innovation, therefore, plays a vital role in providing such a technology driven comparative edge to a country.

Table 1

Growth of Seats in Different Programmes in Technical Institutions

Year	*Engineering*	*Management*	*MCA*	*Pharmacy*	*Architecture*	*HMCT*	*Total*
2005–06	4,99,697	1,22,663	61,991	32,708	4,379	4,435	7,25,873
2006–07	5,50,986	1,44,372	63,394	39,517	4,543	4,242	8,07,054
2007–08	6,53,290	1,85,780	78,692	52,334	4,543	5,275	9,79,914
2008–09	8,41,018	2,27,989	82,578	64,211	4,543	5,794	12,26,133
2009–10	10,71,896	2,73,732	1,21,123	72,836	4,133	6,387	15,50,107
2010–11	13,24,246	3,78,907	1,35,173	1,03,867	4,933	7,061	19,54,482

Engineering, management, pharmacy, architecture and other professional education like medicine are much sought after career options after 10+2 in India. Indian parents have the ambition and desire to give a quality professional education to their children to make them employable. They are willing to invest in their education even if they have to make personal sacrifices of their own comforts. Thus, there is almost an assured supply of talented students to quality institutions in technical education. This is a very positive demand environment.

Growth of Infrastructure

The technical education system comprises central government-funded institutions, state government/state-funded institutions and self-financed institutions. Fast growth of infrastructure is observed in the self-financed/private institutions, marginally state-funded institutions as compared to centrally-funded institutions. There are only 81 centrally-funded institutions as given in the following Table 2.

Table 2

Central Government-Funded Institutions

S.No.	*Type of Institution*	*Number*
1.	Indian Institutes of Technology	15
2.	Indian Institutes of Management	13
3.	Indian Institute of Science	1
4.	Indian Institutes of Science Education and Research	5
5.	National Institutes of Technology	30
6.	Indian Institute of Information Technology	4
7.	National Institutes of Technical Teachers Training and Research	4
8.	Others (SPA, ISMU, NERIST, SLIET, NITIE & NIFFT, CIT)	9
	Total	81

The central and state governments are planning to expand better infrastructure in the field of technical education, since fast growth of self-financed institutions was observed in the post-liberalization era which resulted in increase in intake capacity and programmes of different courses.

Presently (2010–2011), there are 7,361 degree providing institutions which run 10,364 programmes with an intake capacity of 19,54,482 students. However, the engineering and technical infrastructure is not uniform and is more skewed towards South-Central, South and North-West region. Andhra Pradesh, Tamil Nadu, Uttar Pradesh and Maharashtra have the largest number of institutes and North-East States have least number of technical institutes.

The emergence of a knowledge-driven economy and the role intellectual capital will play in enterprises in the future give an additional reason for the developing countries to focus on the improvement of quality of technical education. The rapid quantitative growth of technical education in terms of number of institutions and enrolments has led to a compromise on quality. Since anything worth doing has quality implications, such a scenario is not sustainable for success in the global and knowledge-driven society.

Quality of any system is possible only by striking an optimal balance among various competing demands of any system. The same is true for quality of technical education. An analysis of the technical education scenario in the country reveals some imbalances that affect the health of technical education here.

Imbalances in Technical Education

The spread of technical education suffers from regional imbalances. After privatization of technical education, a large number of new private colleges appeared in a few states while many stales that urgently needed development could not get as many. A balanced growth of technical education in the country is desirable. Even within the same state, there are intrastate regional imbalances leading to 'vital few' and 'ignored many' regions in respect of such colleges. While it is understandable that certain locational advantages attract more private participation than others, yet the under-represented regions do need technical education institutions all the more. Such institutions may be raised then by the government or by the private players attracted by the state offered package of incentives or by means of public-private partnership.

There is also a quantity versus quality imbalance. The near exponential growth of numbers has eroded quality because of acute shortage of intellectual resources such as faculty, laboratory technicians and equipment, facilities, computational and other academic resources required to match the quantitative expansion.

Ownership imbalance is another important factor. Much of the growth has been in privately-funded organizations while investments by the state/central government in creating new state-funded colleges are scanty. State-funding of technical education has not shown any sign of increase, while private investments have multiplied manifold.

There is a gross imbalance in the branches of engineering preferred by the incumbents. An analysis of branch-wise enrolments will indicate that most of the enrolments (nearly 80%) are confined to a few branches. Not many enrolments take place in the core technological disciplines such as electrical, mechanical, civil, chemical, textile, agricultural, metallurgical, aeronautical, paper, leather and other vitally needed technologies. Since the discipline of Information Technology requires fewer investments and has currently a good market, myopic perspectives make them most attractive cash cow whereas balanced technological development suffers a setback. This would cause serious skill shortages in the core branches of engineering.

In many cases, there is also great imbalance between physical and intellectual resources of the institutions. Many private colleges have created good physical infrastructure in buildings, offices, laboratories and hostels but they have an acute shortage of intellectual, academic and learning resources, such as laboratory facilities and the faculty. This mismatch of physical and intellectual resources is a cause for serious concern. Acute shortage of faculty is due to an unreasonable gap in the compensation packages the faculty receives as compared to what their counterparts get in industry. The age profile of the faculty is also not conducive to quality. One comes across either fresh graduates in engineering from these colleges or retired senior professors. A balanced age structure with strong middle cadre is missing.

Graduate versus vocational education imbalance is another feature. Most of the growth in technical education has been at the degree level engineering institutions, while diploma level and vocational trades have not shown corresponding increase. Logically, the diploma level and trade level education and training have to match graduate level education in engineering. However, private investors have not found diploma or lower level training an attractive investment proposition. Additionally, there is no integration of technical education with vocational, polytechnic and research level institutions. Integration from Industrial Training Institutes to Indian Institutes of Technology may be a worthwhile goal.

Training process imbalances are also significant. The focus of technical education should be on developing technical personnel who may contribute to national development process and are globally employable. This calls for a holistic development of personality profile with a judicious mix of theory, practice, industrial exposure, project-based learning, research training, co-curricular activities together with soft skills such as professional and personal communication, teamwork, leadership development, managerial skills, time, project, quality, productivity, cost management training. Values such as concern for others, compassion for underprivileged, concern for the society and the country also need to be installed. Involving industry in curriculum development is a serious yet missing dimension. Thus, there is a serious imbalance of knowledge, skills and attitudes needed to improve global employability of our technical graduates. NASSCOM has opined that the current immediate employability of IT graduates in India may be around 20–25 per cent of those graduating. Hence, global employability enhancement of technical/engineering graduates and others need to be a part of any strategy to improve the quality of technical education in the country.

Faculty Shortage: A Key Constraint: Faculty constitutes the single most critical success factor in pursuit of academic excellence. Regrettably, the best brains in the society are not opting for teaching and research as their preferred choice in career options is engineering and technology.

Salary differentials of unreasonable magnitude, low status of teaching and research, low investment in R&D and non-challenging academic ambience in colleges are, perhaps, responsible for the talent not interested in teaching and research. In the context of this challenge, we need to give the highest priority to attract talent to teaching. As a nation, we need to promote investments in education, research and planning, as all these require intellectual resource inputs. We need to proactively nurture intellectual talent by providing right kind of academic ambience, empowerment, work culture, autonomy with accountability and lucrative emoluments. Faculty development in technical education should become a priority in quality enhancement process. Academic leadership and institutional ownership must strive towards developing their faculty to enable them to motivate, inspire, involve and transform their students in a 'holistic' sense to make them globally employable

Emergence of Global Knowledge Economy: Information technology and the electronic revolution have made the concept of globalization a reality. Consequently, the entire world has shrunk to a global village with interactive communication with anyone, anywhere, anytime. In the increasingly knowledge-driven economy and society we witness today, India has the core competency to become a knowledge super power. We should endeavour to provide enormous opportunities to expand all kinds of technical talent to be developed to lead the knowledge society. There is a paradigm shift in the global competition. If we do not produce such a globally competent engineer or technician someone else will. That someone else would be from anywhere: China, Vietnam, Malaysia, Indonesia, etc. Hence, global trends in the knowledge society are an opportunity as well as a challenge. If we focus on quality, it is an opportunity. It we do not, it will be our loss. Hence, it is a critical moment to introspect and take a vital decision to balance the short-term objectives with the long term ones in order to balance quantity with quality and remove the various kinds of imbalances listed above.

The Indian Advantage in Knowledge Era: On the positive, we have many major strengths. India is a youthful nation with more than 50 per cent of its population under 25 years of age or 65 per cent of population less than 35 years of age. While developed world is already ageing, these would look towards India as a major potential supplier of various kinds of talent. This is a major demographic dividend which we can encash if we make investments in developing globally employable quality technical talent.

Indians intrinsically make a very creative, analytical, innovative, curious and intelligent human resource. We are very strong on integrative complexity and can find innovative solutions to complex problems provided we find a purpose in it. In the era of knowledge process outsourcing, India offers great potential in R&D, software engineering, service process outsourcing due to easy availability of relatively inexpensive (by global standards) talent which is sharp, creative and brilliant. Once again it is only possible if we nurture this talent to achieve high-quality training in engineering, technology, science and mathematics.

Technical Education System in India: A SWOT Analysis

A SWOT framework for Indian Technical Education System provides insights and necessitates soul searching. A brief framework is as follows:

Major Strengths

1. Very young demographic profile with more than 55 per cent of population under 25 years of age.
2. Intrinsically intelligent human resources.
3. Large-trainable population.
4. Engineering and technology still a preferred career option.
5. Parents in India willing to sacrifice their personal comforts for the sake of child's education.
6. Private equity participation is an attractive proposition.

Major Weaknesses

1. Faculty shortage – both in terms of numbers as well as their quality and commitment.
2. Low concern for quality and high concern for increasing intakes in private colleges.
3. Mushrooming of private colleges with inadequate concern for quality.
4. Imbalances – branch wise, geographical and regional.
5. Low focus on practicals, experiments or project work.
6. Very little industrial interaction/collaboration.
7. Low autonomy to academics and academic leadership, irrespective of the source of funding.
8. Little focus on research, consultancy, publications, R&D and product innovation.
9. Teaching mostly based on rote learning/examination centric.
10. Low immediate employability of graduates.

Major Opportunities

1. Rectify imbalance in location, enrolments, branches and compensation packages in technical education.
2. Integrate research, postgraduate, undergraduate, diploma and vocational education with one another to have a holistic development of technical education.

3. Regulatory bodies should take pro-active nurturing role to promote quality and excellence rather than playing just obstructive role.
4. Holistic development of students as a part of nation-building process – improving communication skills, soft-skills, human values, integrity, positivity and professional ethics.
5. Faculty development initiatives, creating an enabling and nurturing academic/learning environment.
6. TQM oriented management of technical education with long term rather than myopic perspective in building institutions.
7. Virtualization, e-learning and using IT-enabled engineering education. Focus on IT in B.Tech programmes rather than only having B.Tech in IT.
8. Networking with reputed academic and industrial organizations for a shared goal of creating outstanding quality, globally employable Indian Talent (new form of IT definition).
9. Sensitizing students to show concern towards others, society, environment, elderly and the under-privileged.
10. Generate healthy sense of competition among colleges by putting their total academic performance, rankings, academic resources/processes on the university website as well as on college websites.

Major Threats

1. Accumulated number of unemployable graduates can cause social upheavals, erode harmony and discipline.
2. Lack of instilling good human values can lead to increased technology-driven cyber crimes.
3. Poor quality graduates will negatively impact national competitiveness index and retard progress. Due to talent shortage, Indian industries and public sector would suffer on productivity, quality and competitiveness.
4. Indian capital may be diverted to foreign universities as parents may decide to get their wards admitted abroad India if quality of Indian Technical Institutions is not perceived to be high.
5. Foreign universities may enter Indian markets and capture education market here.
6. Increasing malpractices, corruption in the process of affiliation, admissions, accreditation and examination processes. This would have a cascading effect and eventually ruin the social and work environment.
7. Low ranking of engineering institutions/graduates as an outcome of persistently poor quality turnout.

It is hoped that the policy makers, promoters, regulatory authorities and academicians would accord a pride of the place to make quality and academic excellence in managing technical education. If that happens, it would transform economic and social environment of this country.

Regulatory Bodies: Agenda for Change

Only inspection-driven, compliance-centric regulatory practices are prone to corruption. Since the purpose of regulation is to promote quality and nurture excellence, it is high time that there is introspection among all regulatory authorities – UGC, AICTE, affiliating universities and the concerned nodal ministry – dealing with technical education to see if current regulatory practices are serving the envisaged purpose. It is a known fact in the quality assurance literature that inspection (particularly the end of line inspection), is a primitive form of quality control. For effective, proactive, objective, transparent and quality regulation, a fundamental shift in the mindset of regulators is required.

We need to create a nurturing rather than inhibiting environment, which should be excellence-driven, holistic and inspiring. For that purpose regulatory bodies have to play the role of facilitators and not regulators. What we need is the following:

- Maintenance of standards.
- Change in admission policy.
- Focus on autonomy: operational, financial and academic autonomy coupled with accountability.
- Focus on quality assurance system.
- Focus on generic skills rather than tailor-made skills.
- Focus on public-private partnership and institution-industry interface
- Involvement of industry in curriculum development and its implementation.
- Appointment and retention of qualified, experienced and competent faculty members.
- Quality improvement of junior faculty members.
- Improvement in institutional infrastructure.
- Improvement in teaching methodology
- More emphasis on laboratory work.
- Revision of curricula to make it more relevant to current needs.
- Development of research culture in the institute.
- Political interference in the appointment of university teachers and administrators should be totally stopped.
- Libraries should be fully equipped with the latest books, journals and periodicals.
- Laboratories should be updated.

- Working facilities and workload of teachers should be as per the norms.
- Teachers should be encouraged to attend various conferences, seminars, workshops in their disciplines.
- Regular monitoring and evaluation.
- To attract bright minds to the teaching profession.
- Focus on e-learning.
- A cell for value education to inculcate human values in the students.

8

Medical Education in India

What Ails Our Institutions?

S.P. KAUSHIK

The medical education system in India is one of the largest in the world. There are 314 medical colleges and institutions in India today. Their number was less than 20 at the time of Independence. The number of graduates and postgraduates coming out annually from these institutions presently stands at 35,000 and 17,935, respectively. The latest figures from the Medical Council of India (June 2012) indicates that the likely number of medical institutions in the country would soon be 355 and that the number of graduates and postgraduates seats would increase to 45,465 and 23,520, respectively. More institutions are likely to be approved in the near future both in public and private sectors. The number is projected to increase to 80,000 of graduates and 45,000 of postgraduates by 2021 in order to achieve the ratio of one doctor per 1,000 population of India.

Nearly 40 per cent of graduates and postgraduates after qualifying from our medical institutions leave the country and go abroad. Majority of the remaining graduates settle down in urban areas leaving India's rural population with very little medical cover.

A number of medical educationists and intellectuals have expressed their concerns about the quality of existing medical education system in India. Prof. Dave (2005), former Director of AIIMS, New Delhi, was amongst the first few educationists to have expressed serious doubts about the relevance of present day medical education for the overall health care needs in the country.[1] Bajaj (2006) emphasized the need for maintaining national standards in our medical education system and supported the idea of a matrix for establishing quality of medical education in the country.[2] Valiathan Committee recommendations (2009) for All India Institute of Medical Sciences, New Delhi, have clearly brought out the urgent need for a change in the present system, including the postgraduate medical teaching and training in the rest of the country.[3] Medical Council of India, after its reconstitution in 2009, has also proposed a number of significant changes in the existing educational system in the country.[4] In a comprehensive review of medical education in India, Sood and Adkoli (2000) have concluded that our medical colleges are not producing graduates who are well equipped to tackle the healthcare needs of the society.[5] Srinivas and Adkoli (2009) underlined the importance of structured faculty development programmes.[6] They have also expressed their disappointment with the government efforts in improving medical education in the country. In their opinion the state of medical education in India presents a scenario marked by rhetoric and wishful thinking rather than by any evidence of concrete steps being taken in the right direction.

A specially set up Task Force by the Ministry of Health and Family Welfare, Government of India, has recommended in 2009 that a National Council of Human Resources in health should be set up as an autonomous body under the ministry. The Council should have the responsibility of developing and strengthening medical education in India in order to meet the country's health needs, monitor the standards of health and of medical education and regulate the nature and contents of educational programmes. Great emphasis has been laid on the absolute and immediate need for public and private partnership in different areas of medical education and health care in our country. A very comprehensive and uniform medical and health care cover could, thus, be provided to the entire population in the country. The report has identified different fields in which public-private partnership could be worked out and be useful for providing required health care services in rural areas.[7] In 2010, Bhaskaran observed that there was hardly any progress in the implementation of the task force recommendations and expressed deep concerns about the insensitivity of Government of India to the views expressed by the medical educationists of the country. It was his opinion that any further delay on part of government in implementing the above recommendations would result in an alarming state of medical education and health care in our country.[8]

The Twelfth Five Year Plan approach paper has focused mainly on restructuring the public health schemes. It has proposed massive expansion of medical education, suggested various reforms in it, and emphasized on public and private partnerships for sharing of resources. The government was expected to act fast, set up six more AIIMS like institutions and upgrade nearly a dozen existing government medical colleges in the country, as already decided. Although some progress in this regard has been made and a number of such institutions have come up in different parts of the country, much greater emphasis is required to be laid on the new and emerging areas in medical education. The priority disciplines which need to be included are specialities like reproductive medicine, plastic surgery, endocrinology, oncology, cardiology and others, as per country's requirement of health care needs of the masses.

India is awfully short of specialist doctors. The current ratio of specialist doctors is only 1 for 10,000 patients. The required ratio ought to be 1 specialist doctor to 1,000 patients. There is, thus, a need for more specialty departments to come up in our medical institutions in order to train more specialists. The enormity of the task to provide educated manpower is further highlighted by the fact that the doctor patient ratio in our country is still 1:1700. To meet the challenges of twenty-first century, the Medical Council of India is no doubt working in the right direction and is increasing the number of medical colleges in the country as well as the number of seats in each institution. However, one needs to remember that there is a limit for increasing number of seats per medical institution because this cannot be permitted to compromise the quality of training of medical graduates and must follow specified norms.

Besides ensuring quality, equal emphasis needs to be placed on the development of skills, use of IT advancements, evolving new disciplines relevant to rural health care and introducing speciality-based postgraduation in the training of medical graduates.

While implementing plans for expansion and revision of medical education, sincere efforts must be made and due attention paid to the quality of medical graduates coming out of our institutions.[9] The quality of product has far reaching implications for our health care programmes and medical services. To improve the quality of our graduates and post graduates one has to give more attention for improving existing infrastructure and bringing accountability in our systems. In other words, there is a strong and urgent need to put our own house in order first. It is widely believed that the performance capabilities of an average Indian doctor today have declined greatly and are not commensurate with the expectations of the society. The quality status, with the exception of a few, does not match the high moral, ethical and professional standards set out for this group of personnel. The service orientation seems to have been largely replaced by greed and a desire to make large amount of money in shortest possible time. Poor quality of medical personnel is bound to affect our performance capabilities at individual, regional and national levels. It is disappointing to know that the United Nation Human Development ranking for India, is 127 out of 177 countries assessed.[10] India has also failed miserably to keep its' commitment under the Alma Ata declaration

'Health for all by the year 2000'. All this speaks poor of the quantity as well as quality of medical manpower in the country.

The Government of India cannot afford to ignore the fact that the standards of medical education in public as well as private medical institutions in the country have deteriorated markedly over the years. The responsibility for improving existing set-ups, however, cannot be left to the government alone. It has to be shared equally by the medical administrators, faculty members, students and the society. Bold steps are required to be taken at all levels. Political interference, if any, has to be resisted and corruption of all kind (money as well as conduct) must be eliminated to bring in honesty and sincerity of purpose in our day-to-day dealings. In order to do so, one needs to identify the ills and deficit areas in the existing system of medical education and explore ways and means to bring it at par with global standards.

Administrative Set-up

Majority of medical educational institutions in India, with the exception of those which are autonomous or in private sector, are under government control. The local administrative set-ups do not seem to have the will to resist interference by political bosses and bureaucratic hierarchy in the day-to-day matters of the institute. Not only this, the chief executives have often surrendered the interests of faculty, students and other staff in order to keep their positions intact. Government must provide certain amount of functional autonomy to them to be able to perform their best and ensure absolute transparency in their functioning. Majority of management bodies and advisory committees, meant to support/guide the chairman/director/principal of the institute/college, have become a mere formality. Differences of opinion are not tolerated, much less given any consideration in decision making. The philosophy of saving one's own chair, get extensions beyond normal term and rule by divisive policies appears to have become the order of the day.

The Infrastructure Support

A strong infrastructure support is often missing in a large number of medical institutions. The equipment is either outdated, old or not necessarily in good functional state. Procurement of new equipment is extremely difficult because of cumbersome government procedures, red tape and financial constraints. By the time the new equipment is delivered, usually the newer and more advanced models are already in the market, making procured equipment obsolete and outdated. The non-functional equipment is neither repaired nor updated for want of expertise and lack of good workshop facilities, besides budgetary constraints. The resultant deficiency is a major factor in frustrating faculty efforts to give their best in routine patient care, in innovating and exploring new techniques and methodologies to achieve better results.

Departmental Set-ups

The hierarchy of lecturers, assistant professors, associate professors, additional professors, professors and heads of the department or lecturers, readers and professors has lost its earlier ethos. There is no cohesive team work in the step ladder pattern, where juniors learn from the experience of seniors and others. The work culture lacks the ethos and spirit with which the system was created by our predecessors. Every faculty member today is autonomous and works by him/herself. There is neither an apex centre of power or control nor the practice of seeking guidance. No wonder, most of the departments have become a battlefield of one up man ship today rather than a happy and healthy work place. Often, the fights get out of the departments/institutions and reach the court rooms, vitiating the atmosphere forever.

The Medical Faculty

The faculty is supposed to play a pivotal role in shaping the quality of the outgoing graduates and/or post graduates. It is a well-known fact that a large number of faculty selections or for that matter creation of new posts, are not unbiased, fair or based on merit alone. Inbreeding, automatic promotions schemes, not taking lateral entries at higher level of faculty positions and the reservations have all taken a toll on the quality of faculty. The faculty development programmes do not exist in a large number of institutions. It is not only the salary structure but also other facilities, like freedom of work, promotional avenues, healthy work culture, active participation in national and international conferences, etc. that make a big difference to the faculty commitment to the institution. For want of such facilities, we have the problem of migration abroad from many institutions, including India's premier institutions.

The poor ratio of teachers and taught is yet another deficiency which is commonly present. The number of teachers is often not adequate as per MCI requirements and it naturally affects teaching, training and research performance of the faculty. The authorities concerned must find ways to attract and retain qualified and good faculty.

Students' Affairs

There is a genuine concern regarding the quality of students entering medical colleges and the proficiency of those passing out after graduation and postgraduation. Admissions to medical colleges have been programmed on the basis of a merit list prepared after successful clearance in a competitive examination. In order to enter a medical college, a student, after 10 + 2 and having attained an age of 17 years, is required to appear and achieve a high rank in the entrance test. However, the ingenious Indian mind is always at work and a certain percentage of back door entries are invariably made by foul means. The post graduate entrance tests are no exception. In the private sector institutions, donations often prevail on merit.

Another setback to the merit pool is the practice of mandatory reservation of seats on the basis of caste. There may well be compelling social and political reasons for such reservations, but the society must consider this issue rather dispassionately if the high quality of students is to be ensured for admission to the vital professional courses. Since the pass percentage of marks for the reserved category of students is lower, the pool of selected candidates consists of two levels, one with high merit and the other with low merit, clubbed together. It is almost impossible for teachers and the taught to improve the low merit over the years and bring the low merit group at par with the high merit students group. The mixture of heterogeneous categories thus results in lowering of standards.

The society, the professionals and the administrators, therefore have to finally and firmly decide now whether to continue with reservation of seats in professional courses in the present form, particularly when the product from a medical institution has such a vital role to play in alleviation of human suffering and is directly responsible for life or death of a patient. If reservations have to stay, the system should be modified in such a manner that the gap between the two uneven merit groups is reduced to the minimum. This could easily be achieved by bringing the cut-off marks for both the categories of students at par so that they compete with each other on equal footing. In order to make it possible for reserved category students to secure high merit marks equal to open category students, their support systems could be upgraded so that they are able to perform better. The state may provide complete financial, social and educational support to them in order to enable them to compete in an open manner. Alternatively, reservations should be provided only at step one and that too only once in life time. This will ensure no dilution of merit at the higher levels of specialization.

The work culture and commitment to teaching and training of students by departmental faculty is another very important factor in achieving excellent quality of end product. It is a pity that a large number of faculty members today either deputise their classes to junior colleagues or come unprepared to the session. Many times the sessions go unattended. The institution of headship stands totally eroded and hopelessly ineffective. A large number of medical institutions in the country, even today, do not have a structured training programme with larger emphasis on practical hands on experience of the trainee. The most adversely affected residents are the surgical trainees. The curricula are often old and unrevised. It is disappointing to see that Minimal Access Surgery has still not formed part of medical curricula in large number of institutions in India. Neither health care ethics is taught as a medical subject. It is even more disappointing to see that programmes made for the students are rarely implemented satisfactorily by many departments and institutions. The final casualty is always the passing-out student and the future of us all.

Private Medical Institutions

A large number of medical colleges have come up in private sector in India during the last 25 years. Although what has been described in the foregone pages is equally applicable to both the public as well as private medical institutions, there are certain specific problems which pertain to private set-ups alone. The faculty shortage is perpetual in all departments in all such establishments and the teaching experience and background of teachers is not one of the best. Often, one day or short-term appointments are made, frequently of doctors working in private non teaching hospitals, in order to put up a show for MCI inspections. Also, the approach in selection of students is based more on the quantum of donation rather than on merit. There is no sustained effort to teach and train young graduates and postgraduates to ensure quality of end product of doctors as well as of specialists.

Concluding Remarks

It is, indeed, appalling that an average qualified Indian doctor today is well below the professional standard and lacks confidence, capabilities and professionalism. All of us have to feel responsible for the same and make efforts to undo the trend. The society must play its role as a pressure group. There is an urgent need for the medical institutions in the country to put their house in order and to make an honest and sincere effort in educating and training the new entrants well. Making any number of changes in curricula, teaching format and pattern is not going to be of any use unless we improve our commitment to work, bring in healthy environment and have sincerity of purpose. The Indian society, academicians, medical administrators and the government must ensure that only the best talented students get the opportunity to enter medical courses, are trained by the best faculty and that the educational institutions are provided with the best infrastructure support and work environment. Only then one hopes to break the shackles of prevailing mediocrity and be able to produce a class of medical graduates and postgraduates, who would be able to perform better and deliver an excellent health care to masses.

Notes

1. P.K. Dave. 'The Relevance of Medical Education for Overall Health Care'. *Ann. Nat. Acad. Med. Scs* (India), Vol. 41, 2005, pp. 77–81.
2. J.S. Bajaj. 'National Standards of Medical Education'. *Ann. Nat. Acad. Med. Scs* (India), Vol. 42, 2006, pp. 85–168.
3. M.S. Valiathan. Valiathan Committee Report Submitted to Lok Sabha on 11December 2009.
4. S.K. Sarin. Medical Council of India: Recommendation for Changes in Medical Curriculum. Personal communication, 2009.
5. R. Sood and B.V. Adkoli. 'Medical Education in India: Problems and Prospects'. *Jour. Ind. Acad. Clin. Med.*, Vol. 1, 2000, pp. 210–12.
6. D.K. Srinivas and B.V. Adkoli. 'Faculty Development in Medical Education in India: The Need of the Day'. *Al Ameen Jour. Med. Sc.*, Vol. 2, 2009, pp. 6–13.
7. Task Force Report, Ministry of Health and Family Welfare, Government of India, 2009. Available at: http/mohfw.nic.in
8. C.S. Bhaskaran. 'Structural Reforms in Planning and Management of Professional Education'. *Ann. Nat. Acad. Med. Scs*, Vol. 46, 2010, pp. 137–53.
9. S.P. Kaushik. 'Quality of Indian Doctors: A Matter for Concern'. *Ann. Nat. Acad. Med. Scs* (India), Vol. 45, 2009, pp. 7–16.
10. A. Supe and W.P. Burdick. 'Challenges and Issues in Medical Education in India'. *Academic Medicine*, Vol. 81, 2006, pp. 1076–80.

9

Legal Education and Legal Profession

The Genesis and the Prognosis

VEER SINGH

Education Matrix: The Changing Horizons

In our knowledge society today, education is a tool of empowerment. It is a facilitator and a force multiplier. The transformation from a production-based economy to knowledge-based economy can very well be called a second renaissance. History is a testimony that societies which did not plan on futuristic education model became static and fossilized. On the other hand, those which invested in education, created knowledge and applied it, witnessed accelerated economic growth and achieved dominant position in the world. Renaissance in Europe after the long Dark Age was by and large an end-product of technology innovation and rationalism nurtured in great universities of Europe. Even today, the global divide between developed and developing worlds in fact is a knowledge divide.

Education in ancient India was very rich in moral and knowledge content but highly elitist and discriminatory. With lack of space for and exclusion of the masses, particularly *shudras*, it suffered an atrophy and could not sustain socio-economic growth. It failed in promotion of innovation and generation of new knowledge and its application. It also reflected itself in our ancient legal system, legal profession and finally, in our poor justice delivery systems paving the way to introduction of English Common Law after the Lex Loci Report of the First Law Commission. However, on account of a dichotomy between ancient Indian conciliatory dispute resolution systems and the adversarial common law system, justice delivery system remains unsatisfactory even today. The common man still feels alienated and finds it difficult to accept and internalize it despite its being in operation for more than 150 years.

In British India, both legal education and legal profession remained a preserve of the elite. The language of law, the court mannerism, the professional robes, the legal jargon and the formalism of legal documentation have been by and large beyond the comprehension of the common Indian. Even the liberal written Constitution and plethora of laws in the post-Independence India could not guarantee effective justice delivery system.

Four Stages of Legal Education in India

The growth and development of legal profession and education in India can be classified into four stages. Each stage has its peculiar characteristics and, therefore, the divide between these stages of development has been clear and perceptible.

The First Phase of development of the legal profession started with the introduction of English Common Law in India after the 'Lex Loci' Report by the First Law Commission. India was deemed to be a 'Legal vacuum' without any 'Law of the Land' (Lex Loci). It only had personal Laws of some religious communities like Hindus, Muslims, Jews and Parsis, the Common Law System in its working in India over the years proved to be rigid, technical and expensive. Moreover, it destroyed the more flexible and inexpensive conciliatory indigenous systems of dispute settlement through people's courts like panchayats. Formal legal education did not exist in India at that time and some Indians used to go to England for legal education. the legal profession was neither formally organized nor regulated through Statutory Laws.

The Second Phase started with our Independence. More or less, it was a continuum of the pre-Independence policies and practices for quite long. Some universities offered two year LL.B. course which was part-time and poorly administered with low paid part-time teachers without almost non-existent infrastructure. As late as 1958, the Law Commission of India observed that legal education was in a pathetic state and lawyers that it produced were 'Drones and Parasites'. Shri M.C. Setalvad, Chairman, Law Commission in 14th Report on Reforms of Judicial Administration 1958 had observed: 'In the period of 10 years which has elapsed since the publication of Radha Krishanan Commission the position in regard to legal Education in this country has, it appears, definitely deteriorated.'

In the Third Phase in 1960s, a need was felt for statutory regulation of the legal profession and legal education, in view of falling standards of both. Consequently, Indian Advocates Act 1961 was enacted which provided for a three-year Law course. In 1980 again, the Bar Council introduced a five-year integrated Law course after 10+2 level. However, the course remained neither integrated nor exclusive. The lateral exit out of five-year course after three years reduced its importance and focus. Moreover, the three-year course also continued and co-existed with the five-year Law course.

Justice A.S. Anand former Chief Justice of India observed:

'In 1958 when the Law Commission voiced its concern, there were hardly 43 institutions preparing 20,159 students for Law examinations. After enactment of Advocates Act 1961, it was noticed that there was a mushroom growth of sub-standard law schools, with hardly any regard to the quality of Legal Education'.[1]

The Fourth Phase started with establishment of new class of National Law Schools. With the advent of globalization, liberalization and privatization, there appeared a paradigm shift in the objectives and content of legal education and legal pedagogy. The driving forces of this change have been the rapid growth of law universities and colleges, emergence of newer and diverse areas of law, trends towards universalization of laws, legal education and the legal profession, needs of socio-legal impact research for perspective welfare planning and service-oriented state governance, growth of faster technology-based means of management, processing and transmission of knowledge, expanding private funding of legal education and insatiable demands of the corporate sector for competent Law professionals and, above all, the falling standards of the Bar. According to the National Knowledge Commission:

'At the time of enactment of the Advocates Act, 1961, it was envisaged that legal education would only produce lawyers for the courts and accordingly the BCI had been entrusted with the limited role of promoting legal education and laying down minimum standards of legal education required for students who are entitled to practice. In the last 50 years, and particularly after liberalization in 1991, the entire concept of legal education has changed considerably. Today, legal education has to meet not only the requirements of the Bar but also the new needs of trade, commerce and industry, in the context of growing internationalization of the profession'.[2]

Legal education is essential part of the larger matrix of a civil society with the guarantee of delivery of justice. There has been a paradigm shift in legal education and legal profession and the establishment of National Law Schools marked a water-shed in its history. We require a new breed of schools that will be able to handle global issues such as climate change, arbitration, mergers and acquisitions. For the same reasons, Ahmed observes:

> Due to expanding role of professionals, our curriculum should be enriched with all inter discreptionary courses which are must to produce the competent law professionsal of 4th generation.[3]

According to Sathe, 'Legal education is essentially a multi-disciplined, multipurpose education which can develop the human resources and idealism needed to strengthen the legal system .... A lawyer, a product of such education, would be able to contribute to national development and social change in a much more constructive manner'.[4]

Globalization of laws and business has led to selection of best students in the law schools in the fist stage followed by quality legal education with right type of teaching and training methodologies. Collaboration between Foreign Law Schools, particularly in Common Law countries and Indian Law Schools at student and faculty levels was a historical imperative on account of commonalities in Indian and western democracies in terms of common law, independent judiciary, common policies and objectives. Considering the sheer member of global law firms that have set up shops in India in the past 10 years, there is an urgent need for truly global legal education. We also need to have a special fleet of lawyers who can represent India in the WTO. The Bar Council of India is doing very little in this regard. The Council should also consider a five-year law course where faculty could consist of accomplished lawyers and researchers. Legal research has to be strengthened as a necessary input for legislation in future, perspective welfare, planning and even for use by judges. Moreover, we need clinical legal education so that students could get real life dealing in the courts and with clients. We may be local in our thinking but the focus would be to create lawyers who can relate to the global situation. Hence, our vision is to increase interaction between our law schools and others world-wide.

Two types of law schools exist in India today: public and private. Law colleges and faculties which are part of multi-faculty central and state universities have very high degree of variation in terms of quality of legal education, faculty and students, teaching methodologies, course content, degrees of autonomy and even financial viability. The mushroom growth of private law schools has further impacted the quality due to excessive commercialization of legal education. In these multi-faculty universities, law faculty enjoys very low priority resulting in either total lack of or poor quality of infrastructure, faculty and students. In some cases, law is taught as a part-time course with low students' motivation and commitment. Traditional course offered by them are more than two decades old and these faculties have failed to capture the far-reaching changes taking place in legal education today. Little wonder that: BUX1 observed that in his first teaching assignments in India, he realized 'with degree of astonishment, if not horror' what passed off as Legal Education in India.[5]

The new experiment of establishment of National Law Schools, starting with the establishment of Bangalore Law School in 1987 was necessitated by obsolescence and irrelevance of existing legal education and falling standards of legal profession. The initiative was timely in the context of demands of globalization with sweeping changes the world over. The advantages and improvements which the new experiment brought about included freedom from constraints of multi-faculty university system, improved quality of students and the faculty, inter-active and inter-disciplinary methods of teaching, focus on lawyering skills through moots and clinical legal work, international competitiveness and better infrastructure, work environment and work culture.

Legal education has to be much more comprehensive and wider in its sweep in view of universalization of laws and business. For this purpose, there is a need to establish global law schools with global faculty and syllabus. Law teaching must be interwoven with emerging contemporary issues, including international and comparative law perspectives. The curricula and syllabi must be based on a multidisciplinary body of social science and scientific knowledge. Curriculum development should include expanding the domain of optional courses, providing deeper under-standing of professional ethics, modernizing clinic courses, mainstreaming legal aid programmes and developing innovative pedagogic methods. Legal education must also be socially engaged and sensitize students on issues of social justice.[6]

Student and faculty exchanges should accelerate so that all law schools benefit from the expertise of others. The law syllabus should ensure that it is suitable for international student and also for home student to provide him with international perspective. Each law school should create a centre of excellence in a particular area of law like IPRs, Cyber Laws, Corporate Laws and faculty expertise of a law school may be available to others to ensure optimum use of the faculty with minimum cost. Flexible learning with inbuilt tertiary education in social sciences and technology-based online self-learning have to be integral parts of diver-sified legal education. Audio-visual technology-based self-assessment by the student and the faculty could also be introduced. Technology-enabled global virtual classroom should be available in all law schools so that legal learning from anywhere is available every where. Legal education should be available to candidates from diverse disciplines cutting across disci-pline boundaries. Law schools may award dual use, hybrid degrees like Law (Management), Law (Agriculture), Law (Technology), Law (Economics), Law (Medicine), Law (Biotechnology), Law (Business), Law (Space).

The National Knowledge Commission recommends:

> 'to attract and retain talented faculty, better incentives, including improving remuneration and service conditions may be introduced. It may be necessary to think of salary differentials within and between universities and law schools along with other means of attracting and retaining talented faculty members. Such salary differentials between and within universities and law schools could be effective without being large. This will help retain talent in legal academia where the problem of inadequate remuneration is far more acute than in other disciplines. Salary differentials could be considered as a means to retain quality talent and also promote a culture of excellence.'

To foster quality and create better incentives, there is also need to remove fetters on faculty that pertain to opportunities in legal practice (such as consultancy assignments and legal practice in courts). These reforms need to be introduced in a balanced, reasonable and regulated manner to ensure adequate incentivization for faculty without compromising on the maintenance of consistent academic quality. As a further incentive, it is necessary to create better opportunities for active involvement of academia in the shaping of national legal education policy.

There is also need to reconsider existing promotional schemes and avenues to promote meritorious faculty members. Other incentives for faculty include fully paid sabbaticals; adequate House Rent Allowance (HRA); instituting awards to honour reputed teachers and researchers at national and institutional levels; flexibility to appoint law teachers without having an LLM degree if the individual has proven academic or professional credentials; faculty exchange programmes with leading universities abroad and upgrading existing infrastructure.[7]

To meet the challenge of paucity of competent faculty, strategies are to be worked out to attract the best talent with academic aptitudes to LLM courses so that some of the LLMs stay back to teach at law schools, law schools should not only recruit and retain competent faculty but also ensure that they are well trained and motivated. To expose them to the best of academic environment, law school in India and abroad may plan for Joint-LLM courses. To retain the faculty, pay scales, service and working conditions have to be comparable to the corporate sector. Faculty exchange programmes have to be strengthened. Teaching facilities at induction level and later on, in service training through Academic Staff colleges, have to be provided for. To strengthen clinical legal education, Judges, senior lawyers and captains of industry should find time to teach some courses. This could also help in revision and updating of content of law courses as per requirement of the legal profession, corporate and public sectors. Horizons of legal education have to expand and law graduates from law schools should not only be well trained as professional lawyers but also as expert consultants, mediators, conciliators, arbitrators and above all, socially relevant so that they play multiple roles in securing social justice and equity. This may also necessitate continuing academic and social audit of the law schools, evaluation of faculty performance and research and follow up studies and research on the performance and commitment of law graduates in the legal profession and other sectors of employment and social service. In the highly competitive and international environment, demands and expectations of various stake holders like government, corporate sector, civil society, students, social action groups, private and public enterprises are expanding very fast.

Another important issue relates to the financial viability of law schools. Presently, the status of law schools is such that in principle they are supposed to be self financing. To keep legal education affordable, fees cannot be enormously high and, therefore, direct state funding or through UGC is essential. National Law Schools have been set up under the state Acts, with national character. As such, they are not central law schools and states provide limited funds for infrastructure only. New funding frameworks and diversification of income streams of law schools have to be planned for. On the other hand, extreme commercialization in private law schools and private law universities has to be checked and compliance with minimum standards – both physical and academic has to be ensured. The role of private players and foreign providers of legal education have been on the increase. In view of proliferation of overseas universities offering courses locally through an agent or with a partner institution, the distinction between private and public universities is fudging. Institutional arrangements for accreditation and assessment have to be created to monitor and regulate working of law schools. Law schools should not be perceived as a market places and legal education as a commodity which could be traded as per market forces of demand and supply. As knowledge spaces, law schools should also strengthen study and research in behavioural sciences so that they produce humane and sensitive lawyers and not professionally trained mercenaries. Legal education has to be transformed into justice education. Singh rightly observes:

> 'The Legal Education and the Profession have to take care for the "invisible man". The Advocate have to become socially more relevant and technically very sound if they have to serve the needs of the society in 21st century'.[8]

Notes

1. A.S. Anand. Savion Memorial Legal Aid Foundation Lecture, Reported (1998) 3SCC(Jour)1.
2. National Knowledge Commission Report, p. 86.
3. Tabrez Ahmed. 'Legal Education in Indian Perspective', 2009, p. 1, www.site.technolixindia.com
4. S.P. Sathe. 'Access to Legal Education and the Legal Profession in India', in R. Dhawan, N. Kibble and W. Twining (eds), *Access to Legal Education and the Legal Profession*, London: Butterworths, 1989, p. 165.
5. Quoted by Arushi Garg, 'Legal Education in India: Laws and Other Things'. A Blog about India's Laws and Legal System, its Courts and its Constitution, 3 June 2011.
6. National Knowledge Commission Report, pp. 87–88.
7. Ibid., p. 88.
8. Ranbir Singh. 'Reforms in Legal Education and Legal Profession in India', *Andhra Law Times*, Vol. 6, 1998, pp.15–18.

10

Management Education in India

Emerging Challenges and Issues

PUNEET SHARMA

'According to an international ranking of universities, no Indian university figures among the top 200 universities of the world.' So said President Pranab Mukherjee on March 17, 2013, while addressing the convocation of the Indian Institute of Management in Uttarakhand. Outlining the dire need for a competent cadre of management professionals, he further remarked: 'The pool of such professionals in our country is unfortunately not enough to meet the demands of the country' (http://presidentofindia.nic.in/ sp170313.html, March 17, 2013). This sums up the current state of management education in India.

This paper intends to trace the evolution and growth of management education in India, its contemporary status vis-à-vis global benchmarks and the challenges and issues facing management education in India.

Growth Points

The origins of management education go back to pre-Independence India when the first college level business school was founded in 1913 in Mumbai to teach the principles of trade and commerce to clerks and supervisors (Indian Management, September 2004). If anything, it concerned itself more with the study of commerce than really with teaching the principles of management. The management education has come a long way since then.

The model of planned development followed by the leaders of post-Independence era focused on the industrialization of the country and, therefore, formal training of managers and supervisors became almost a necessity. Though accounts vary, it is safe to assume that the first business school (B-school) post-Independence was set up in early 1950s in Kolkata and was called Indian Institute of Social Welfare and Business Management. In tune with the thinking that all policies, including planned industrialization of the country should have social welfare as their goal, it is but obvious that management education and social welfare be taught together. The first Indian Institute of Management (IIM) was set up in 1961 at Kolkata and was soon followed by others.

For tracing the growth of management education in post-Independence era, it may be analytically valuable to project it in two phases – pre-liberalization and post-liberalization. To begin with pre-liberalization phase, the socialist influence was the dominating theme defining policies of the government during this period. The government believed that it knew what was best for the economy. With resources scarce, the intention was to employ these resources in a way that would result in the maximum good of maximum people. Therefore, the economy was tightly regulated and for most of the ventures, licenses and permits were needed from the government. Up to 1980, government agencies had to be satisfied before private enterprise could start a business. The enterprises needed people who could manage the government officials and get the work done more than the managers to run the business. With production quotas allocated by the government and availability of ready market, a situation almost akin to monopoly, the businesses did not really feel the need for effective managers. No wonder the period from 1950 to 1995 saw addition of a meagre 9.38 B-schools in India per year (Dayal, 2002). In terms of functional specialization, this period also saw greater emphasis on finance, production (operations), marketing and industrial relations. The business theory was geared more to the study of these areas with little emphasis on human resource development.

Moving on to the post-liberalization phase, India was faced with a serious balance of payments crisis in the year 1991. The government was left with little option but to undertake dramatic reforms to save the country from going insolvent. This led to opening up of many sectors for private participation. The red tape in the approval processes was systematically removed. The production quotas were done away with. The certainty of markets was no longer there and consequently, the businesses started feeling the need for trained managers. The average annual addition to B-schools in India jumped up to 64 for the period 1995 to 2000 (ibid.). The policies of liberalization continued to gather steam and India soon became a global hub for outsourcing of services. A rapid rise in the number of B-schools in India was all but inevitable. In the last five years (2007 to 2012), the number of B-schools in India has trebled to almost 4,500. This explosive growth, in part, is explained by the tremendous opportunity seen by the private sector in the field of professional and technical education. The Working Group on Management Education (WGME) set up by National Knowledge Commission (NKC) notes in its report that the accelerated growth in the number of B schools in India 'speaks also for the entrepreneurial initiative of promoters to seize commercial opportunities in education' (http://knowledgecommission. gov.in/downloads/documents/wg_managedu.pdf, 2007). The steep rise in the number of B schools in India is further explained by a rapid rise in the economic growth rate of the country. As intuitive as it may be, it is clearly borne out by facts too. The average annual economic growth of India moved up from 3.6 per cent in the period 1950–1980 to 8.03 per cent in the period 2007–2012 and so did the number of B schools in India which grew from 118 to about 4,500 at the end of 2012 (http://planningcommission.nic.in/data/datatable/1503/databook_1.pdf). Liberalization also brought about a change in the character of management education. With Indian economy becoming more service-centric, the emphasis on the study of human resource development increased greatly. At the same time, the study of public policy made inroads into management education as a result of the changed thinking in the government that public programmes need to be managed rather than administered which was the case for most part of the pre-liberalization period.

State of Quality

In its preamble, the Association to Advance Collegiate Schools of Business (AACSB), which monitors quality management education worldwide through accreditation, thought leadership and value added services has identified three core areas that it bases its accreditation on. These are: innovation, impact and engagement (http://www.aacsb.edu/accreditation/2013standards/). In a fast changing and highly competitive world, it is no surprise that AACSB puts premium on innovation. Impact, in a narrow sense, refers to the contributions of business management education to business theory, teaching and practice. In a broader sense, it refers to the difference that management education makes to advancing the frontiers and standards of business and to the socio-economic advancement of mankind. Engagement refers to a meaningful interaction between academic and professional organization without which the learning is incomplete and theory does not contribute to practice.

On all the three criteria, management education in India appears to be under-performing. Part of the reason is the misplaced emphasis on over-regulation where the focus is on norms for inputs such as land, faculty and other infrastructure. Contrast this with the accreditation measures used by the AACSB which focus on governance for building processes that will ensure quality output rather than on control which insists simply on inputs. No wonder, India has only two management education institutions accredited by AACSB compared to 13 of China. Global accreditation apart, the state is dismal even by the local accreditation standards. Lamenting this, UGC chairman remarked in November 2006 that only 20 per cent of Indian engineering programmes are accredited. The proportion of management programmes accredited is much lower (http://knowledgecommission.gov.in/downloads/documents/wg_managedu.pdf, 2007: 10).

Regulatory framework notwithstanding, the quality of management education leaves much to be desired in India. In a country where an MBA degree is considered a passport to good employment, many unscrupulous promoters, with no commitment to the cause of management education, have set up management education institutions with the sole purpose of exploiting the lucrative financial opportunities the field offers. This view is endorsed by WGME in its report. It notes: 'The imbalance between demand and supply for management graduates has led to an overly commercial and exploitative environment in management education. It is not clear how many of the recently started institutions are merely speculative and how many are seriously committed to the cause of management education. It is not also clear how many actually meet the norms and standards established by All India Council for Technical Education.'

This should, however, not worry us overly. Free markets are a great leveler. In fact, some of the private management education institutions have started shutting shop after their failure to attract students. There were no takers for students being churned out by dubious institutions as they added no value to the corporates. Sluggish economy too played its part. So much so, that in a recent report, *The Economic Times* pointed out that even the IIMs were facing problems in placing their students (Basu and Sengupta, 2013).

The quality of management education is a function of inputs, processes and output. The inputs include students, faculty, curriculum and infrastructure. While a lot has been written about the current state of faculty, curriculum and infrastructure, student selection and student aspiration has not been given enough importance. While the top management education institutions like the IIMs have a structured testing procedure for selection of students, the same cannot be said about the other institutions, especially the private ones which are happy to offer the student a seat as long as one is willing to pay. It is also important to understand what drives the students to opt for management education. In a study of the socio-economic background of management education seekers, it was found that 77 per cent of the applicants opted for it in order 'to become a professional' (Sidhu and Jyoti, 2005). It is highly debatable whether the respondents, indeed, knew what that meant except the commonly understood meaning, i.e. a white collar job that guarantees money and status. The lure of the lucre, of course, has been the driving factor for taking up management education. Nothing wrong with that. The problem arises when majority of the aspirants either do not have the aptitude or the required drive to learn and then to practice what they learn. And that seems to be the bane of the current management education which is under the siege of the private sector.

The issues of unqualified/under-qualified faculty and inadequate infrastructure have been highlighted by various reports. The NKC, in its recommendations to the Prime Minister's Office (PMO), notes: 'Non availability of adequate proficient faculty is a major constraint for sustainable growth of quality management education in India' (http://knowledgecommission.gov.in/recommendations/management.asp, 2007). Ruing the inept faculty in management education institutions in India, N. Ravichandran, Director of IIM, Indore, observes: 'In the western world, competency is a pre-requisite to become a tenured faculty in a decent university .... Over a period of time, our management educational system has degenerated into information sharing. Often the teacher is two hours ahead of the taught on the subject matter' (Ravichandran, 2009).

The state of curriculum is no better. History of management education in India shows that it is the western model of management education which has been imported and supplanted here. Most of the management education institutions simply copy and paste the curriculum being followed in the West. Neither do they have the resources nor the willingness to develop curricula relevant to Indian conditions. Further, with businesses in a constant flux, the skills required by the industry are changing rapidly. Under such circumstances, the curricula must be updated regularly to keep pace with the changing requirements. Nothing of the sort is being practiced in reality except by a few top notch management education institutions in India. Commenting on the same, WGME, in its report to the NKC, states: 'Most institutions depend on curricula developed elsewhere and have not developed an intrinsic capacity to respond and evolve to the changing needs of various sectors of industry and services, student interests, non-governmental organizations, or the economy and society. Many are unable to fulfill the mandatory changes imposed on them, such as upgrading of the curriculum by the universities or the Board of Management Studies' (http://knowledgecommission.gov.in/downloads/documents/wg_managedu.pdf, 2007: 11).

To get an idea of the pathetic state of infrastructure of the Management education institutions in India here is a quote from the Report to the Nation presented by the NKC: 'There are several instances where an engineering college or a business school is approved promptly, in a small house of a metropolitan suburb without the requisite teachers, infrastructure or facilities, ...' (www.knowledgecommission.gov.in/reports/report06/asp, 2006: 54). This is an extreme situation highlighted more for its dramatic effect but the fact still remains that most management education institutions in India have inadequate infrastructure to support learning, research and engagement with industry.

Turning to the processes, it is pretty much the same story. We have by and large adopted the same pedagogy and methodology as in the west with emphasis on multiple ways of instruction, including lecturing, case study method and industry interaction. The problem is that the system has been copied and implemented here with little thought given to its relevance. It is important that the processes be so designed as to promote excellence in teaching methodology and research and to promote an open mind. Unfortunately, while the pedagogy has been copied, the nuances that build quality into the process have been completely ignored. There are very few management education institutions that have documented processes to promote quality. For instance, while the case study method of pedagogy has been lapped up by management education institutions, little effort has been made to generate case studies relevant to the Indian context except by a few premier management institutions. Almost all management education institutions have no formal process or system that promotes and rewards research by faculty members. To put this in proper perspective, 'At London Business School, an average of 300 research papers, articles and books are published every year', says Laura Tyson, Dean of the LBS. In comparison, IIM Ahmedabad published 139 papers in 2001–02 and IIM Kolkata around 195 (Sharma, 2005). The story down the order is miserable with the numbers woefully small and quality highly questionable. While industry exposure has been made a part of the curriculum, little effort is made to ensure the exposure contributes to learning. There are no formal processes in place that reward innovation which is so critical today for the continued success of any business. Given its importance, encouraging innovation in any process, even when it fails to produce desired results, is considered a key element for accreditation by the AACSB.

Coming to the output, needless to say that the true measure of quality is in the output produced by the optimal mix of inputs and processes. Weakness in either the inputs or the processes will reflect in the output. Our output is well below the standard. Except for some leading management education institutions, most others have been producing students/practitioners who the industry finds not suited to its requirements. The disenchantment of the industry with the product is apparent from the poor placement records of most management education institutions in India and their lowly rankings in the international arena.

Challenges and Issues

India today is at the cusp of transformation. As India transforms itself into a global economic powerhouse, industry today has a crying need for trained and skilled management graduates to drive this transformation. Given this, it is imperative that we identify the challenges and issues facing management education in India.

Challenges

Manpower Planning

India has more than 50 per cent of its population below the age of 25 and more than 65 per cent below the age of 35. It is expected that, in 2020, the average age of an Indian will be 29 years, compared to 37 for a Chinese and 48 for a Japanese. By 2030, India's dependency ratio would be just over 0.4. When this is viewed along with the fact that the Indian economy which is already growing at a healthy rate, will be the fastest growing economy of the world shortly, the future looks extremely rosy. But is it really so? Such a large proportion of young population in the total population is a great asset if managed properly. If, however, mismanaged, it can turn into a disaster of catastrophic proportions. In order to manage the tremendous growth opportunity the future provides and to ensure that India does not run into socio-economic problems, a very careful manpower planning is required.

The fast growing Indian economy requires adequate number of management professionals of global standards suited to the requirements of various industries. There are three key phrases here. 'Adequate' refers to the appropriate number, neither more nor less based on projected rates of growth. 'Global standards' refers to the quality of such professionals. Since we live in a highly integrated world where businesses are facing intense competition globally, the quality of management professionals assumes paramount importance. Quality is a construct of inputs and processes both of which must be of global standards to give us an outstanding output. 'Suited' refers to the suitability of such professionals to the specific industry. It is very likely that the skill-set required for the management of health services or public policy is very different from the one needed for manufacturing industry. The adequacy, quality and suitability of our management professionals in turn depend upon the adequacy, quality and suitability of our management education.

Diversity

A singular focus on management school rankings, combined with a copied model of management education in India, pushes all management schools to have similar structure, processes and value system. This produces students who are trained to think alike adversely impacting diversity of views so essential for innovation and reaching the next level. One of the reasons advanced for appointing Carlos Ghosn, a non-Japanese, as Chairman and CEO of Renault Nissan was to promote diversity of views within the organization. Many in Japan blame the lack of diversity of backgrounds of most of the Japanese CEOs and political leaders for the problems of the Japanese economy. A large number of Japanese business and political leaders are the products of the schools with similar structure, culture and processes. Therefore, the challenge before the management educators is to provide enough room for diversity in student backgrounds, curriculum and pedagogy without diluting the focus of management education.

Research

As the economy is expanding, the industry is getting exposed to fierce global competition. There is a tremendous requirement of insights into consumer behaviour. Insights provided by cutting edge management research are the need of the hour. Unfortunately, there is a woeful lack of candidates who wish to pursue research in management despite it being one of the most critical areas for expansion of knowledge in the field of management. De Angelo, De Angelo and Zimmerman (2005) talk of a communal lack of scholarly focus in management research, a malady that has been afflicting management research in India. Bennis and O'Toole (2005), on the other hand, believe that the scholars have lost focus on the industry. They seem to communicate among themselves in an esoteric language in the name of scholarly focus which is not easily understood by the industry (Greenbaum, 2005). Be that as it may, the policy makers, educators and the industry are faced with the daunting challenge of attracting talent into management research which is so crucial for the success of businesses today.

Innovation

An equally daunting challenge facing management education is integrating innovation in management education curriculum, pedagogy and processes. Innovation is the key for businesses to effectively compete in the market place. Innovation is a construct of a free thinking mind. Unfortunately, our whole education system, and not just management education, does precious little to promote free thinking and creativity so essential for innovation. We are trained to think in silos. The costs of ignoring this one element can be enormous as innovation will be the critical element in segregating winners from the losers.

Industry Interface

Industry interface is yet another major challenge for our management educators. There has to be a two-way connect between the management education institutions and the industry with each contributing to the other and learning from it. Barring the top few management education institutions in India, there is hardly any meaningful contribution made by one to the other. On the face of it, almost all management education institutions tout industry training as an integral part of their curriculum but dig just a little deeper and the reality springs forth. The student training in most cases is a farce with no clearly laid down objectives, no specification of process and in most cases no evaluation of the result. Similarly, with under performance of faculty and curriculum and suspect research in most management education institutions, the industry has very little to draw upon from the management education institutions. Commenting on the same, Rahul Gandhi during his recent address to Indian business leaders at CII lamented: 'Our university structures are closed. They are silos. The university is a network. It has to be connected to the industry' (*Times News Network*, 2013).

Social Responsibility

The issue of social responsibility has gained in salience as businesses have grown bigger, some larger than even GDPs of certain countries. They are touching billions of lives today and are making a profound impact on both the people and the environment. There are essentially two components of social responsibility. One is the obligation towards all stakeholders, including suppliers, employees, customers and shareholders and the other is the obligation towards the public at large. It is not uncommon to find business organizations whose goals at times are in conflict with their social responsibility. For instance, tobacco companies are known to spend billions of dollars to resist legislation that would impact their business knowing fully well that they will be harming their customers by not letting such a legislation go through. Similarly, the very recent case of Glivec, an anti-leukaemia drug made by Novartis, where 90 per cent of funding for R&D came from public sources but the patent was cornered by Novartis making billions of dollars worldwide in sales by pricing the drug well beyond the means of majority of the population of the world is another such example. There are, on the other hand, large business organizations that have been able to integrate social responsibility in their business processes. Many like Levi Strauss, Gap Inc, etc. have written down codes of conduct for their vendors to follow both in terms of how they treat their employees and also how the waste product is disposed of so that least harm is done to the environment. With the size and scale that the corporate sector has today and the profound impact it has on the lives of the general public, every action of theirs is under public scrutiny. While social responsibility is the buzzword today among corporates, it is practised more in its breach. The challenge before the educators today is to build the issue of social responsibility in management curricula in such a way that the students are trained to strike an optimal balance between the business objectives and social responsibility.

Issues

Model of Management Education

An unplanned growth of management education institutions is not the solution to meet the requirements of the industry. The solution lies in the adequacy, quality and suitability of management education. The issue is whether the model being followed in the West may be copied and pasted here or if we need to look for alternative models. The businesses do not operate in silos. They operate in a social milieu and are very much a part of the cultural matrix which affects the way they operate. There is a need to rethink the model of management education being followed here.

Bureaucratic Framework

Most of our management education institutions work within the framework of the university system and, therefore, have to follow the rules and regulations of the university. There is a bureaucratic process for effecting any changes in the inputs and processes. The issue is that with industry's requirements changing continuously, is it possible to operate within the university's framework without compromising quality of management education? The good news is that the issue of flexible curriculum is already being debated and discussed in the press. Though not yet in the university circles.

Private Institutions

Majority of management education institutions in India are privately-funded and operated. It is not uncommon to point fingers at them for the sorry state of management education in India. The issue is how to ensure that these institutions align their goals with those of the industry. So far the market forces have failed to yield the desired results and, therefore, the question is about the kind of model that must be followed to make them industry relevant. Should it be the regulatory model or the governance model or a judicious mix of the two?

Ethics

Business history is replete with examples of ethical, moral and legal violations, sometimes of the scale that have submerged the whole world into a financial crisis. Who can forget the sub-prime crisis which began in the U S and led to the crash of global financial markets sending the global economy into recession? Corporates and individuals manipulating systems or even transgressing the legislative boundaries to pander to their greed are only increasing in incidence. Ethical indiscretions on the part of individual managers are far too common to ignore. Rajat Gupta's case in the US or Satyam scam closer home are not one off or peculiar examples. Unethical practices are rampant cutting across industries from pharmaceuticals to tobacco to the financial sector. Pfeffer, 2004, argues that management educators have lost their souls (Greenbaum, 2005). Managers are being trained to play to the stock markets and short-termism dominates even at the level of top leadership where financial results have become more important than the purity of means.

There are, however, varying opinions whether ethics can be taught in B-schools. Wonders Stuart I. Greenbaum (2005), 'Just how 18 months (two or three years part-time) in pursuit of an MBA can reverse 25 to 30 years of cultural conditioning remains a mystery'. Speaking in the same vein, David Wilson, President and CEO, GMAC, argues that teaching ethics does not make the students ethical. It has to be a part of the DNA (*The Economic Times*, 2013). While there is merit in the above argument, it is equally true that the thrust of management education is more on enhancing efficiency and affluence than on inculcating ethics and morals, more on the methods of profit maximization than on imbibing the professional code of conduct. Hence, the need to incorporate ethical component into management education which in all likelihood would make a difference to the situation.

Last but not the least, management is an application-based profession and, therefore, integration of management education with industry is critical. The two must draw upon each other for the expansion of knowledge so critical for the unhindered growth of both and that of the economy. The issues are why there is such a disconnect between management education and industry and how the two may be brought together to exploit each other's strengths. If we look hard enough, the answers may not be too difficult to find.

References

Basu, Sreeradha and Devina Sengupta. 2013. 'A Management Lesson? 13 IIMs Unlucky for Placements'. *The Economic Times*, New Delhi, March 18.

Dayal, I. 2002. 'Developing Management Education in India'. *Journal of Management Research*, Vol. 2, No. 2, August, p. 101.

Greenbaum, Stuart I. 2005. http://apps.olin.wustl.edu/workingpapers/pdf/2005-11-004.pdf

http://knowledgecommission.gov.in/downloads/documents/wg_managedu.pdf

http://knowledgecommission.gov.in/recommendations/management.asp

http://planningcommission.nic.in/data/datatable/1503/databook_1.pdf

http://presidentofindia.nic.in/sp170313.html

http://www.aacsb.edu/accreditation/2013standards/

Ravichandran, N. 2009. 'A Perspective on Management Education in India'. *The Financial Express*, Internet edition, October 12.

Sharma, K.K. 2005. 'Management Education in India: The Changing Scenario', in S.K. Chadha and P.P. Arya (eds), *Quality of Management Education: The Challenge of Changing Scenario*, New Delhi: Deep and Deep Publications.

Sidhu, A.S. and Jyoti. 2005. 'Socio-Economic Background of Management Education Seekers: A Case Study', in S.K. Chadha and P.P. Arya (eds), *Quality of Management Education: The Challenge of Changing Scenario*, New Delhi: Deep and Deep Publications.

The Economic Times Q&A. 2013. 'Ethics can't be Taught in a B-School'. March 19, p. 6.

Times News Network. 2013. 'Rahul Gives India Inc a "Bee" School Lecture'. *The Times of India*, April 5, p. 1.

www.knowledgecommission.gov.in/reports/report06.asp

11

Higher Education in Punjab

Under-representation of Rural Students

RANJIT SINGH GHUMAN

Rationale for Higher Education

Access to higher education and the broad range of services it can render to society is part and parcel of any sustainable development programme in which human expertise and professional skills are required (UNESCO, 1995). It is the substrate on which research and development flourish, which is the ultimate guarantee of national self-reliance. It provides people with an opportunity to reflect on the political, social, economic, cultural, moral and spiritual issues facing the humanity (GoI, 1986). Tomorrow's world will demand highly qualified specialists and increasingly flexible generalists (The World Bank, 2000: 69). It is in this context that 'the real wealth of a nation is its people' (UNDP, 1990).

The modern growth theories have established beyond doubt that economic growth and development cannot attain an optimum and self-sustenance path without the development of human resources (Romer, 1990; Lucas, 1993; Benhabib and Spiegel, 1994; Barro and Sala-i-Martin, 1995; Barro, 2001; Krueger and Lindahl, 2001). Actually, higher education enhances skills and capacities of the people and brings them to the centre stage of economic development of a country (Agarwal, 2006). All those countries, who had focused on human capital formation in the past, have achieved high growth trajectory in their national and per capita income (OECD/UNESCO, 2002). And, higher education is certainly associated with high economic returns and rising stock of human capital (Qian and Smyth, 2007).

The seminal work of Schultz and Becker have virtually revolutionized the main contours of development economics and led to resurgence of economics of education as the most important discipline of research in the knowledge economy (Schultz, 1961; Becker, 1964). Alfred Marshall, the great classical economist, also stated that although the nature's production system is subject to decreasing returns, yet the men's skills and knowledge have the capacity to produce increasing returns (Marshall, 1920). Many empirical studies, conducted by various social scientists, have shown that a country would remain underdeveloped so long as her people are deprived of higher education (The World Bank, 2002; Tilak, 2004a, b). Kothari Commission also highlighted the key role of higher education in economic and social development of India (GoI, 1968). The Planning Commission of India (GoI, 2008) emphasized the role of higher education in achieving better socio-economic development and emancipation of the individuals as well as the society. India's National Knowledge Commission (NKC) re-emphasized its commitment to promote higher education in India (GoI, 2007). Many recent research studies show that the remarkable economic success of East Asian Countries has been the result not only of abundance of natural resources but also of their highly developed human resources (Tilak, 2001). The significance of higher education to develop the personality, inculcate the rationality and quality of the individual to fulfill certain political and cultural functions are well documented in the form of externalities (Tilak, 2002).

However, in the race towards growth, it is often forgotten that people are the real wealth of nations. '... Mesmerized by the rise and fall of national incomes (as measured by GDP), we tend to equate human welfare with material wealth. The importance of the GDP growth and economic stability should not be understated: both are fundamental to sustain human progress .... But the ultimate yardstick for measuring progress is people's quality of life ...' (UNDP, 2006: 263). The famous philosopher Aristotle argued, 'Wealth is evidently not the good we are seeking: for it is merely useful and for the sake of something else' (Aristotle, quoted in UNDP, 2006: 263). The development is eventually about expanding human potentialities and enlarging human freedoms. It is about developing and enhancing the capabilities of the people. This, in turn, empowers the people to make choices and lead the lives they have reason to value (Sen, 2000: 293). Expansion of freedom is, thus, viewed as both the primary end and the principal means of development. 'Even a very rich person, who is prevented from speaking freely, or from participating in public debates and decisions, is deprived of something that she has reason to value. The process of development, when judged by the enhancement of human freedom, has to include the removal of this person's deprivation' (ibid., pp. 36–37).

As a matter of fact, human development is closely connected with the GDP growth rate, and vice-versa. If growth is not reflected in raising the level of educational attainment and health standards (which is the substrate of human development) then the very growth and development process needs a serious review. The low level of human development is a drag on the growth and development. At the same time, if growth and development adversely impact the environment then the environment, in turn, would have unfavourable impact on growth. If environment gets polluted and the social development is not taking place then it falls back on the human choices. It would limit the human choices instead of widening them. And any process of growth and development which is not environment friendly and which does not widen the human choices and capabilities would not be sustainable. In other words, the kind of push that growth and development would get from better human resources and unpolluted environment would be missing. That, in turn, would limit the possibilities of future growth potentialities. And eventually the growth, we are now boasting upon, would get stuck and even the growth machine may get into the reverse gear.

In the words of Martin Luther King Jr., 'Human progress is neither automatic nor inevitable. We are faced now with the fact that tomorrow is today. We are confronted with the fierce urgency of now. In the unfolding conundrum of life and history there is such a thing as being too late .... We may cry out desperately for time to pause in her passage, but time is deaf to every plea and rushes on. Over the bleached bones and jumbled residues of numerous civilizations are written the pathetic words: *Too Late*.'[1] The human development, thus, goes beyond 'growth' and development. Human development is an umbrella which encompasses both growth and development. The growth and development could be sustainable only on the substrate of human development and vice-versa. And, of course, unsustainable growth would eat up every thing, which nature has bestowed upon mankind on which future generations have the legitimate right. 'The pioneering example of enhancing economic growth through social opportunity, especially in basic education, is of course Japan.[2] It is sometimes forgotten that Japan had a higher rate of literacy than Europe had even at the time of Meiji restoration in the mid-nineteenth century, when industrialization had not yet occurred there .... The so-called East Asian Miracle involving other countries in East Asia was, to a great extent, based on similar connections' (Sen, 2000: 41).

'Three great development waves have swept over Asia in the last five decades. The first wave started in Japan in the 1940s and 1950s when Japan combined its cheap labour with education and technical skills and took over rapidly the global markets in the export of low and medium technology consumer goods. Then came the second wave, as the low-income East Asian societies stepped into this growing void in the 1960s and 1970s following the same simple but brilliant model where low wages became a powerful engine of competition and growth as they are combined with an educated and skilled labour force and open economies. The third wave emerged in China in the 1980s and 1990s, and still continues unabated, based on simple human development models, as followed by Japan and East Asian countries in the past. An intriguing question remains: will the fourth great wave of development touch the shores of South Asia? Can South Asia become the next economic frontier in the 21st century' (Haq, 1998)?

The paradigm shift under the General Agreement on Trade in Services (GATS) brought education in the purview of World Trade Organization (WTO).[3] Education, being a service, is now being governed by the basic rules of GATS, viz.; national and most favoured nation (MFN) treatment to all the foreign institutions of education. Under the WTO regime, every country's education system is going to be closely linked at the global level. A country can supply its education service through four modes. They are: cross-border supply; consumption abroad; commercial presence in the territory of any other member country and presence of natural persons of a member country in the territory of any other member.[4]

The recent reforms initiated in India have brought out an unprecedented demand for skilled workforce relevant to the needs of industrial and business sectors. This has generated a considerable pressure on the government to reform the higher education sector so as to make it 'demand driven' for meeting the emerging needs of the economy and to keep its highly skilled and qualified people within the country (Kaul, 2006). The institution of the National Knowledge Commission, the Yashpal Committee Report and the proposed overarching National Council for Higher Education and Research are all steps towards revolutionary reforms in the education sector in India. All the stakeholders in India must get prepared to face the challenges and reap the benefits of opportunities under the changed global scenario. If India is to compete at the global level then it would have to establish world class higher education institutions. That would require huge investment in the higher education sector.

It is significant to note that the gross enrolment ratio (GER) in India is far below the GER in the developed countries of the world. The GER in India is hovering around 13 per cent. The Government of India is envisaging raising it to 30 per cent by 2020. The average world GER was 24 per cent in 2007. The average GER in high-income countries is 67 per cent and that in the upper and lower middle-income countries, it is 40 per cent and 23 per cent, respectively (The World Bank, 2008). Clearly, India has to cover a lot of distance to make up the gap in the enrolment ratio. This is equally applicable to Punjab where the GER is much below the national average.

Evolution of Higher Education in Punjab

The higher education in Punjab has a very long historical past with a strong colonial legacy. However, its expansion had been very limited and elite oriented. Its accessibility and affordability to the general masses was highly marred, on the one hand, by the supply constraints (very few institutions in urban locations) and, on the other, by the poor socio-economic conditions of people (Kaur, 1992). After Independence, the Union as well as provincial governments started allocating a sizeable proportion of public funds to establish new higher education institutions in the country. Consequently, enrolment in higher education institutions in Punjab also increased at a higher speed (Ghuman, Singh and Brar, 2006, 2009). The structure of higher education developed in the Punjab state mainly followed the national pattern of imparting higher education in the general (Arts, Science, Commerce and Home Science), professional and technical subjects through the universities and their affiliated colleges (Mittar, Singh and Brar, 2002). Many research studies reveal that the state government has allocated more funds to higher education during the 1970s and mid-1980s (Gill, Singh and Brar, 2005) and the budgetary expenditure on the general education in the state was quite high (Ghuman, Singh and Brar, 2005).

Table 1 presents the evolution of higher education in Punjab. There were 188 colleges (62 rurally located colleges; 32.98%) in Punjab in 1981. Their number rose to 202 (67 rurally located colleges; 33.17%) in 1991, which further increased to 524 (204 rurally located colleges; 38.93%) during 2006–07. It means a large number of the colleges in the state were established during 1991–2006. And, large majority of them came up in the urban areas. The expansion of higher education during the latter period mainly came in professional and technical education and that, too, in the private sector.

The state of Punjab has a number of universities imparting higher education in general, professional and technical courses. These are: Punjab Agricultural University (PAU), Ludhiana; Punjabi University (PUP) Patiala, Guru Nanak Dev University (GNDU), Amritsar; Punjab Technical University (PTU), Jalandhar; Baba Farid University of Health Science (BFUHS), Faridkot; Guru Angad Dev Veterinary and Animal Sciences University (GADVAU), Ludhiana. These universities are funded by the government of Punjab. However, the government funding, these days, is not able to cover even the 20 per cent of their budgets. The Rajiv Gandhi National University of Law, Punjab, Patiala is partially funded by the Union Government and partially by the government of Punjab. Thaper University, Patiala, is mainly funded privately whereas Lovely Professional University, Phagwara, is purely private university. Three other private universities (Chandigarh University, Gharuan; DAV University, Jalandhar; and Desh Bhagat University, Gobindgarh) have recently been approved by the State Assembly. A couple of more private universities are in the wings. Sant Longowal Institute of Engineering and Technology, Longowal is a deemed university and is mainly funded by the Union Government. The Central University of Punjab, Bathinda, has been recently established by the Union Government. Panjab University, Chandigarh, though situated in Chandigarh, has its affiliated colleges in Punjab. The Union Government has also announced to set up a world class university in Punjab near Amritsar. It is, thus, clear that the state of Punjab has all types of higher education institutions imparting education in diverse streams.

Table 1

Number of Recognized Colleges/Institutions in Punjab by Types and Location (selected years)

Type of College	*1981*		*1991*		*2006–07*	
	Total	*Rural*	*Total*	*Rural*	*Total*	*Rural*
Arts, Science, Commerce and Home Science	162 (86.17)	58 (35.20)	171 (84.65)	63 (36.42)	232 (44.28)	71 (30.60)
Teachers' Training (B.Ed./M.Ed.)	18 (9.57)	3 (16.67)	18 (8.91)	3 (16.67)	124 (23.66)	68 (54.84)
Engineering, Architecture and Pharmacy	3 (1.60)	1 (33.33)	4 (1.98)	1 (25.00)	66 (12.60)	28 (42.42)
Medical, Dental, Ayurvedic, Homeopathy, Nursing, etc.	5* (2.66)	—	9 (4.46)	—	55 (10.50)	17 (30.91)
Management/Computer Science/Law	—	—	—	—	47 (8.97)	20 (42.55)
Total	188 (100)	62 (32.46)	202 (100)	67 (32.68)	524 (100)	204 (38.93)

Note: *Allopathic medical colleges only. Figures in parentheses (...) are percentages and in index brackets (...) are rural proportions.

Sources: 1. Statistical Abstract of Punjab, Economic and Statistical Organization, Chandigarh, various issues.
2. Economic Survey, Punjab, Economic and Statistical Organization, Chandigarh, various issues.
3. Social and Educational Statistics of Punjab, Economic and Statistical Organization, Chandigarh, various issues.

The PUP, GNDU, PTU, BFUHS and PU are all affiliating universities and all the colleges in the state are affiliated to one or the other university. The affiliating jurisdiction of the PUP, GNDU and PU is confined to specified districts of Punjab. The affiliating jurisdiction of the PTU and BFUHS is the whole of Punjab. It is significant to note that these two universities have been simply the examining bodies, so far. They did not have their own faculty and teaching and research departments.

The universities are primarily responsible for quality control in higher education. Apart from imparting instructions, they are also responsible to undertake research and intervene in the policies of the state. 'A University is a place where new ideas germinate, strike roots and grow tall and sturdy. It is a unique space, which covers the entire universe of knowledge. It is a place where creative minds converge, interact with each other and construct visions of new realities. Established notions of truth are challenged in the pursuit of knowledge' (Yashpal Committee, 2009).

Ownership-cum-Management of Colleges in Punjab

Table 2 shows that the majority of general education colleges are privately managed. The higher professional education facilities are overwhelmingly in the hands of for-profit private sector. The responsibilities of the state government and that of the universities of the state, therefore, increase manifold to monitor and regulate the quality of higher professional education and fees and funds being charged by these private unaided service providers.

Table 2

Distribution of Recognized Colleges in Punjab by Type of College and Management

<table>
<tr><th rowspan="4">Type of College</th><th colspan="3">1998–99</th><th colspan="4">2006–07</th></tr>
<tr><th colspan="3">Type of Management</th><th colspan="4">Type of Management</th></tr>
<tr><th rowspan="2">Government</th><th rowspan="2">Private Aided and Non-Aided</th><th rowspan="2">Total</th><th rowspan="2">Government</th><th colspan="2">Private</th><th rowspan="2">Total</th></tr>
<tr><th>Aided</th><th>Non-Aided</th></tr>
<tr><td>Arts, Science, Commerce and Home Science</td><td>48
(23.30)</td><td>158
(76.70)</td><td>206
(100)</td><td>52
(22.41)</td><td>125
(53.88)</td><td>55
(23.71)</td><td>232
(100)</td></tr>
<tr><td>Teachers' Training (B. Ed./M. Ed.)</td><td>3
(15.00)</td><td>17
(85.00)</td><td>20
(100)</td><td>4
(3.23)</td><td>15
(12.10)</td><td>105
(84.67)</td><td>124
(100)</td></tr>
<tr><td>Engineering, Architecture and Pharmacy</td><td>4
(22.22)</td><td>14
(77.78)</td><td>18
(100)</td><td>6
(9.09)</td><td>2
(3.03)</td><td>58
(87.88)</td><td>66
(100)</td></tr>
<tr><td>Medical, Dental, Ayurvedic, Homeopathy, Nursing, etc.</td><td>6
(22.22)</td><td>21
(77.78)</td><td>27
(100)</td><td>10
(18.18)</td><td>—</td><td>45
(81.82)</td><td>55
(100)</td></tr>
<tr><td>Management/Computer Science/Law</td><td>N.A.</td><td>N.A.</td><td>N.A.</td><td>6
(12.76)</td><td>1
(2.13)</td><td>40
(85.11)</td><td>46
(100)</td></tr>
<tr><td>Total</td><td>61
(22.51)</td><td>210
(77.49)</td><td>271
(100)</td><td>78
(14.89)</td><td>143
(27.29)</td><td>303
(57.82)</td><td>524
(100)</td></tr>
</table>

Source: 1. Office of Director Public Instructions (Colleges), Punjab, Chandigarh.
2. Prospectus-*cum-Counselling* Brochure, State Level Entrance Tests Conducted by Different Universities of Punjab, 2007.

Growing Enrolment of Students

Punjab has enjoyed an envious position in terms of the highest per capita income for many years (for about 25 years starting from 1970 onwards) among the major Indian states. Its people are expected to prefer to send their wards for higher education. As a result, the number of students enroled in the higher education has increased many times. In the case of professional education, students' enrolment in engineering and medical courses has displayed a moderate rise between 1981–82 and 1991–92, but during 1991–92 and 2006–07, the students' enrolment has increased at a faster rate. That process has brought out the significant structural changes in favour of professional higher education in the state.

It is clear from Table 3 that the enrolment of students in higher education in Punjab increased from 1.34 lakh in 1981–82 to 1.77 lakh in 1991–92 and further to 2.67 lakh in 2006–07. It has increased further during the more recent years. The share of students in non-professional education declined from 92 per cent in 1981–82 to 81.3 per cent in 2006–07. Clearly, more and more students have now developed a tendency to join professional courses. This is largely because of the growing demand for skilled man-power in the job-market.

Table 3

Number of Students by Gender and Type of College

Type of College		*1981–82*	*1991–92*	*2006–07*
Arts, Science, Commerce and Home Science	B	74,403 (60.40)	81,778 (49.78)	n.a
	G	48,778 (39.60)	82,497 (50.22)	n.a
	T	1,23,181 (100.00) (92.03)	1,64,275 (100.00) (92.90)	2,17,086 (81.31)
Teachers' Training (B. Ed./M.Ed.)	B	1,191 (34.10)	921 (27.27)	n.a.
	G	2,302 (65.90)	2,456 (72.73)	n.a.
	T	3,493 (100.00) (2.61)	3,377 (100.00) (1.91)	6,206 (2.32)
Engineering, Architecture and Pharmacy	T	1,869 (1.40)	2,737 (1.55)	30,415 (11.39)
Medical, Dental, Ayurvedic, Homeopathy, Nursing, etc.	T	3,148 (2.35)	4,380 (2.48)	11,715 (4.39)
Veterinary and Agriculture	T	2,159* (1.61)	2,044** (1.16)	1,549 (0.58)
Total	T	1,33,850 (100.00)	1,76,813 (100.00)	2,66,971 (100.00)

Note: B= Boys, G= Girls, T= Total. *For 1982–83, **For 1990–91, n.a. = not available. Figures in capital brackets are percentage shares in the respective category and in the small brackets the percentage share in various streams of education.

Source: As Reported in Table 1.

Rural Students in Higher Education in Punjab

Though higher education has expanded at a fast pace in Punjab yet the rural students have remained marginalized and excluded from higher education. Two recent studies (Ghuman, Singh and Brar, 2006, 2009) of Punjabi University, Patiala, have made significant revelations in this context.[5]

During the academic session 2005–06, the total number of students in four universities (Guru Nanak Dev, Punjabi, Panjab and PAU) of Punjab state was 22,360 (Table 4). Out of this, the proportion of boys and girls was 53.40 per cent and 46.60 per cent, respectively. At the campus departments, the boys and girls were almost evenly divided (50.44% boys and 49.56% girls), and at the regional centres, the boys constituted more than two-thirds share (68.05%) and the rest were the girls (31.92%). The rural students in the universities and their regional centres constituted a meagre proportion of 4.07 per cent (911 students). The share of rural boys and rural girls in universities' overall boys and overall girls was 4.96 per cent and 3.06 per cent, respectively. The proportion of rural students in the universities of Punjab is, thus, far below than that of the proportion of rural population in the state (66.05% as per Population Census of 2001 and 62.51% according to Census 2011). The proportion of girl students from the rural areas is rather dismal. Amongst the total students enroled in the universities of Punjab, the share of girl students is 46.60 per cent, whereas the share of rural girls among the total rural students is 35.20 per cent. Thus, as compared to their urban counterparts, the share of rural girls in the universities of Punjab is much lower.

Table 4

Number of Rural Students in the Universities of Punjab (2005–06)*

	Total Enrolment			*Rural Students*					
				Number			*Percentage*		
	Persons	*Male*	*Female*	*Persons*	*Male*	*Female*	*Persons*	*Male*	*Female*
(a) Campus	18,598 (100)	9,381 (50.44)	9,217 (49.56)	696 (100.00)	451 (64.80)	245 (25.20)	3.74	4.81	2.66
(b) Regional Centres	3,762 (100)	2,560 (68.05)	1,202 (31.95)	215 (100.00)	141 (65.58)	74 (34.42)	5.72	5.51	6.16
Total (a+b)	22,360 (100)	11,941 (53.40)	10,419 (46.60)	911 (100.00)	592 (64.98)	319 (35.02)	4.07	4.96	3.06

*Universities of Punjab here means four universities, viz. Punjabi University, Patiala, Panjab University, Chandigarh, Punjab Agricultural University, Ludhiana, and Guru Nanak Dev University, Amritsar.

Note: Figures in parentheses are percentages.

Source: Ghuman, Singh and Brar, 2006.

The university – specific scenario of rural students presents an interesting picture (Table 5). Punjabi University had the highest proportion of rural students (8.16%; 10.47% for boys and 5.81% for girls) among all the universities of Punjab. Punjab Agricultural University, with a share of 4.73 per cent (4.99% for boys and 4.37% for girls), occupied the next place. Guru Nanak Dev University and Panjab University had 3.01 per cent (3.38% for boys and 2.55% for girls) and 2.20 per cent (2.95% for boys and 1.38% for girls) rural students on their rolls, respectively. The higher share of rural students in Punjabi University may be attributed to the feeding area, which has relatively higher proportion of rural population compared to the jurisdictional areas of other universities. The lower proportion of rural students in Punjab Agricultural University, which caters to the entire Punjab, and whose students are mainly trained to serve the agriculture and allied agricultural activities, is a rather disappointing phenomenon. It is also true about other universities of the state.

Table 5

University-Wise Scenario of Rural Students

	Total Enrolment			*Rural Students*					
				Number			*Percentage*		
	Persons	*Male*	*Female*	*Persons*	*Male*	*Female*	*Persons*	*Male*	*Female*
PUNJABI UNIVERSITY PATIALA									
(a) Campus	4,251	2,067	2,184	342	217	125	8.05	10.50	5.72
(b) Regional Centres	1,030	597	433	89	62	27	8.64	10.39	6.24
Total (a+b)	5,281	2,664	2,617	431	279	152	8.16	10.47	5.81
GURU NANAK DEV UNIVERSITY, AMRITSAR									
(a) Campus	4,883	2,370	2,513	144	89	55	2.95	3.76	2.19
(b) Regional Centres	2,059	1,472	587	65	41	24	3.16	2.79	4.09
Total (a+b)	6,942	3,842	3,100	209	130	79	3.01	3.38	2.55
PANJAB UNIVERSITY, CHANDIGARH									
(a) Campus	7,584	3,842	3,742	121	90	31	1.60	2.34	0.83
(b) Regional Centres	673	491	182	61	38	23	9.06	7.74	12.64
Total (a+b)	8,257	4,333	3,924	182	128	54	2.20	2.95	1.38
PUNJAB AGRICULTURAL UNIVERSITY, LUDHIANA									
Campus	1,880	1,102	778	89	55	34	4.73	4.99	4.37

Source: Ghuman, Singh and Brar, 2006.

Across the universities, the proportion of rural students enroled in their respective regional centres is much higher than that of those who enroled in the respective campus departments at Amritsar, Patiala and Chandigarh. This phenomenon is very prominent in the case of Panjab University, where the share of rural students at its regional centres was 9.06 per cent compared to just 1.60 per cent at its campus departments. It may be due to proximity of such centres to the villages and/or due to lower academic merit of students admitted in the regional centres. Nevertheless, it lends support for the establishment of regional centres or neighbour-hood campuses by the universities in the rural areas.

Among all the campus departments of the universities, the share of rural female students is substantially lower compared to the share of rural male students. The difference is more prominent in the case of Punjabi University (10.50% for boys and 5.72% for girls) and Panjab University (2.34% for boys and 0.83% for girls) compared to Guru Nanak Dev University (3.76% for boys and 2.19% for girls). All these facts call for special initiatives for promoting rural female students' enrolment in higher education. Moreover, among the regional centres of the universities, the share of rural girls has been at the highest in the case of Panjab University (12.64%), followed by the Punjabi University (6.24%) and Guru Nanak Dev University (4.09%). It shows that urban girl students prefer generally the university campuses and rural girl students prefer nearby regional centres.

Further, the share of total girls among the total students in various universities has been much higher than that of rural girl students. The overall share of girl students was 49.55 per cent (Punjabi University), 44.66 per cent (Guru Nanak Dev University), 47.52 per cent (Panjab University) and 41.38 per cent (PAU). As compared to it, the proportionate share of rural girl students out of total girl students was a meagre 5.81 per cent, 2.55 per cent, 1.38 per cent and 4.37 per cent, respectively. Clearly, there is a long way before the state to cross the road that could raise the enrolment ratio of rural girl students in the universities of Punjab.

Faculty-Wise Rural Students

The faculty-wise scenario of rural students getting higher education in the university campus departments and regional centres is presented in Table 6. The data shows that the proportion of rural students in the faculty of Education and Information Science was the highest (12.14%), followed by the faculties of Art and Culture (8.87%), the Social Sciences (6.76%), and the Agriculture and Agricultural Engineering (6.21%). The enrolment of rural students in the remaining faculties ranges from 1.41 per cent in the Professional Courses to 4.51 per cent in the Languages. As compared to it, the enrolment of rural students in the regional centres of the universities is the highest in the case of Social Sciences (16.51%), followed by the Languages (13.33%) and the Professional Courses (4.88%).

Table 6

Rural Students in Universities of Punjab: Faculty-Wise

	University Campus								
	Total Enrolment			Rural Students					
				Number			Percentage		
Name of Faculty	*Persons*	*Male*	*Female*	*Persons*	*Male*	*Female*	*Persons*	*Male*	*Female*
Social Sciences	2,380	905	1,475	161	119	42	6.76	13.15	2.85
Art and Culture	293	135	158	26	21	5	8.87	15.56	3.16
Life Sciences	2,829	896	1,933	105	45	60	3.71	5.02	3.10
Physical Sciences	2,518	1,069	1,449	72	41	31	2.86	3.84	2.14
Languages	1,750	675	1,075	79	40	39	4.51	5.93	3.63
Education and Information Science	692	275	417	84	54	30	12.14	19.64	7.19
Professional Courses	6,800	4,450	2,350	96	76	20	1.41	1.71	0.85
Veterinary Sciences	386	304	82	14	11	3	3.63	3.62	3.66
Agriculture and Agricultural Engg.	950	672	278	59	44	15	6.21	6.55	5.40
Campus Total	18,598	Male	9,217	696	451	245	3.74	4.81	2.66
			Regional Centres						
Social Sciences	109	41	68	18	7	11	16.51	17.07	16.18
Languages	405	206	199	54	27	27	13.33	13.11	13.57
Education and Information Science	53	26	27	0	0	0	0.00	0.00	0.00
Professional Courses	3,195	2,287	908	143	107	36	4.48	4.68	3.96
RC Total	3,762	2,560	1,202	215	141	74	5.72	5.51	6.16
Grand Total	22,360	11,941	10,419	911	592	319	4.07	4.96	3.06

Source: Ghuman, Singh and Brar, 2006.

In nutshell, the scenario about the share of rural students in the four universities of Punjab and their regional centres, emerging from the preceding discussion, is a disappointing one. More so, it is a pointer to the deteriorating quality of education in rural schools and, by proxy measure, may be an indicator of deteriorating economic position of the ruralities. To enhance the number and proportion of rural students in higher education is of utmost importance. It is more so because the rural students (when trained in such a skill and expertise) would be able to interact with the farmers in a more effective manner. Besides, being familiar to the rural conditions and needs, they would feel more concerned with the rural economy in general and agriculture and dairying in particular. Apart from this, it would contribute to the upliftment of human resources in the rural Punjab.

In fact, the negligible proportion of rural students in the university education in general and engineering science and other professional courses in particular is a cause of worry and needs immediate attention. There is a need for short-term and long-term strategies to tackle such a serious phenomenon. In the short run, there is a need to create additional seats for ruralites, or even reserve a substantial number of existing seats for the rural students. In order to provide a level playing field for the rural students, there is a need to improve the quality of school education in the rural Punjab. Again, this requires both short-term and long-term strategies on the part of the government. Along with this, there is an immediate need to establish a Rural Education Commission with a specific focus on rural education and enhancing the enrolment of rural students in higher education, particularly in the university level education. These universities have established some neighbourhood campuses and regional centres. Such a phenomenon needs to be strengthened.

Caste Composition of Rural Students

The scheduled castes comprise 28.85 per cent population in Punjab (GoP, 2005), whereas the proportion of rural SC students in the total rural students in the universities of Punjab is comparatively low, i.e. 14.60 per cent (Table 7). However, the proportion of SC girls is very small (7.52%) as compared to the SC boys (18.41%). Further, the proportion of female students from the other backward classes is rather dismal (0.63%). Contrary to it, the proportion of female students in the general category is higher (84.95%) than that of the male students (70.44%).

Table 7

Caste Composition of Rural Students

Category	*Persons*		*Male*		*Female*	
	No.	*%*	*No.*	*%*	*No.*	*%*
General	688	75.52	417	70.44	271	84.95
SC	133	14.60	109	18.41	24	7.52
BC	66	7.24	44	7.43	22	6.90
OBC	24	2.63	22	3.72	2	0.63
Total	911	100.00	592	100.00	319	100.00

Source: Ghuman, Singh and Brar, 2006.

Ownership, Affiliation and Location of Schools

Table 8 presents a picture about ownership of schools from where the rural students in the universities acquired their education. As regards primary and middle schools, 63 to 67 per cent students studied in government/aided schools. This proportion in the case of high and senior secondary schools was 71.57 and 70.14 per cent, respectively. Clearly, a very sizeable proportion of students studied in the government and government aided schools. Contrary to the popular perception and belief, the proportion of rural girls came from private rural schools at all levels of school education, has been higher than that of the boys. This is in spite of the fact that the private schools are more costly than the government/aided schools. This is something, which negates the gender discrimination on the part of the parents of the rural students and moreover, these girl students are from relatively rich and educated rural parents.

Table 8

Rural Students in Universities of Punjab by Type of School Background Pattern of Schools

Ownership Pattern	*Persons*		*Male*		*Female*	
	No.	*%*	*No.*	*%*	*No.*	*%*
Primary Schools						
Government/Aided	572	62.79	405	68.41	167	52.35
Private	339	37.21	187	31.59	152	47.65
Total	911	100.00	592	100.00	319	100.00
Middle Schools						
Government/Aided	611	67.07	425	71.79	186	58.31
Private	300	32.93	167	28.21	133	41.69
Total	911	100.00	592	100.00	319	100.00
Secondary Schools						
Government/Aided	652	71.57	444	75.00	208	65.20
Private	259	28.43	148	25.00	111	34.80
Total	911	100.00	592	100.00	319	100.00
Senior Secondary Schools						
Government	639	70.14	435	73.48	204	63.95
Private	272	29.86	157	26.52	115	36.05
Total	911	100.00	592	100.00	319	100.00

Source: Ghuman, Singh and Brar, 2006.

Education Level of Parents of Rural Students

Education level of the parents is another important determinant of access to and choice of the course at the university level education. Educated parents encourage their children to go in for higher education and willingly bear the cost of education. Table 9 shows that 8.78 per cent fathers and 20.97 per cent mothers of rural students were uneducated. A good proportion (37.87% fathers and 34.14% mothers) of parents was having education beyond middle level but up to high/higher secondary level. Another 23.16 per cent fathers and 7.90 per cent mothers were having graduation degree. The proportion of fathers and mothers having postgraduate and professional degrees was 5.38 per cent and 1.87 per cent; and 11.31 per cent and 3.95 per cent, respectively. In fact, the situation was quite improved during the post-Independence era, i.e. during 1950s, 60s and 70s. Probably, this improved education level was due to public and philanthropic investment in education sector up to 1970s in Punjab. That must have caused awareness among the parents who preferred to send their wards to the universities for attaining higher education.

Table 9

Rural Students in Universities of Punjab by Educational Level of Parents

Education Level	*Persons*		*Male Students*		*Female Students*	
	Father	*Mother*	*Father*	*Mother*	*Father*	*Mother*
No Education	80 (8.78)	191 (20.97)	58 (9.80)	157 (26.52)	22 (6.90)	34 (10.66)
Primary	45 (4.94)	117 (12.84)	33 (5.57)	90 (15.20)	12 (3.76)	27 (8.46)
Middle	61 (6.70)	118 (12.95)	48 (8.11)	87 (14.70)	13 (4.08)	31 (9.72)
High/Higher Secondary	345 (37.87)	311 (34.14)	230 (38.85)	173 (29.22)	115 (36.05)	138 (43.26)
Graduate in Arts/Science/Commerce	211 (23.16)	72 (7.90)	137 (23.14)	40 (6.76)	74 (23.20)	32 (10.03)
Postgraduate in Arts/Science/Commerce	49 (5.38)	17 (1.87)	31 (5.24)	7 (1.18)	18 (5.64)	10 (3.13)
Profession	103 (11.31)	36 (3.95)	48 (8.11)	14 (2.36)	55 (17.24)	22 (6.90)
Others	17 (1.87)	49 (5.38)	7 (1.18)	24 (4.05)	10 (3.13)	25 (7.84)
Total	911 (100.00)	911 (100.00)	592 (100.00)	592 (100.00)	319 (100.00)	319 (100.00)

Note: Figures in parentheses are percentages.

Source: Ghuman, Singh and Brar, 2006.

Occupation of the Parents of Rural Students

Occupation of parents, too, has a relationship with the education of their children. As is evident from Table 10, about 44 per cent rural students came from the families whose parents are cultivators. Nearly 82 per cent of the male students' mothers were doing household work. As regards the service, the fathers of 35 per cent students are in service whereas only 16.25 per cent students' mothers are in service. The low proportion of students from the business class is mainly because of the low proportion of this section in the rural area. Moreover, they mainly belong to petty shop-keeper households and such other low-earning activities. The proportion of students whose fathers are in business, etc. is nearly 10 per cent. The proportion of students coming from the labourer class is just 4.39 per cent. It is important to note that the proportion of girls is very low from the labourer's class. The labour class would hardly afford to bear the cost of education.

Table 10

Rural Students in Universities of Punjab by Occupational Status of Parents

Occupation Status	*Persons*		*Male Students*		*Female Students*	
	Father	*Mother*	*Father*	*Mother*	*Father*	*Mother*
Cultivation	402 (44.13)	0 (0.00)	258 (43.58)	0 (0.00)	144 (45.14)	0 (0.00)
Household Work	0 (0.00)	751 (82.44)	0 (0.00)	514 (86.82)	0 (0.00)	237 (74.29)
Service	320 (35.13)	148 (16.25)	197 (33.28)	72 (12.16)	123 (38.56)	76 (23.82)
Ex-Service	46 (5.05)	0 (0.00)	37 (6.25)	0 (0.00)	9 (2.82)	0 (0.00)
Business/Shop	93 (10.21)	0 (0.00)	60 (10.14)	0 (0.00)	33 (10.34)	0 (0.00)
Labour	40 (4.39)	0 (0.00)	35 (5.91)	0 (0.00)	5 (1.57)	0 (0.00)
Others *	10 (1.10)	12 (1.32)	5 (0.84)	6 (1.01)	5 (1.57)	6 (1.88)
Total	911 (100.00)	911 (100.00)	592 (100.00)	592 (100.00)	319 (100.00)	319 (100.00)

*It includes artisans also.

Note: Figures in parentheses are percentages.

Source: Ghuman, Singh and Brar, 2006.

The distribution of students coming from households with different income levels is given in Table 11. About 10 per cent students are coming from such households whose income is less than ₹ 50,000 per annum. Nearly 34 per cent students are from an income range between ₹ 51,000 and ₹ 100 thousand per annum. Another 30.41 per cent students are from income bracket between ₹ 101 thousands and ₹ 150 thousands per annum. Thus, a sizeable proportion of students (64.33%) are coming from an income range of ₹ 51 thousands and ₹ 1.5 lakh per annum. The proportion of students from the income range of ₹ 151 thousands and ₹ 200 thousands is 13.28 per cent. The proportion of students coming from the income bracket above ₹ 200 thousands is nearly 12 per cent.

Table 11

Rural Students in Universities of Punjab by Family Income Level

Family Income (in Thousand ₹)	*Persons*		*Male Students*		*Female Students*	
	No.	*%*	*No.*	*%*	*No.*	*%*
>50	93	10.21	61	10.30	32	10.03
51–100	309	33.92	199	33.61	110	34.48
101–150	277	30.41	187	31.59	90	28.21
151–200	121	13.28	78	13.18	43	13.48
201–250	42	4.61	26	4.39	16	5.02
251–300	21	2.30	12	2.03	9	2.82
301+	48	5.27	29	4.90	19	5.96
Total	911		592	100.00	319	100.00
Mean Family Income (₹)	1,46,460		1,46,789		1,45,850	

Source: Ghuman, Singh and Brar, 2006.

Higher Professional Education in Punjab

Though the higher (graduate and postgraduate degree) professional and technical education is being imparted by almost all the universities and their affiliated colleges in Punjab, yet there are some universities which are mainly imparting professional and technical education. These universities are listed in Table 12. This table presents university-wise and gender-wise total number of students in higher professional education in Punjab.

In all 56,240 students were studying in all the five universities during the academic session 2007–08 mentioned in Table 12. Out of them, 65 per cent were males and nearly 35 per cent were females. The percentage share of males and females in PTU was 70 and 30, respectively. The respective share of males and females in BFUHS was 32 per cent and 68 per cent. The male-female ratio in Thaper University was 81 per cent and 19 per cent, respectively. The share of male and female students in SLIET was 82 per cent and 18 per cent, respectively. The male and female proportion in RGNUL was 65 per cent and 35 per cent. The average share of males and females was almost 65 per cent and 35 per cent, respectively.

Table 12

Tcial Enrolment of Students in Professional Education in Selected Universities of Punjab by Gender (2007–08)

Universities	*Total Enrolment*		
	Persons	*Male*	*Female*
PTU	42,837(76.17) (100.00)	30,070 (70.20)	12,767 (29.80)
BFUHS	8,761 (15.58) (100.00)	2,823 (32.22)	5,938 (67.78)
(a) B.Sc. Nursing	2,201 (3.91) (100.00)	51 (2.32)	2,150 (97.68)
(b) Medical Courses	6,560 (11.66) (100.00)	2,772 (42.26)	3,788 (57.74)
TU	3,324 (5.91) (100.00)	2,696 (81.11)	628 (18.89)
SLIET	1,158 (2.06) (100.00)	954 (82.38)	204 (17.62)
RGNUL	160 (0.28) (100.00)	104 (65.00)	56 (35.00)
Overall	56,240 (100.00) (100.00)	36,647 (65.16)	19,593 (34.84)

Note: 1. Figures in parentheses are percentages.
2. Figures in square brackets (..) show the column-wise percentage share.
3. PTU stands for Punjab Technical University, Jalandhar; BFUHS stands for Baba Farid University of Health Sciences, Faridkot; TU stands for Thaper University, Patiala; SLIET stands for Sant Longowal Institute of Engineering and Technology, Longowal; and RGNUL stands for Rajiv Gandhi National University of Law, Punjab, Patiala.

Source: Ghuman, Singh and Brar, 2009.

As regards rural students, there were 2,085 students (Table 13). It constituted only 3.71 per cent of the total enroled students in all the surveyed colleges and universities. The proportion of rural students was the highest in BFUHS (8.88%) and the lowest in Thapar University (0.30%). The proportion of rural students in the rest of the universities was as follows: PTU (2.97%); SLIET (1.81%); RGNUL (1.88%). It is to be noted that the overall proportion of rural students in BFUHS was the highest because of very high proportion of rural students in the B.Sc. Nursing course (22.63%). The share of rural students in other medical courses was only 4.27 per cent.

The gender-wise break-up shows that the proportion of rural female students (5.27%) was more than that of rural male students (2.87%). The university-cum-gender wise break-up of rural students further shows that the proportion of girls was the highest in BFUHS (11.10%) and no rural female student was enroled in any course of Thapar University and RGNUL. The proportion of rural male students was the highest in BFUHS (4.22%) and the lowest in Thapar University (0.37%). Within total rural students (2,085 students), the proportion of girls was 49.49 per cent and that of boys 50.50 per cent. University-wise, the proportion of rural girls was in the following manner: PTU (28.75%); BFUHS (84.70%); SLIET (33.33%) (Table 13).

Table 13

Gender-wise Number and Proportion of Rural Students in Professional Education in Selected Universities of Punjab (2007–08)

Universities	*Rural Students*					
	Number			*Percentage Share*		
	Persons	*Male*	*Female*	*Persons*	*Male*	*Female*
PTU, Jalandhar	1,273 (61.06)	907 (86.13)	366 (35.47)	2.97	3.02	2.87
BFUHS, Faridkot	778 (37.31)	119 (11.30)	659 (63.86)	8.88	4.22	11.10
(a) B. Sc. Nursing	498 (23.88)	5 (0.47)	493 (47.77)	22.63	9.80	22.93
(b) Medical Courses	280 (13.43)	114 (10.83)	166 (16.09)	4.27	4.11	4.38
Thapar University, Patiala	10 (0.48)	10 (0.95)	0 (0.00)	0.30	0.37	0.00
SLIET, Longowal	21 (1.01)	14 (1.33)	7 (0.68)	1.81	1.47	3.43
RGNUL, Patiala	3 (0.14)	3 (0.28)	0 (0.00)	1.88	2.88	0.00
Total	2,085 (100.00)	1,053 (100.00)	1,032 (100.00)	3.71	2.87	5.27

Note: Figures in parentheses indicate share in respective university.

Source: Ghuman, Singh and Brar, 2009.

Out of the total rural students, as many as 500 students (23.98%) belong to the rural areas of the other states, as is evident from Table 14. Excluding the rural students of states other than Punjab, the proportion of rural students of Punjab further declined to 2.84 per cent (1.82% for boys and 4.76% for girls).

Table 14

Rural Students in Professional Education in Punjab by Native State (2007–08)

State	Number			Percentage Share		
	Persons	Boys	Girls	Persons	Boys	Girls
Punjab	1,585	658	927	76.02	62.49	89.83
Neighbouring States	405	310	95	19.42	29.44	9.21
Other States	95	85	10	4.56	8.07	0.97
Total	2,085	1,053	1,032	100.00	100.00	100.00

Note: (i) Neighbouring States include Haryana, Himachal Pradesh, Jammu & Kashmir and Rajasthan.
(ii) Other States include UP, West Bengal, Bihar, Orissa, Jharkhand, Kerala, Delhi, Manipur and Tripura.

Source: Ghuman, Singh and Brar, 2009.

The two empirical studies (Ghuman, Singh and Brar, 2006, 2009), thus, strongly indicate towards the exclusion of rural students from the higher education, both in general and professional education.

The collapse of rural school education, particularly in the government and government aided schools, along with the high drop-out rate, has been the main reason behind exclusion of rural students from higher education in Punjab. It has been noticed that the drop-out rate from 1st to 10th standard was 48.10 per cent during the academic session 2002–03 in Punjab (Gill, Singh and Brar, 2005). The educational attainment of poor households declined across all the grades from 1st to 9th during 1992–93 and 1998–99 (The World Bank, 2004). Another study based on the census survey of 36 villages of Punjab (located in 12 districts) found out that about 69 per cent of all the rural households and 90 per cent of all the rural labour households did not have even a single member with matriculation level (10th standard) of education (Ghuman, Singh and Singh, 2007).

The underperformance of education sector has crippled the education base of the workforce in the State. During 1999–2000, the education level of the workforce in Punjab was as follows: illiterate (33.50%); primary (22.10%); middle (13%); secondary and above (31.50%). Nearly 48 per cent of the agricultural workforce was illiterate (Chadha, 2004).

This sorry state of affairs has been the result of neglect of rural education by the successive governments in Punjab. The government schools in the rural Punjab have been facing a perennial shortage of teachers, and school heads, to the tune of around 40,000 during the last about two decades. The monitoring and regulatory mechanism has come to a naught (Ghuman, 2008). As a result, the affluent and aware parents have started sending their wards to the private schools in search of quality education. Some studies have revealed that a very high proportion (ranging from 60 to 85%) of students in rural government primary schools in Punjab belong to the SC (Scheduled Castes), BC (Backward Classes) and other weaker sections of rural society (Joshi, 2003; Kaur, 2004; Rani, 2007).

Social and Educational Profile of Parents of Rural Students in Professional Education

The distribution of rural students according to the social category shows that as high as 76.59 per cent of them belong to the General Category. The proportion of the rest of the categories was as follows: SC/ST (11.56%); BC (6.38%); and OBC (5.47%). Across the gender, the proportion of the General Category rural girls (80.62%) was higher than that of the General Category rural boys (72.65%) (Table 15). It is significant to note that the proportion of SC rural students in professional courses in total rural students is far less than the proportion of SC population in rural Punjab, 33.04 per cent (Census 2001).

Table 15

Caste Composition of Rural Students in Professional Education

Category	*Number*			*Percentage Share*		
	Persons	*Male*	*Female*	*Persons*	*Male*	*Female*
Gen	1,597	765	832	76.59	72.65	80.62
SC/ST	241	114	127	11.56	10.83	12.31
BC	133	78	55	6.38	7.41	5.33
OBC	114	96	18	5.47	9.12	1.74
Total	2,085	1,053	1,032	100.00	100.00	100.00

Source: Ghuman, Singh and Brar, 2009.

Type of Schooling of Rural Students in Professional Colleges

It is a well recognized fact that the rural school education in Punjab has collapsed due to the apathy of the successive state governments. The vacuum has been filled by the unrecognized and unregulated private schools. But, they charge very high fee and funds which is beyond the reach of weaker sections of rural society (Brar, Singh and Ghuman, 2008).

It has been found that about 53 per cent of rural students passed their secondary school examination from the private schools. And, the remaining 47 per cent passed the same from the government owned schools. But, at the senior secondary level, the situation is almost different (Table 16).

Table 16

Percentage Distribution of Rural Students in Professional Education by Type of School

Ownership Pattern	*Secondary*			*Senior Secondary*		
	Persons	*Male*	*Female*	*Persons*	*Male*	*Female*
Government/Aided	46.91	52.71	40.99	61.06	65.72	56.49
Private	53.09	47.29	59.01	38.94	34.28	43.51
Total	100.00	100.00	100.00	100.00	100.00	100.00

Source: Ghuman, Singh and Brar, 2009.

Education Level of Parents

Education stock at the level of households play crucial role in the formation of the human capital and determination of inter-household levels of inequalities. The familial advantages have been identified as the important determinant of the educational attainments of the children. Table 17 highlights educational status of the parents of rural students. The education level of fathers and mothers of the rural students indicates that both the parents of the rural students were well educated as the share of the graduates and above was quite significant. It is apparent that the rural students who entered the higher professional courses are from relatively well educated parents.

Table 17

Percentage Distribution of Rural Students in Professional Education by Educational Level of Parents

Education Level	*Father*			*Mother*		
	Persons	*Male*	*Female*	*Persons*	*Male*	*Female*
Illiterate	4.14	4.71	3.55	8.84	11.31	6.34
Middle	6.48	7.16	5.78	17.59	20.04	15.11
Matriculation	31.46	32.65	30.22	38.81	40.94	36.65
Senior Secondary	16.20	16.96	15.42	10.68	9.30	12.09
Graduation	23.03	20.88	25.25	17.40	14.09	20.76
Post Graduation	9.82	8.92	10.75	4.25	2.97	5.56
Professional	3.19	3.53	2.84	0.48	0.58	0.39
M.Phil/PhD	0.45	0.69	0.20	0.24	0.10	0.39
Others	5.23	4.51	5.98	1.69	0.67	2.73
Total	100.00	100.00	100.00	100.00	100.00	100.00

Source: Ghuman, Singh and Brar, 2009.

Occupational and Income Profile of Parents of Rural Students

The data reveal that nearly 51 per cent of the fathers of the rural students were reported to be in the service in the organized sector and a little less than one-third (31.80%) were engaged in cultivation for their livelihood (Table 18). The share of remaining occupations in the case of fathers in the descending order was as follows: business (12.51%); ex-employee (3.54%), labour (1.50%). The proportionate share of mothers of rural students engaged in service was 17.40 per cent. Thus, the employment of fathers in the service sector has been the single largest category from which rural students found access in the higher professional education.

Table 18

Percentage Distribution of Rural Students in Professional Education by Occupational Status of Their Parents

Occupation Status	*Father*			*Mother*		
	Persons	*Male*	*Female*	*Persons*	*Male*	*Female*
Service (government and private)	50.65	53.24	47.97	17.40	12.75	22.12
Agriculture	31.80	28.33	35.40	0.00	0.00	0.00
Business	12.51	13.33	11.66	0.14	0.00	0.29
Ex-Employee	3.54	3.24	3.85	0.14	0.10	0.19
Labour	1.50	1.86	1.12	0.05	0.10	0.00
Housewife	0.00	0.00	0.00	82.26	87.06	77.39
Total	100.00	100.00	100.00	100.00	100.00	100.00

Source: Ghuman, Singh and Brar, 2009.

Table 19

Rural Students in Professional Education by Source of Income

Source of Income	*Number*			*Percentage Share*		
	Persons	*Male*	*Female*	*Persons*	*Male*	*Female*
Agriculture Land Only	494	268	226	23.69	25.45	21.90
Salary Only	629	336	293	30.17	31.91	28.39
Businesses Only	160	88	72	7.67	8.36	6.98
Wages Only	25	16	9	1.20	1.52	0.87
Pension Only	15	8	7	0.72	0.76	0.68
Any Other	2	1	1	0.10	0.09	0.10
More than one Income Source	760	336	424	36.45	31.91	41.09
Total	2,085	1,053	1,032	100.00	100.00	100.00

Source: Ghuman, Singh and Brar, 2009.

The perusal of Table 19 shows that in the case of nearly 24 per cent of the rural students, agricultural land constituted the only source of income. For another 30 per cent of the rural students, the salary constituted the only source of income. Thus, the agricultural land and salary were the two main sources of the income of households of the rural students. Further, more than one-third of rural students' households (36.45%) were having more than one source of income.

The level of income has a strong connection with the students' access to the high cost higher education, as is evident from Table 20. In the case of 25 per cent of the rural students, income level of households was less than ₹ 100,000 per annum. Another 46.43 per cent rural students reported an annual income of their parents between ₹ 100,001 and ₹ 200,000. For another 18.85 per cent, the annual income was between ₹ 200,001 and ₹ 300,000.

Table 20

Rural Students in Professional Education by Their Family Income Level

Family Income (₹)	*Number*			*Percentage Share*		
	Persons	*Male*	*Female*	*Persons*	*Male*	*Female*
Up to 100,000	521	267	254	24.99	25.36	24.61
100,001–200,000	968	508	460	46.43	48.24	44.57
200,001–300,000	393	187	206	18.85	17.76	19.96
300,001–400,000	116	50	66	5.56	4.75	6.40
400,001–500,000	49	24	25	2.35	2.28	2.42
500,001 and more	38	17	21	1.82	1.61	2.03
Total	2,085	1,053	1,032	100.00	100.00	100.00

Source: Ghuman, Singh and Brar, 2009.

Expenses on Education: University-Wise

The various types of expenditure flows have been worked out in a comprehensive manner and arranged in a systematic manner in order to put forward a wider spectrum of payments made by the students.

In the case of colleges affiliated to PTU, per student per annum average expenditure, excluding hostel expenses, was equivalent to ₹ 63,873 (Table 21). The tuition fees and funds accounted for nearly 83 per cent of the total expenses. Per student expenditure was found out to be the highest in the case of Engineering Courses (₹ 71,267) and the lowest for the BBA (₹ 35,094).

Table 21

Average Expenditure by Rural Students in PTU by Course (₹ per annum)

Course	Fee and Funds	Books/ Stationery/ Photocopy	Telephone/ Mobile	Canteen Bill	Cloths and Garments	Others	Total
Engineering Courses	59,707 (83.78)	3,832 (5.38)	2,208 (3.10)	1,264 (1.77)	3,347 (4.70)	909 (1.28)	71,267 (100.00)
Architecture	58,541 (82.77)	3,118 (4.41)	2,409 (3.41)	1,388 (1.96)	3,769 (5.33)	1,500 (2.12)	70,725 (100.00)
B. Pharmacy	59,281 (86.05)	3,359 (4.88)	1,758 (2.55)	961 (1.39)	2,873 (4.17)	659 (0.96)	68,891 (100.00)
MBA	60,297 (85.30)	3,093 (4.38)	2,096 (2.96)	1,107 (1.57)	3,258 (4.61)	841 (1.19)	70,692 (100.00)
MCA	54,503 (82.33)	3,590 (5.42)	2,171 (3.28)	1,220 (1.84)	3,395 (5.13)	1319 (1.99)	66,198 (100.00)
BBA	26,350 (75.08)	2,383 (6.79)	2,792 (7.96)	670 (1.91)	2,772 (7.90)	127 (0.36)	35,094 (100.00)
BCA	25,829 (73.29)	2,858 (8.11)	2,019 (5.73)	839 (2.38)	2,966 (8.42)	730 (2.07)	35,241 (100.00)
Total	53,080 (83.10)	3,475 (5.44)	2,124 (3.33)	1,122 (1.76)	3,213 (5.03)	859 (1.34)	63,873 (100.00)

Source: Ghuman, Singh and Brar, 2009.

Table 22

Average Expenditure by Rural Students in BFUHS by Course (₹ per annum)

Course	Fee and Funds	Books/ Stationery/ Photocopy	Telephone/ Mobile	Canteen Bill	Cloths and Garments	Others	Total
MBBS	67,520 (77.14)	5716 (6.53)	3151 (3.60)	3594 (4.11)	3505 (4.00)	4039 (4.61)	87,525 (100.00)
BDS	41,026 (69.75)	5,866 (9.97)	2,598 (4.42)	2,613 (4.44)	4,213 (7.16)	2,500 (4.25)	58,816 (100.00)
Nursing	41,927 (73.52)	4,666 (8.18)	2,040 (3.58)	2,138 (3.75)	3,767 (6.61)	2,491 (4.37)	57,029 (100.00)
BHMS	36,864 (66.05)	4,781 (8.57)	4,094 (7.34)	2,444 (4.38)	3,880 (6.95)	3,750 (6.72)	55,813 (100.00)
BAMS	53,871 (75.79)	4,987 (7.02)	2,493 (3.51)	2,278 (3.20)	4,293 (6.04)	3,160 (4.45)	71,082 (100.00)
BPT	40,432 (69.97)	4,770 (8.25)	2,984 (5.16)	2,666 (4.61)	4,079 (7.06)	2,857 (4.94)	57,788 (100.00)
Total	45,573 (73.87)	4,883 (7.92)	2,356 (3.82)	2,345 (3.80)	3,847 (6.24)	2,688 (4.36)	61,692 (100.00)

Source: Ghuman, Singh and Brar, 2009.

In the case of colleges affiliated to the BFUHS, per student average expenses were ₹ 61,692 per annum (Table 22). The share of tuition fee and funds was 73.87 per cent. Per student expenditure was found to be the highest in the case of MBBS (₹ 87,525) and the lowest for BHMS (₹ 55,813).

It is interesting to note that the average tuition fee and other funds in private colleges are much higher than that in the government college for the same degree course. For instance, an MBBS student had to pay only ₹ 13,471 per annum as tuition fee and other charges in the government medical college compared to ₹ 113,463 per annum in a private college. Similarly, a BDS student had to spend ₹ 13,000 per annum as tuition fee and other charges in the government medical college compared to ₹ 65,396 per annum in private college. And, in the case of B.Sc. Nursing course, a student paid ₹ 13,528 per annum tuition fee and other funds in the government nursing college compared to ₹ 43,877 in the private nursing college (Table 23). It lends support to the conclusion that there exist wide variations in the structure of tuition fee and other funds in public-funded institution and private non-aided institution.

Table 23

Average Tuition Fee and Funds Per Annum Paid by Rural Students in BFUHS by Ownership and Course

Courses	*Per Annum Average Tuition Fee and Funds Paid (₹)*		
	Government Owned	*Private Owned*	*Total*
MBBS	13,471	113,463	67,520
BDS	13,000	65,396	41,026
Nursing	13,528	43,877	41,927
BHMS	na	36,864	36,864
BAMS	na	53,871	53,871
BPT	na	40,432	40,432
Total	13,383	49,574	45,573

Source: Ghuman, Singh and Brar, 2009.

In the case of courses run by the Thapar University, per student average expenditure made by the rural students was equivalent to ₹ 93,193 per annum. The share of tuition fee and funds is 86.46 per cent. Per student expenditure was found out to be higher in the case of Bachelor of Engineering (BE) ccurses (₹ 1,21,450) and the lowest for Master of Engineering (ME) courses (₹ 81,082) (Table 24).

In the case of SLIET, per student average expenditure was equivalent to ₹ 47,235 per annum. The share of tuition fee was 79.90 per cent (Table 25).

Table 24

Average Expenditure by Rural Students in Thapar University by Course (₹ per annum)

Course	*Fee and Funds*	*Books/ Stationery/ Photocopy*	*Telephone/ Mobile*	*Canteen Bill*	*Cloths and Garments*	*Others*	*Total*
BE	109,100 (89.83)	3,400 (2.80)	2,300 (1.89)	2,750 (2.26)	3,150 (2.59)	750 (0.62)	121,450 (100.00)
ME	68,345 (84.29)	2,640 (3.26)	2,180 (2.69)	3,667 (4.52)	3,000 (3.70)	1250 (1.54)	81,082 (100.00)
Total	80,572 (86.46)	2,868 (3.08)	2,216 (2.38)	3,392 (3.64)	3,045 (3.27)	1,100 (1.18)	93,193 (100.00)

Source: Ghuman, Singh and Brar, 2009.

Table 25

Average Expenditure by Rural Students in SLIET by Course (₹ per annum)

Courses	*Fee and Funds*	*Books/ Stationery/ Photocopy*	*Telephone/ Mobile*	*Canteen Bill*	*Cloths and Garments*	*Others*	*Total*
CSE	37,500 (81.74)	3,000 (6.54)	1,500 (3.27)	1,525 (3.32)	1,925 (4.20)	425 (0.93)	45,875 (100.00)
ECE	37,364 (77.09)	4,200 (8.66)	1,638 (3.38)	2,300 (4.75)	2,300 (4.75)	667 (1.37)	48,469 (100.00)
Instrumentation Engineering	38,184 (81.36)	2,500 (5.33)	1,544 (3.29)	1,275 (2.72)	2,675 (5.70)	750 (1.60)	46,928 (100.00)
Total	37,741 (79.90)	3,243 (6.87)	1,571 (3.33)	1,713 (2.62)	2,389 (5.06)	578 (1.22)	47,235 (100.00)

Source: Ghuman, Singh and Brar, 2009.

Interestingly, cost of acquiring an engineering degree in the SLIET is quite low compared to the cost of engineering degree of the other two universities, namely, PTU and Thapar University. The main reason behind this is that SLIET is central government university funded and fee and funds have been kept low. And, the colleges affiliated with PTU are overwhelmingly unaided private colleges, who charge heavy fee and funds. The Thapar University is privately financed and managed university. However, it is interesting to note that the SLIET has very few rural students (21 students; 1.81%) who had passed either their matriculation or senior secondary examination or both from the rurally located schools anywhere in India.

In the case of RGNUL, per student average expenditure was ₹ 68,184 per annum. The share of tuition fee and funds was 86.53 per cent (Table 26). The RGNUL is another state-funded university and was established in 2006.

It is significant to note that across the courses and universities, the share of tuition fee and funds was very high which ranged between 74 per cent (BFUHS) and 80 per cent (RGNUL). The per student hostel expenses in all the institutions under study ranged from ₹ 22,709 (SLIET) to ₹ 29,759 (TU) per annum.

Table 26

Average Expenditure by Rural Students in RGNUL by Course (₹ per annum)

Course	*Fee and Funds*	*Books/ Stationery/ Photocopy*	*Telephone/ Mobile*	*Canteen Bill*	*Cloths and Garments*	*Others*	*Total*
BA LLB	59,000 (86.53)	3,250 (4.77)	1,067 (1.56)	1,267 (1.86)	2,833 (4.15)	767 (1.13)	68,184 (100.00)
Total	59,000 (86.53)	3,250 (4.77)	1,067 (1.56)	1,267 (1.86)	2,833 (4.15)	767 (1.13)	68,184 (100.00)

Source: Ghuman, Singh and Brar, 2009.

Cost of Higher Education and Affordability Question

In the absence of public funding of higher education or public-aid to private institutions of higher education, the cost of education would have to be met by the students. In view of the ever-rising cost of education, the question of affordability has come to acquire the central-stage. Mainly, the private cost (cost to the individual student or to the parents) consists of two types of costs – institutional charges and the incidental charges. The institutional charges are those which the education institution charged from the students in terms of fees and other funds. Apart from the institutional charges, the student has to incur expenses on many other heads, such as, expenditure on books, stationery, transport, boarding or loading, study for, entertainment, etc. depending on the nature and type of the course and the institution. All these together comprise incidental charges.

The affordability of the private cost of education by the student (by the parents, as student is invariably not an earning hand) is largely determined by the income of the parents, their past savings and their creditworthiness. By juxtaposing the per student private cost of education on the NSSO (National Sample Survey Organization, Government of India) household expenditure data of Punjab, it has been worked out that nearly 40 per cent of the rural households in Punjab cannot afford to bear the private cost of general education (B.A./B.Sc. etc.) even for one child. In the case of urban households, about 31 per cent parents cannot afford to pay the cost of general education, even for a single child (Ghuman, Singh and Brar 2005, pp. 94–100).

As regards cost of professional and technical education, the affordability condition is at the razor's edge. About 85 per cent households in Punjab cannot afford the cost of higher professional education of a single child, even if they spend their entire income on education. This is something which is not possible by any stretch of imagination. The corresponding proportion in rural area may go well beyond 95 per cent. Many of the courses in medical education (such as MBBS, BDS, BHMS and BAMS) may simply be not in the affordable reach of 90 per cent of urban households and 95 per cent of rural households (Ghuman, Singh and Brar, 2005). It is significant to note that no household can afford to spend its entire income on education of their children. In view of the rising cost of education and increasing cost of living, the affordability question is becoming all the more serious. It is, thus, clear that the existing cost structure of higher education and the existing structure of income distribution would tantamount to exclude a very larger section of Punjab's population from the higher education. This would mean two things: one, exclusion of merit out of education and, thus, create a mediocre society; two, serious drag on the development of the state. These two things would become a serious constraint on the potential development of Punjab.

The issue of affordability has also been highlighted by the Yashpal Committee (2009). The Committee revealed that the quantum of fees charged has no rational basis. The illegal capitation fees range from ₹ 1–10 lakh for the engineering courses; ₹ 20–40 lakh for MBBS courses; ₹ 5–12 lakh for dental courses; and ₹ 30,000–50,000 for courses in arts and science colleges, depending on the demand.

Public Expenditure on Education in Punjab

The low amount of resource mobilization has been a serious constraint on state's capacity to intervene in the development process and give the desired direction to it. It has, often, resulted in an ever declining allocation of resources even to the vital sectors, especially the social sector, of the economy. Table 27 presents such a scenario since the latter half of the 1960s (coinciding with the reorganization of Punjab and the advent of green revolution). The expenditure share of general services in the state budget (on revenue account) has substantially increased from 1990s. It varied between 35 and 40 per cent in the earlier period and was quite low (23.40%) in 1991–92. In 2000–01 it shot up to about 58 per cent and to 59 per cent in 2003–04. The share of general services as a percentage of NSDP increased from 3.18 in 1970–71 to 4.84 in 1991–92 and spurted up to 13 per cent in 2003–04. It, however, declined to 10.80 per cent during 2005–06.

As compared to it, the percentage share of expenditure on social services declined substantially since 1980s, from around 31 per cent in 1970–71 to 22.47 per cent in 1991–92. It went up to 25.55 per cent in 2000–01 but declined again to 21.45 per cent in 2003–04. During 2005–06, it declined to 19.74 per cent. In the process, education and health became the victims. The share of education declined from 22 per cent in 1970–71 to 13.55 per cent in 1991–92 and to 13.25 per cent in 2003–04 and further to 12.57 per cent in 2005–06. Such a sharp decline in expenditure on education would have very serious implications for the future growth and development of the state of Punjab (Brar, 2008). The share of education is not looking up even in the latter years. Similarly, expenditure on health decreased from 7.24 per cent in 1970–71 to 4.32 per cent in 1991–92 and to 3.88 per cent in 2003–04 and further to 3.82 per cent during 2005–06. It further declined during the succeeding years. The public expenditure on education, sports and culture, as a percentage of NSDP, however, increased from 2.18 per cent in 1970–71 to 3.08 per cent in 1980–81 and further to 3.93 per cent in 2003–04. It, however, declined to 2.35 per cent during 2005–06. Clearly, it is much below the ideal 6 per cent level. The share of health sector in state's NSDP always remained less than one per cent, except for 1980–81, throughout this period. It is clear from the foregoing analysis that education and health are sliding down on the state's priorities, during all these years. There is, thus, an urgent need to raise the share of social services (particularly education and health), both in the state budget and in the NSDP.

Table 27

Composition of Expenditure in the Punjab Government Budget for Selected Years: 1970–2008 (on Revenue Account, at Current Prices, %age Share)

		1970–71	*1980–81*	*1991–92*	*2000–01*	*2003–04*	*2005–06*	*2006–07*	*2007–08*
A	General Services	34.74 (3.18)	39.53 (3.42)	23.40 (4.84)	55.76 (11.10)	59.55 (12.94)	57.76 (10.80)	55.75	51.33
B	Social Services	31.35 (3.09)	30.66 (5.11)	22.77 (4.72)	25.55 (5.09)	21.45 (4.66)	19.79 (3.70)	22.13	20.18
(i)	Education, Sports and Culture	22.17 (2.18)	17.12 (3.08)	13.55 (2.80)	15.87 (3.16)	13.25 (3.93)	12.57 (2.35)	12.50	12.33
(ii)	Health and Family Welfare	7.24 (0.71)	5.49 (1.09)	4.32 (0.89)	5.44 (1.08)	3.88 (0.84)	3.82 (0.71)	3.72	3.33
C	Economic Services	33.91 (2.89)	29.81 (3.72)	53.08 (10.98)	17.93 (3.57)	18.72 (4.07)	20.40 (3.81)	20.35	25.44
	Development Expenditure (B+C)	65.26 (5.98)	60.47 (8.83)	75.85 (15.70)	43.18 (8.66)	40.17 (8.73)	40.19 (7.51)	42.48	45.62

Note: Figures in parenthesis indicate share in NSDP.

Source: Government of Punjab, Statistical Abstract of Punjab (various years).

The share of economic services in state budget witnessed an upward trend (from 30% in 1967-68 to 53% in 1991-92) during 1967-68 to 1991-92, but nose dived to around 18 per cent in 2000-01. As regards the share of economic services in NSDP, it increased from around 3 per cent in 1970-71 to nearly 11 per cent in 1991-92. However, it again declined to 3.57 per cent in 2000-01 but went up to 4 per cent in 2003-04. It, however, declined to 3.81 per cent during 2005-06.

The social and economic services together are, often, categorized as development expenditure. These two heads, together, accounted for 65.26 per cent in 1970-71 and 75.85 per cent in 1991-92. Their share in the state budget, however, substantially decreased to 43 per cent, in 2000-01 and further to 40 per cent in 2003-04. It did not improve during the latter years. Development expenditure, as percentage share of NSDP, increased from 6 per cent in 1970-71 to 9 per cent in 1980-81 and further increased to 15.7 per cent in 1991-92. It, however, declined to 8.66 per cent in 2000-01. It further declined to 7.51 per cent during 2005-06.

It is clear from the foregoing analysis that State's priorities have undergone a sea-change since 1990s, i.e. since the advent of the reform-period. In 1991-92, 60 per cent of state budget was spent on development. The situation totally reversed by the year 2005-06 when around 58 per cent of state budget was spent on general services. There was nearly 8 percentage point increase in the share of general services as percentage of NSDP in 2003-04 as compared to 1991-92. Compared to it, there was about 7 percentage point decline in the share of development expenditure during the same period. Clearly, the state's priorities have been shifted in favour of general services, from social and economic services, ever since the shift in the policy regime in 1991, as far as the expenditure on revenue account is concerned. Such a shift in priority may result in marginalizing the already marginalized sections of population.

The higher education sector, within the education sector, is facing a serious resource crunch. As a result, the state-funded universities, government colleges and government-aided private colleges are not able to fill up their vacant positions and have introduced many self-financing courses. The fee and other charges of these courses are so high that they are literally beyond the reach of majority of people (Ghuman, Singh and Brar, 2005). The share of universities and higher education in Punjab in government's budgetary allocation for education is very very small. Consequently, they are facing a huge budgetary deficit.

Table 28 reflects on the extremely low share of higher education in the public expenditure on education in Punjab.

Table 28

Public Expenditure on University and Higher Education in Punjab During Selected Years (on Revenue Account, Both Plan and Non-plan, at Current Price)

(₹ million)

Year	*Education (Total)*	*University and Higher Education*	
		Total	*Share*
2000–01 (actual)	20,561	2,119	10.31
2005–06 (actual)	22,341	2,255	10.09
2006–07 (R.E.)	24,812	1,821	7.34
2007–08 (Budgeted)	27,521	2,485	9.03

Source: Government of India, Ministry of Human Resource Development, Budget Expenditure on Education (various annual budgets), New Delhi.

It is clear from Table 28 that the share of universities and higher education in the budget allocation for education in Punjab has remained around 10 per cent during 2000–01 and 2005–06. During 2006–07, it declined to 7.34 per cent. The budgeted allocation during 2007–08 was 9 per cent. Clearly, there is a need to allocate a higher share to universities and higher education in Punjab, but not at the cost of school education. There is a need to substantially raise the allocation to education (at last it should be doubled) and out of which at least 30 per cent should be allocated to universities and higher education. Unless that is done the public-aided universities and other aided institutions of higher education would not be able to sustain and survive. And in due course of time they shall die a natural death.

It is significant to note that the National Knowledge Commission's Report (GoI, 2007) has also recommended a higher public spending on higher education. The Commission is of the view that access to higher education for all deserving students must be ensured. This would require well-funded scholarship scheme and affirmative action on the part of both government and private sector.

It is significant to mention that a large number of faculty positions are lying vacant in the state universities, government and government aided colleges. About 26 to 30 per cent posts of teachers in Guru Nanak Dev University have been lying vacant during the last five years (Table 29). The percentage of vacant post of teachers in Punjabi University varied between 32 per cent to 45 per cent, during 2004–05 and 2008–09.

Table 30 presents the faculty position in the universities which are directly related to the rural and agricultural economy of Punjab. Nearly 29 per cent to 39 per cent positions of teachers have been lying vacant in Punjab Agricultural University, Ludhiana, during 2004–05 and 2008–09. In the case of Guru Angad Dev Veterinary and Animal Sciences University, the proportion of vacant posts of teachers varied between 19 per cent to

34 per cent. During the last three years, the proportion of vacant positions of teachers has been between 33 per cent to 34 per cent.

Table 29

Number of Teaching Faculty in Guru Nanak Dev University and Punjabi University: 2004–05 to 2008–09.

Year	*Guru Nanak Dev University*				*Punjabi University*			
	Number		*Vacant Positions*		*Number*		*Vacant Positions*	
	Sanctioned	*Filled*	*Number*	*%*	*Sanctioned*	*Filled*	*Number*	*%*
2004–05	534	376	158	29.59	716	456	260	36.31
2005–06	534	378	156	29.21	853	578	275	32.24
2006–07	539	422	117	21.71	914	512	402	43.98
2007–08	539	396	143	26.53	929	509	420	45.21
2008–09	539	400	139	25.79	980	561	419	42.76

Source: 1. For Guru Nanak Dev University, information was supplied to the Punjab Governance Reforms Commission (PGRC) by Deputy Registrar Establishment vide letter no. 8593/Estt., dated 04.05.2010. The said information was supplied to the author by Research Officer, PGRC vide his letter no. PGRC/2010/169, dated 05.05.2010.
2.The information about Punjabi University was supplied to the PGRC by the Director Planning and Monitoring vide his letter no. 730/A-2/PMU, dated 03.03.2010. The same has been supplied to the author by the Director PGRC, vide his letter no. PGRC/2010/168, dated 23.04.2010.

Table 30

Number of Teaching Faculty in Punjab Agricultural University (PAU) and Guru Angad Dev Veterinary and Animal Sciences University (GADVASU), Ludhiana University; 2004–05 to 2008–09.

Year	*Punjab Agricultural University*				*Guru Angad Dev Veterinary and Animal Science University*			
	Number		*Vacant Positions*		*Number*		*Vacant Positions*	
	Sanctioned	*Filled*	*Number*	*%*	*Sanctioned*	*Filled*	*Number*	*%*
2004–05	1,645	1,161	484	29.42	136	110	26	19.12
2005–06	1,698	1,109	589	34.69	132	105	27	20.45
2006–07	1,456	895	561	38.53	227	151	76	33.48
2007–08	1,382	851	531	38.42	260	175	85	32.69
2008–09	1,344	833	511	38.02	267	176	91	34.08

Source: The information about PAU was supplied to the PGRC by the Registrar vide his Memo No. Admn. 1. Au. 2010/3951 and the information about the GAD VASU was supplied to the PGRC by the Registrar vide his Memo No. GADVASU/2010/E-1/4559, dated 31.03.2010. The said information has been supplied to the author by the Director PGRC vide his letter no. PGRC/2010/168, dated 23.04.2010.

The position in the government and government-aided private colleges is even worse. For the last so many years, there has been no recruitment of teachers on regular basis in the government colleges. As a result, nearly 25–40 per cent positions of teachers have been lying vacant. Many of them have been filled in by part-time contract/guest faculty. These teachers are grossly under-paid but have to do full teaching work. Nearly 50 per cent of the government colleges in Punjab are without regular principals (*The Tribune*, 2010). The situation in government-aided private colleges is rather worse. For the last so many years, the government has imposed a ban on the filling in of covered posts of teachers in such colleges. All such colleges, established after 1981, are not getting any government grant-in-aid. Similarly, new posts of teachers created after 1981 have not been covered by grant-in-aid. These colleges have filled in most of the vacant/newly created posts by part-time/contract/guest faculty at a much less salary. Such a high proportion of vacant positions have adversely affected the quality of teaching and research.

The other two important state universities – Punjab Technical University and Baba Farid University of Health Sciences – have taken very long period to have their own campuses, mainly because of apathetic attitude of the successive governments in the state of Punjab. As a matter of fact, higher education sector as a whole is facing a serious resource crunch and if this trend continued, these state-funded institutions would head towards their natural death. Significantly, all these universities have been established by the various Acts of the State Assembly wherein the State of Punjab has taken the responsibility to give adequate grant-in-aid to these universities. It is disappointing to note that the successive governments in the state have conveniently forgotten the responsibility of the state towards education sector. Such a withdrawal has taken place mainly because of the shift in the government's priorities towards education. Over the last three decades, more particularly during the last two decades, the bureaucracy and political leadership have made an understanding that education is a non-merit and non-public good. Hence, there is no need of public funding to this sector. In the process, the share of education in the State for Budget has been shrinking. The lack of financial resources with the government is cited as the main reason for cutting down grant-in-aid to the universities, government and the government-aided colleges.

The resource crunch with the government is mainly because of the low-mobilization of resources by the government and the competitive political populism among the political parties. The competitive political populism has been manifesting in non-judicious use of available financial resources and resulting in lower mobilization of resources. The various Finance Ministers in the State of Punjab have been quoted by various news papers that the potentialities to mobilize resources for the state exchequer are much higher than what is being actually mobilized.

The size of black/parallel economy is estimated between 45 per cent and 50 per cent in India. And there is no reason that it should not be the same in Punjab. As per the quick estimates, the gross domestic product (GDP) in Punjab was ₹ 1,65,804 crores in 2008–09 (GDP, 2010). Going by 50 per cent proportion, the size of black economy in Punjab may be ₹ 82,902 crores during 2008–09. If we are able to lower the size of black economy even by 25 per cent, the government would be able to mobilize additional resources to the tune of ₹ 20,725 crores annually. If this seems to be a big task even 10 per cent would generate an additional ₹ 8,290 crores annually.

Further, 10 per cent of ₹ 8,290 crores would come up ₹ 829 crores. This amount, if invested in education, would be enough to fill in all the vacant posts and create necessary infrastructure in the education sector, including higher education. Change in the attitude, towards education, of the bureaucracy and political leadership, along with will to do, would change this seemingly impossible task into a possible one. As a matter of fact, the strong and vibrant higher education systems in most of the developing countries have been built mainly by the government and with public funds (Tilak, 2010).

Summing Up

Higher education is sine qua non for the holistic development of every society. As such the availability and access to quality higher education at an affordable cost is imperative to empower the youth in the eligible age group. Punjab would have to make conscious and long-drawn efforts to raise its gross enrolment ratio (GER) in higher education. Its GER is still hovering around 9 per cent which is below the national average.

Human capital is all the more important for Punjab in view of the deceleration of agricultural growth, lack of natural resources (particularly minerals and metals) and being a land-locked-border state. It is in this context that the state needs to groom its human resources with an utmost care.

Though the higher education sector in Punjab has been growing at a much faster rate during the last one decade or so, yet most of the new institutions are coming up in the for-profit private sector. Majority of the households in Punjab cannot afford to bear the cost of education in the privately-run-institutions.

The state universities, government and government-aided colleges are facing a serious resource crunch due to withdrawal symptoms by the successive governments. The successive governments in Punjab have been withdrawing funding to education sector in general and higher education sector in particular, over the last three decades. Consequently, the universities, government and government-aided colleges are facing an acute shortage of faculty and physical infrastructure. In the process education – both in terms of quality and quantity – has become the victim of resource crunch and poor governance in these institutions. There are hardly any finances available for research which is one of the main responsibilities of a university. Even the Punjab Agricultural University, who is solely responsible for research and development in agriculture, is not having any funds for research. This is in spite of the fact that agriculture is the mainstay of Punjab.

As a result, the poor people, particularly the ruralites are being pushed out of higher education. The share of rural students in the universities (imparting liberal education) is around 4 per cent. Their share in the professional higher education is 3.7 per cent. The share of rural population, as per 2001 census, is 66 per cent. Clearly, the rural students stand excluded from higher education. This would enhance the existing rural-urban divide. Devoid of higher education, the rural people will stand deprived off the enormous amount of benefits of higher education. It is significant to note that the negligible share of rural students in higher education has much to do with the collapse of school education in the rural areas, particularly in the government rural schools. The apathetic attitude and lack-luster approach by the successive governments (particularly since 1980s) in Punjab have been solely responsible for the collapse of rural schools and the consequent negligible share of rural students in higher education.

As regards affordability of the cost of higher education, nearly 40 per cent of the rural households and 31 per cent of urban households in Punjab cannot afford the cost of general education (B.A./B.Sc. and M.A./M.Sc., etc.) even for the one child. In the case of professional and technical education, about 85 per cent of the households in Punjab cannot afford to bear the cost of education of a single child. The corresponding proportion of rural area households may well go beyond 90 per cent. Many of the courses in medical education may simply be not in the affordable reach of 90 per cent of urban households and 95 per cent of the rural households.

In view of the rising cost of education, and increasing cost of living, the affordability question is becoming all the more serious. In fact, a very large section of population in Punjab would get excluded from the higher education. This would have serious implications for the society and economy. It would tantamount to (i) exclusion of potential meritorious students out of education and creation of a mediocre society; (ii) a serious drag on the socio-economic and political development of the state.

In order to reap the benefits of the emerging knowledge economy and venture into meritorious society, the state of Punjab would have to translate the challenges into opportunities. It is all the more important for a border state like Punjab whose main stake is on its human resources as agricultural growth rate is decelerating and the state does not have much of the natural resources. Translation of challenges into opportunities would need highly skilled and educated manpower. There is, thus, an immediate need to revamp and strengthen the higher education sector in Punjab in view of the changing scenario at the national and global levels.

The government, thus, has the primary responsibility to impart education at all the three levels, viz.; primary, secondary and tertiary. Education at all the levels deserves a substantial public funding due to its social benefits, public returns and enormous amount of externalities. As such, public investment in education sector should not be treated as a wasteful expenditure. It is, rather, the most productive investment in human capital. Even the World Bank Studies advocate public funding of education. The government must not withdraw from the education sector considering it a soft-target. The history of economic development of various countries testifies that investment in human capital has played a key role in their socio-economic development.

Resource crunch must not be used as an excuse to justify government withdrawal from social sectors, especially, education. Instead the state should resort to additional resource mobilization through better tax-compliance (plug tax evasion), bringing more services under tax-net and lowering the size of black economy in the state. It has been often conceded by the successive Finance Ministers of Punjab that there is an under mobilization of tax potentials of the state. Realization of the latent potential, along with downsizing the extent of black economy, would generate enough resources to finance education and other development activities in the state. The voluntary, philanthropic, diasporas and community funding of education can also supplement the public efforts.

The ongoing education system has definitely been showing the strong signs of exclusion process, particularly from the quality education, and that too of the weaker sections consisting of landless labourers; marginal, and small farmers; factory workers; slum dwellers, low level technicians, and low income earners in informal self employment activities. There is a need to mitigate the educational vulnerability of such sections by strengthening the public provisioning along with the more effective ways of motivation and involvement of the stakeholders.

Education of ruralities in the state is sine qua non for shifting the workforce from agriculture to non-agricultural sectors and for reaping the benefits/dividends of changing global economic scenario. As such, education sector in general and rural education in particular should not be left to the mercy and vagaries of the market forces alone. Public funding and policy intervention, along with public-private partnership (in an accountable and transparent manner), is of great necessity.

The inclusion of students from rural area and marginalized sections is a must for inclusive and balanced social growth. There is a strong need to provide special incentives to students from the weaker sections, particularly from the rural areas so as to make their entry into higher education. To begin with, it is necessary to create at least 20 per cent additional seats in degree level professional and technical courses for rural and weaker sections.

The vertical socio-economic mobility without education is beyond imagination. As such the marginalized sections of population need to have access and affordability to education. The freebies alone in the form of free electricity, etc. would not help them to attain vertical socio-economic mobility. What they need is quality education and skill. To save them form further marginalization, the government must take immediate policy measures.

There is a need to establish a State Education Development and Regulatory Authority (SRD) to prevent excessive commercialization and profiteering in the non-aided for-profit private institutions. This statutory body should regulate the fee structure, service conditions of teaching and non-teaching staff, and profiteering in such institutions.

Quality control of higher education is a sine qua non and all higher education institutions must be regulated on this count. The quality control of higher education must be left to universities with zero political and bureaucratic interference. Political leadership, civil bureaucracy, policy makers, judiciary and all other stake holders need to be sensitive about the relevance and importance of higher education.

The government of Punjab and all the institutions in higher education sector must prepare themselves for the competition and challenges from foreign universities going to enter India under GATS (General Agreement on Trade in Services). These challenges would become more formidable with the passing of Foreign Educational Institutional Bill.

Notes

1. Delivered in a sermon on social justice four decades ago, Martin Luther King's words retain a powerful resonance (quoted in UNDP, *Human Development Report 2007/2008*, p. 1).
2. There is an implicit prejudice in the policy circles that 'human development' (as the process of expanding education, health care and other conditions of human life is often called) is really a kind of luxury that only richer countries can afford. Japan and other East Asian countries' early expansion of education at a massive scale occurred before even they broke the restraints of general poverty. The priority to human resources

for economic development applies particularly to the early history of Japanese economic development beginning with the Meiji era (1868–1911) (Sen, 2000: 41).

3. The World Trade Organization became operative with effect from 1 January 1995. Prior to that international trade was governed by the General Agreement on Tariffs and Trade. The basis of WTO was General Agreements on Tariffs and Trade (GATT) Agreements concluded in April 1994.
4. Article 1 of General Agreement on Trade in Services (GATS), states that trade in services is defined as the supply of service:
   (a) From the territory of one member into the territory of any other member: This mode is often called as the *cross border supply* of the service. In education, it may be affected through distant education/internet or any type of testing service and educational materials that can cross national boundaries.
   (b) In the territory of one member to the service of consumer of any other member: This mode is termed as *consumption abroad.* Under this mode students of one member country move to another member country to attain education.
   (c) By a service supplier of one member, through *commercial presence* in the territory of any other member: This refers to actual presence of foreign supplier in a host country. This would include universities or education providers of a member country 'A' setting up courses through branches or franchises or entire institutions in another member country 'B'. Thus, country 'A' would be deemed to be exporting education service to country 'B'.
   (d) By a service supplier of one member through *presence of natural persons* of a member in the territory of any other member: This refers to when teachers of a member country 'A' move to teach in another member country 'B'. Country 'A' would be deemed to be exporting education service to country 'B'.
5. The Hon'ble High Court of Punjab and Haryana have also recognized the educational inequality of rural students vis-à-vis their counterparts in the urban schools. And hence, on the basis of a scientific study (Ghuman, Singh and Brar, 2006) done by the Punjabi University, Patiala, it upheld the weightage of five additional marks given to rural candidates by Government of Punjab while preparing merit list in the selection of school teachers in Punjab and dismissed the writ petitions against this additional weightage (The High Court).

References

Agarwal, P. 2006. 'Higher Education in India: The Need for Change'. Working Paper No. 180, Indian Council for Research on International Economic Relations, New Delhi.

Barro, R.J. 2001. 'Human Capital and Growth'. *American Economic Review*, Vol. 91, No. 2, pp. 12–17.

Barro, R.J. and X. Sala-i-Martin. 1995. *Economic Growth*. New York: McGraw-Hill.

Becker, Garry S. 1964. *Human Capital: A Theoretical and Empirical Analysis with Reference to Education*. Chicago: University of Chicago Press.

Benhabib, J. and M. Spiegel. 1994. 'The Role of Human Capital in Economic Development: Evidence from Aggregate Cross Country Data'. *Journal of Monetary Economics*, Vol. 34, pp. 143–51 and 158–61.

Brar, J.S. 2008. 'Public Expenditure on Education: An Evaluation', in S. Dhesi and Gurmail Singh (eds), *Rural Development in Punjab: A Success Story Going Astray*, New Delhi: Routledge.

Brar, J.S., S. Singh and R.S. Ghuman. 2008. 'Costs of Higher Education in Punjab: Levels, Patterns and Efficiency Issues'. *Journal of Educational Planning and Administration*, Vol. 22, No. 2, pp. 153–77.

Chadha, G.K. 2004. 'Human Capital Base of the Labour Force: Identifying Worry Spots'. *The Indian Journal of Labour Economics*, Vol. 47, No. 1, pp. 3–38.

Ghuman, R.S. 2008. 'Socio-Economic Crisis in Rural Punjab'. *Economic and Political Weekly*, Vol. 43, No. 7, pp. 12–15.

Ghuman, R.S., Inderjeet Singh and Lakhwinder Singh. 2007. *Status of Local Agricultural Labour in Punjab*. Mohali: The Punjab State Farmers Commission.

Ghuman, R.S., S. Singh and J.S. Brar. 2005. *Unit Cost of Higher Education in Punjab: A Study of Universities and their Affiliated Colleges*. A Report Submitted to Association of Indian Universities (AIU), New Delhi.

——. 2006. *Rural Students in Universities of Punjab*. Patiala: Punjabi University.

——. 2009. *Professional Education in Punjab: Exclusion of Rural Students*. Patiala: Punjabi University.

Gill, S.S., S. Singh and J.S. Brar. 2005. *Financing of Secondary Education: Grants-in-Aid Policies and Practices in Punjab*. A Report Submitted to National Institute of Educational Planning and Administration (NIEPA), New Delhi.

Government of India. 1968. *Education and National Development: Report of the Education Commission, 1964–66*. Ministry of Education, New Delhi.

——. 1986. *National Policy on Education, 1986*. Ministry of Education, New Delhi.

——. 2007. *Report to the Nation 2006*. National Knowledge Commission, New Delhi.

——. 2008. Eleventh Five Year Plan 2007–12. Vol. II, New Delhi.

——. *Census 2001*.

Government of Punjab. 2008. *Statistical Abstract of Punjab, 2007*. Economic and Statistical Organization, Chandigarh.

——. 2010. *Statistical Abstract of Punjab, 2009*. Economic and Statistical Organization, Chandigarh.

Haq, Mahbub ul. 1998. *Dawn*. 27 April 1998 (quoted in *Human Development in South Asia 2007: A Ten Year Review*, Karachi: Oxford University Press).

Joshi, M. 2003. 'Primary Education in Rural Punjab: A Case Study of Ropar District'. M.Phil. Dissertation (Unpublished), Punjabi University, Patiala.

Kaul, S. 2006. 'Higher Education in India: Seizing the Opportunity'. Working Paper No. 179, Indian Council for Research on International Economic Relations, New Delhi.

Kaur, C. 1992. *Education in Punjab: A Historical Study*. New Delhi: Intellectual Publishing House.

Kaur, Jaswinder. 2004. 'Changing Scenario of Primary Education in Rural Punjab: A Case Study of Ferozepur District'. M.Phil. Dissertation (Unpublished), Punjabi University, Patiala.

Krueger, A.B. and M. Lindahl. 2001. 'Education for Growth: Why and for Whom?'. *Journal of Economic Literature*, Vol. 39, No. 4, pp. 1101–36.

Lucas, R.E. Jr. 1993. 'Making a Miracle'. *Econometrica*, Vol. 61, No. 2, March, pp. 251–72.

Marshall, A. 1920. *Principles of Economics*. Eighth edition, London: Macmillan Publishers.

Mittar, V., S. Singh and J.S. Brar. 2002. *Changing Structure of Education in Punjab: Some Issues and Policy Recommendations*. Patiala: Publication Bureau, Punjabi University.

OECD/UNESCO. 2002. *Financing Education – investment and Returns: An Analysis of the World Education Indicators*. www.oecd.org and www.unesco.org/publications.

Qian, X. and R. Smyth. 2007. 'Education and Economic Growth: Complementarities or Threshold Effects? Some Empirical Evidence from China'. *The Indian Economic Journal*, Vol. 55, No. 2, July–September, pp. 24–38.

Rani, Kavita. 2007. 'A Socio-Economic Analysis of Primary Education in Rural Punjab: A Case Study of District Bathinda'. M.Phil. Dissertation (Unpublished), Punjabi University, Patiala.

Romer, P.M. 1990. 'Endogenous Technological Change'. *Journal of Political Economy*, Vol. 94, No. 5, pp. 1002–36.

Schultz, T.W. 1961. 'Investment in Human Capital'. *American Economic Review*, Vol. 51, January.

Sen, Amartya. 2009. *The Idea of Justice*. New York: Penguin Books.

——. 2000. *Development as Freedom*. London: Oxford University Press.

The High Court of Punjab and Haryana at Chandigarh. 2010. CWP No. 6801 of 2008, Date of Decision: 20 April 2010.

The Tribune. 2010. 'Half of Government Colleges Sans Principals'. Chandigarh, April 25.

The World Bank. 2002. *Constructing Knowledge Societies: New Challenges for Tertiary Education*. Washington, DC.

——. 2000. *Higher Education in Developing Countries: Peril and Promise*. Washington, DC.

——. 2004. *Punjab Development Report*. Poverty Reduction and Economic Management Sector Unit, South Asia Region, IBRD, Washington, DC, June 26.

——. 2008. *World Development Indicators*.

Tilak, J.B.G 2001. 'Education and Development: Lessons from Asian Experience'. *Indian Social Science Review*, Vol. 3, No. 2, July–December, pp. 221–67.

——. 2002. 'Determinants of Household Expenditure on Education in Rural India'. Working Paper No. 89, National Council of Applied Economic Research, New Delhi.

——. 2004a. 'Public Subsidies in Education in India'. *Economic and Political Weekly*, Vol. 39, No. 4, January 24, pp. 343–59.

——. 2004b. 'Education in the UPA Government Common Minimum Programme'. Economic *and Political Weekly*, Vol. 39, No. 43, October 23, pp. 4717–21.

——. 2010. 'The Foreign Education Institutions Bill: A Critique'. *Economic and Political Weekly*, Vol. 45, No. 19, May 8–14, pp. 12–15.

UNDP. 1990. *Human Development Report 1990*.

——. 2006. *Human Development Report 2006*.

UNESCO. 1995. *Policy Paper on Change and Development of Higher Education*. www.unesco.org.

Yashpal Committee. 2009. *Report of the Committee to Advise on Renovation and Rejuvenation of Higher Education*. Submitted to Ministry of Human Resource Development, March 1, p. 9.

Part III

Public-Private Partnership

12

Public-Private Partnership in Education

KULDEEP MATHUR

Universalization of education is now accepted as one of the key triggers of development. It is widely recognized that poor countries are also the countries that have poor education levels. India has not done too well in providing access to education to all its citizens. The challenge before the country is how to redeem its pledge made in the Constitution. One way to do it is involve the private sector in provisioning education. There is surprising support to the idea that private schools are run better and cooperation with the private sector will help improve the quality of education in schools run by the government. The government has also pleaded that it does not have the resources to universalize education and partnership with the private sector will help fill this financial and technological gap.

Thus, the idea of public-private partnership has emerged as the key policy instrument for provisioning education to its citizens in the country. This partnership is being thought of at all levels and for all types of education. The Ministry of Human Resources Development has also brought out a Concept Note on Public-Private Partnership in Education and projects it as an approach used by government to deliver quality services to its population by using the expertise of the private sector. It goes on to point out that this approach has been used in India from a long time. The most common form that it has undertaken is that of government aided schools system in the country. In 2006–07, 30.05 per cent of higher secondary schools and junior colleges, 27.15 per cent of high schools, 6.75

per cent of upper-primary schools, 3.19 per cent of primary schools and 5.15 per cent of pre-primary schools were run by private institutions with substantial financial assistance from the state governments.

However, the government is moving towards different forms of public-private partnerships and also establishing more schools only in this mode. The HRD Minister recently announced that the government was planning to set up over 2,500 model and 200 central schools on public-private partnership (PPP) basis in the country in next two years (*Indian Express,* 29 August 2009). He added that the schools would be set up in public-private partnership as part of our efforts to strengthen the human resource base and then went on to ask the corporate houses to invest in a big way in the education sector emphasizing that developing human resources is key to success of any nation. This commitment to public-private partnership in education had been articulated earlier in a session on knowledge economy at the Pravasi Bharatiya Divas meeting. Admitting that it was not capable of meeting the challenges of the education sector on its own, the government invited the participation of overseas Indians in the field (*Indian Express,* 9 January 2008).

Federation of Indian Chambers of Commerce and Industry has been holding summits in higher education from 2004.[1] It has been organizing them as annual international events with the support of Ministry Human Resources Development and the Planning Commission, Government of India. From the last two years, Ernst and Young has joined FICCI to prepare the background paper in these meetings. In the paper prepared for the 2009 summit, titled 'Leveraging Partnerships in India in Education Sector' the need for PPPs in higher education sector is underlined. This is necessary to meet the financial constraints of the government and to meet the demand of skilled persons of the industry. It identifies various types of partnerships and also recommends collaboration with foreign universities for research and student exchange.

Other institutions and researchers have also joined in stressing the need of introducing PPPs in education sector for similar reasons and also for fulfilling the commitment of raising literacy levels. In a World Bank study, Jagannathan (2001) has explored the working of six NGOs that extend primary education to rural children in India. She argues that these NGOs have demonstrated effective grassroots action to enhance the quality of basic education and have also influenced mainstream education through replication of their models and through policy dialogue with the government. While suggesting that NGOs are best suited for small projects and micro-level interventions, she strongly advocates sustainable and enduring partnership with the voluntary sector that will strengthen the government's efforts to actualize the goal of universal elementary education. In their official documents, both World Bank as well as Asian Development Bank have been advocating the policy of 'pppization'.

Centre for Civil Society launched a School Choice Campaign in 2007 arguing that what the poor need today 'is not just Right to Education, but the Right to Education of Choice.' It advocates public-private partnership through the use of voucher system. At a conference in 2009, the speakers included representatives of the World Bank and the private sector and stressed the need of quality education by providing choices to the poor. This scheme aimed at funding the students and not the schools and giving choice to the students through a voucher system.[2]

Thus, the international donor agencies and some civil society organizations are demanding greater public-private partnership in the education sector. Having articulated its commitment to provide education for all through the enactment of the Right to Education Act, the government is also becoming receptive to these ideas. For, it is facing resource crunch and lack of capacity to run a responsive and efficient educational system.

But government is still at the stage of experimentation. For one thing, the forms that partnerships can take in education are diverse. Government aid to schools is a form of partnership that has existed from a long time but does not fit into the current mould. In this partnership, a private entrepreneur or trust provided the school buildings and infrastructure while the government paid for the salary of teachers and regulated the curriculum and quality of teaching. There are now many other openings like financing of services such as those of IT, underwriting mid-day meals or handing over of a school to the private sector to provide management services. The Concept paper mentioned above has set up several alternative forms of partnership for greater debate and discussion.

At the higher education level it can take such forms as establishing research collaboration between government and industry, giving space to private entrepreneurs to enter the field, and providing for partnership with foreign universities. For quite sometime, large business has been a big player in the field of higher education like engineering and medical education. These institutions were primarily colleges affiliated to universities which exercised control over their academic norms. By the mid-1990s, promoters of private colleges saw the regulatory control of the affiliating universities and state governments as cumbersome, impeding the full utilization of the colleges' market potential. Thus, they wanted university status to wriggle out of the control of state governments and the affiliating universities. This resulted in the proliferation of private universities and private deemed universities. Now, state legislatures have established 10 private universities and 70 private deemed universities. Earlier, the deemed university provision that empowered an institution to award its own degree was sparingly used to allow leading institutions to offer programmes at an advanced level in a particular field or specialization. The Indian Institute of Science in Bangalore and the Indian Agricultural Research Institute in Delhi were the first two institutions to be declared deemed universities in 1958. This number increased to 29 in 1990/91 and 38 in 1998 and now stands at 110. Most of the post-1998 deemed universities are private.[3] The current Minister of HRD is soliciting partnerships with universities in the US and UK to enhance the quality of education India.

It is the resource deficiency that is driving the government to seek partnership with private sector in the field of higher education but at the primary school level this is not the only reason. It is also inefficiencies in the delivery system. Thus, in both health and education, government is seeking partnership – at the local and grassroots level with the NGOs and at higher level with the private sector.

Using the public-private partnership mode is, however, not an easy task. At the primary level, there has to be free schooling which is not an attractive proposition for the private sector. NGOs have come into this arena but the task is truly herculean. Private sector has been attracted to secondary, technical and higher education as it provides both visibility as well as opportunity to run the institutions on their own revenue and earn profit. This is the major challenge. How do you provide services in this mode when the issue of justice and equity are involved and when quality education has to be provided free. The jury is still out.

Notes

1. http://www.ficci-hes2009.com/htm/e&y-executive-summery.pdf
2. Speeches available on its website: http://schoolchoice.in/scnc2009/index.php
3. This experiment seems to have had uncertain success. A recent newspaper report, *The Times of India* (19 January 2010) announces government's decision to derecognize 44 deemed universities for unsatisfactory performance.

13

Public-Private Partnership Model in Higher Education in India

B.S. GHUMAN, AKSHAT MEHTA AND RANJEET SINGH

Education plays a significant role in development of a nation, particularly in the context of knowledge economy. It is increasingly being recognized as a source of growth and as an equalizer in the distribution of growth. Traditionally, education has been mainly in public domain. But, as the state had limited finances, private capital gained momentum in the field of higher education. The experiment of privatization of education in certain areas did not yield good results. As education is a merit good, it led to the realization that presence of government is all the more necessary in the field of education. The government can make its presence felt in education through three modes, (i) Ownership; (ii) Regulation; and (iii) Public-Private Partnership (PPP).

Emergence of PPP Model

The debate for quite a long period of time has been that of Public vs. Private. However, the answer perhaps is in mixing the two. Public-Private Partnership (PPP) model has emerged as an important innovation in various sectors. This model draws strength from the synergy of government sector and private sector in fulfilling the essential infrastructural tasks, which are urgently needed in a developing country like India. The physical infrastructure, including roads, ports, power, telecommunications, etc. have got a fillip, courtesy PPP. The potential for PPP model in the field of education particularly higher education, is being increasingly recognized. In the recent past, the Five Year Plan documents,

N.R. Narayana Murthy Committee (Planning Commission, 2012) and K.B. Pawar Committee (Government of India, 2011) have made policy pronouncements and mooted models for effectively translating the potential of PPP Model in higher education.

First policy pronouncement in this regard, though in implicit form was made in the Tenth Five Year Plan. The Plan underlined the need to establish a large number of centres for excellence for producing quality manpower in the areas relevant to industry and society with the 'triangular partnership of academia, industry and government'. The Plan felt that these institutes were required to make India a knowledge superpower and retain its competitive edge in the global economy (Planning Commission, 2002: 64).

Government of India in its *Approach Paper on Defining Public-Private Partnerships* also states that 'provision of public services and infrastructure has traditionally been the exclusive domain of the government. However, with increasing population pressures, urbanization and other developmental trends, government's ability to adequately address the public needs through traditional means has been severely constrained. This has led the government's across the world to increasingly look at the private sector to supplement public investments and provide public services through Public-Private Partnerships' (Government of India, 2010: 3).

The Twelfth Plan also proclaims that new models of Public-Private Partnerships (PPP) in higher education will be encouraged particularly in the establishment of research and innovation institutions. The document further states that drawing from the Eleventh Plan experience of setting up of IIITs and Polytechnics in PPP mode, a framework, to encourage the spread and growth of PPP models, enhance the quality of education and improve the utilization of resources, will be put in place (Planning Commission, 2013: 100–1).

Tilak, in his analysis of Public-Private Partnership in education, opines that, 'the Public-Private Partnership (PPP) model is projected as an innovative idea to tap private resources and to encourage the active participation of private sector in the national development. It is more forcefully advocated when public resources are projected to be inadequate to meet needs. PPP is already adopted in several infrastructure development sectors, such as development of airports, railways, roads and so on. But going by media reports, these have mixed outcomes. The policy initiatives are no longer confined to these; they are being extended to human development sectors such as education and health' (Tilak, 2010).

The present paper is organized in five parts. Part I provides the rationale for Public-Private Partnership in education. Part II covers the policy pronouncements relating to PPP model in the field of education. Part III describes the PPP models in higher education. In Part IV, a couple of practices at international level have been briefly described. Part V makes an attempt to draw lessons from the PPP experience in school education.

I
Rationale

The rationale for Public-Private Partnership in education is understandable interims of various factors. The first and foremost of these is the poor access to education, especially higher education. The access to higher education in India is very low at 18 per cent, while the world average is 27 per cent. The comparative figures for other emerging countries such as China and Brazil are 26 per cent and 36 per cent, respectively, in the year 2010 (E&Y and FICCI, 2012). This comparative picture clearly shows that India needs to undertake several policy initiatives to catch up with the rest of the world.

The expenditure on education in India as percentage of Gross Domestic Product is around 4 per cent and that on higher education is only 1.25 per cent (University Grants Commission, 2012). Even in case of Eleventh Five Year Plan, though the Government of India has allocated ₹ 850 billion on higher education, it is for short of the identified resource gap of ₹ 2.2 trillion (E&Y and FICCCI, 2008; Anand, 2012). There are several competing demands and financial limitations, which the government is facing and as such, there is an urgent need to innovate. The PPP model is one such innovative mechanism.

The second related factor is the emerging need for expansion of higher education as well as its diversification and qualitative improvement. The number of higher educational institutions and the number of students pursuing higher education is shown in Table 1.

Table 1

Expansion of Higher Education in India Over the Past Four Decades

Year	*Number of Universities*	*Number of Colleges*	*Students Enroled (in million)*
1970–71	103	3,604	2.0
1980–81	133	4,722	2.8
1990–91	190	7,346	4.9
2000–01	256	12,806	8.4
2006–07	387	21,170	16.6
2011–12	659	33,023	25.9

Source: UGC, 2012; E&Y and FICCI, 2012.

As can be seen in Table 1, India has been witnessing a rapid expansion in the number of higher educational institutions as well as student and enrolment. The number of universities has grown more than six times and the number of students by 12 times in the last four decades. One-third of the colleges in India have been set up in the last five years. In addition to these institutions, there were 12, 748 diploma granting institutions in the country as of 2011–12 (E&Y and FICCI, 2012).

Third and major rationale for PPP model in higher education emerges from the need for inclusive growth. The Indian higher education scenario reveals that there are huge variations in terms of gender, caste, locale, and income (University Grants Commission, 2008). In case of gender, the figures show that the GER for females is 15.2 per cent in comparison to 19 per cent for the males. Similarly, the GER for SCs is only 11.6 per cent, for STs a meagre 7.7 per cent, for OBCs 14.8 per cent. The rural-urban divide, with only 11.1 per cent of the students from the rural background as against 30 per cent from the urban areas. Location-wise also there is wide disparity in the GER of higher education across states with 47.9 per cent in Delhi and only 9 per cent in Assam (E&Y and FICCI, 2012).

Further, privatization of higher education has delivered mixed outcomes. It has helped the cause of expansion but generated the problem of inequity and poor quality. The role of public sector is to provide a cushion and moderate these harsh impacts. It is for this reason that discussion paper on PPP in higher and technical education the Planning Commission it has argued that in Public-Private Partnership, the government retains full responsibility for providing educational services. The legal ownership of assets created under PPP would rest with the government. The nature and scope of services are contractually determined between the government and the private service providers and the risks and rewards are shared between the government and the service providers. This way, the PPP mode is much better than the privatization model (Mahadevan, 2008).

II
Policy Pronouncements

The Government of India has been making some significant policy pronouncements and coming out with certain policy documents, which have laid emphasis on PPP mode for higher education. These included the Narayana Murthy Committee Report set up by the Planning Commission; Consolidated Working Group Report of the Department of Higher Education for Twelfth Five Year Plan on higher education, technical education and private sector participation including PPP in higher education; and the policy pronouncement relating to the setting up of 20 new Indian Institutes of Information Technology (IIITs). These three have been briefly discussed as under:

(i) *Narayana Murthy Committee, Planning Commission:* The NR Narayana Murthy Committee Report (also known as 'Committee on Corporate Participation in Higher Education) has called for quick and hassle free process for establishing public, private and PPP universities and higher education institutions under both the central and state governments. It also calls for the need to define a flexible PPP developmental framework in order to build synergies and to leverage existing resources/capabilities to their full potential (Planning Commission, 2012: 13–16).

(ii) *The Consolidated Working Group Report of the Department of Higher Education for Twelfth Five Year Plan on higher education, technical education and private sector participation including PPP in higher education, Department of Higher Education,* Ministry of Human Resources Development – The department has finalized a legislation for creating a framework for setting up of 'Universities for Innovation' aiming at world class standards, in public sector, private sector as well as in PPP mode (Government of India, 2011: 27). The report further talks about 'Incentivization Scheme', in which it is proposed to initiate a Centrally-Sponsored Scheme, wherein states would be incentivized to invest resources in creating new higher education institutions and expand existing ones. The scheme would be applicable for all districts where GER is less than 15 per cent. The states would be free to mobilize part percentage of their share from private partners by means of 'innovative PPP schemes'. The states can set up and expand: (i) State Universities; (ii) State Engineering Colleges; (iii) State Colleges (Others); (iv) Diploma Level Institutions; and (v) Vocational Institutions (ibid., p. 53).

(iii) *Setting up of 20 new Indian Institutes of Information Technology (IIITs):* At present, there are four IIITs in the country and the government proposes to add 20 more on not-for-profit PPP mode to address the challenges faced by the Indian IT industry and meet the growth objective. The capital cost of each IIIT would be ₹ 128 crores. The contribution of central government, state government and industry for setting up an IIIT is to be in the ratio of 50:35:15 in all places except in the North-Eastern Region, where the contribution of the central government is to be 57.5 and that of industry at 7.5. The provision has also been made for Faculty Development Programme to the tune of ₹ 50 crores and up to ₹ 10 crores recurring expenditure for the first four years. Each IIIT will be expected to meet its operating expenditure on its own within five years of commencement out of students' fees, research and other internal accruals (Vats, 2011; currenteventsworld.com, 2012).

III
PPP Models in Higher Education

K.B. Pawar Committee (Government of India, 2011) constituted by the UGC has recommended the following four models of PPP in higher education:

(i) Basic Infrastructure Model;
(ii) Outsourcing Model;
(iii) Equity/Hybrid Model; and
(iv) Reserve Outsourcing Model.

Their salient features are outlined in Table 2.

Table 2

Four Models of PPP in Higher Education Proposed by the K.B. Pawar Committee Constituted by the UGC

S.No.	*PPP Model*	*Features*
1.	Basic Infrastructure Model	The private sector would invest in infrastructure whereas the government would run the operations and management aspects. The government in this model is also to make annualised payments to the private investor.
2.	Outsourcing Model	The private sector not only invests in the infrastructure but also runs the operations and management part. In this model, the role of the government is limited to paying the private investor for the specified services.
3.	Equity/Hybrid Model	The investments in infrastructure are shared between the government and private sector. This model, however, states that the responsibility for operations and management aspects vests with the private investor.
4.	Reserve Outsourcing Model	The government invests in the infrastructure, while the responsibilities for operations and management are to be handled by the private investor.

Source: Government of India, 2011, pp. 68–69.

An advisory and research company that caters to education sector (Indalytics) has suggested that in the Indian scenario, the first model is best suited for real estate, infrastructure companies and financial institutions. The second model is suitable for real estate and infrastructural companies, who operate educational institutions like DLF and Jaypee Group. The third model would be beneficial for existing private players in the field of higher educational institutions such as Amity, ICFAI, Manipal groups and the fourth model is best suited for school management companies, which have experience in managing and operating schools on contracts like Navneet Publications and BVM Global (Indalytics, 2012).

The efficacy of these models remains to be tested. However, considering the merit good characteristics of education sector, the resource constraints of the public sector as well as the involvement of private sector, it could be reasoned that the Outsourcing and Equity/Hybrid model would be more suitable in the field of higher education. Not many players in the private sector would be eager to be part of the first model, wherein private sector invests in the infrastructure and government is involved in operations and management. Similarly, in case of the fourth model, the resource constraints would make government reluctant to come forward and invest in infrastructure and leave the operations and management to private sector. In contrast, the outsourcing model with suitable monitoring would be beneficial for all. Similarly, the equity/hybrid model with sharing of investment in infrastructure provision makes it win-win situation for both the parties. It is pertinent to mention here that for any of these models to succeed, it is vital to have adequate safeguards and regulatory checks in place.

IV
Practices

The *Consolidated Working Group Report of the Department of Higher Education for XII Five Year Plan on Higher Education, Technical Education and Private Sector Participation Including PPP in Higher Education* observes that very few PPP models have been tried in the field of higher education in India so far. While the aided colleges are one of the conventional forms of PPP, their impact has been felt more on addressing issues of access and expansion, with limited or no impact on quality. The need for scaling up the new scheme of setting up of 20 IIITs through PPP mode has also been emphasized. The Report further calls for the need to explore new forms of PPP and mentions Private Finance Initiative; Modified Voucher System for below poverty line students belonging to SC/ST; Charter Colleges; and Outcome-Based Financing for sponsored students as possible formats in which PPP could be explored (Government of India, 2011: 69).

The Indian Institutes of Information Technology (IIITs) at Hyderabad, Kerala and Bangalore are functional and the centre recently has cleared the proposal to set up three new IIITs under the PPP mode at Assam, Tripura and Rajasthan. According to the Government of India, 11 states have identified land and are in the process of identifying the industry partners (currenteventsworld.com, 2012).

The Twelfth Plan has highlighted that the Ministry of Human Resource Development under the Coordinated Action on Skill Development has taken initiatives to set up 300 polytechnics through PPP by the state governments/union territories in consultation with CII, FICCI, ASSOCHAM and PHD Chamber of Commerce (Planning Commission, 2013: 144).

The select PPP initiatives undertaken by some of the state governments in the field of higher education have been shown in Table 3.

Table 3

PPP in Higher Education Across States

S.No.	*State*	*Completed, Ongoing/In Pipeline PPP Initiatives*
1.	Andhra Pradesh	Andhra Pradesh is the leading state in promoting largest number of Infrastructure projects under PPP (130 projects with investment of ₹ 45,678 Crores). It has promoted PPPs in Education Sector through International Finance Corporation (IFC). In this regard, ISB has been provided Institutional support and NALSAR has been provided legal support by the state government.
2.	Assam	An Engineering College to be set up under PPP mode is at the Bid Stage in Assam.
3.	Haryana	Technical Institutes at 14 different locations and Technical Institute at Khilor (Sonepat) are the ongoing/in pipeline PPP initiatives in the State of Haryana.
4.	Gujarat	Gujarat Power Education and Research Foundation (GPERF) has been set up in the state of Gujarat. 15 Poly-techs, ITIs and Gujarat Power Engineering and Research Institute are the ongoing/in pipeline PPP initiatives.
5.	Jharkhand	The state government has signed an MoU with the Techno India Group for running two technical institutions on PPP mode. These institutions are Ramgarh Engineering College and Silli Polytechnic Institute.
6.	Madhya Pardesh	Setting up of a Special Education Zone in Madhya Pradesh (Technical Education); a Medical College at Ratlam; and 39 colleges under GoI Scheme are the ongoing/in pipeline PPP initiatives in the state of Madhya Pradesh.
7.	Punjab	3 Polytechnics on BOT basis at Anandpur Sahib, Muktsar and Sultanpur Lodhi have been completed. 2 Polytechnics at Rahon and Nanowal; and Punjab Institute of Medical Sciences at Jalandhar (Health) are the ongoing/in-pipeline PPP initiatives.

Cont'd...

...Cont'd

8.	Sikkim	Sikkim Manipal University (SMU) is the result of a unique partnership between the Government of Sikkim and Manipal Education. Established in 1995, it is the first government-private initiative in the region. SMU is recognized by the University Grants Commission and approved by the Government of India.
9.	Uttarakhand	A Medical College at Haldwani; Aarohi: A Computer Literacy and CAL Project; and Shikhar: A Job oriented IT Professional Education project have been completed.
10.	Uttar Pradesh	The State has decided to run 2 State Medical Colleges at Azamgarh and Banda as well as a Paramedical College at Safai on PPP Model. The State is also planning to implement the public-private partnership (PPP) in technical education by considering the establishment of two more branches of the Indian Institute of Information Technology (IIT) in the state. The proposed IIITs will have special emphasis on postgraduate programmes and research and development. The companies like IBM, TCS were being considered by the state government. The public sector undertakings (PSUs) are also included for the venture.

Source: http://pppinindia.com/round-table-files/states/andhra_pradesh_ppp_nov2008_kochi_meet.pdf; http://pppinindia.com/round-table-files/states/assam_ppp_nov2008_kochi_meet.pdf; http://pppinindia.com/state-presentation/Haryana_PPP_Review_23Mar2009.pdf; http://www.gperi.ac.in/; http://pppinindia.com/state-presentation/Gujarat__PPP_Review_23Mar2009.pdf; Chaudhary, 2012; http://pppinindia.com/pdf/mp_ppp_projects_in_pipeline.pdf; http://pppinindia.com/state-presentation/Madhya_Pradesh__PPP_Review_23Mar2009.pdf; http://smude.edu.in/about-us/sikkim-manipal-university; http://pppinindia.com/pdf/uttarakhand_PPP3Jan2008.pdf; http://pppinindia.com/ppp-initiatives-punjab.php; https://udyogbandhu.com/topics.aspx?mid=Medical Education; and http://articles.timesofindia.indiatimes.com/2013-02-05/lucknow/36763294_1_iiits-ppp-model-technical-education

International Practices in Higher Education

Cheng, in his research work says, 'The public sector has traditionally enjoyed a near monopoly in the provision of higher education in most countries of the world, except for some in East Asia and Latin America where private universities have long been established. This situation changed in the 1990s when many countries in different regions experienced the emergence and expansion of private universities and institutions of higher education ... . The PPP has become a major item on the agenda of education reform in many countries. It carries the connotation that the private sector is recognized as a social necessity and contributes to societal developments' .... It is no longer easy to have purely public or private entities in higher education. Public institutions are involved in various ways in private or market engagements. There are also various ways that private institutions receive public support' (Cheng, 2009: 51–52).

Table 4 depicts select international practices in higher education, including the various ways in which public-private partnerships have emerged.

Table 4

Select International Practices in Higher Education

S.No.	*Country*	*Practices in Higher Education*
1.	China	Most of the public institutions are expected to generate income from self-financing and commercial activities. These include fee-charging courses, sales of services or research products and the operation of private enterprises for profit. Shantou University in Guangdong is an example in this regard.
2.	France	There are over 1,000 institutes of higher education, but only 15 of them are private institutions.
3.	Indonesia	Out of more than 2,900 institutions of higher education only 32 are public. The government has the policy of encouraging appointment of higher qualified teachers in these private institutions by providing a subsidy.
4.	Japan	Since 2001, public institutions of higher education have been corporatized and they have become Independent Administrative Institutions who are given block grants and institutional autonomy in return for competition and accountability for results.
5.	Netherlands	There are 14 government-supported universities and 45 government-supported institutes of applied sciences and only two private universities.
6.	Pakistan	Private sector is favoured in new development in higher education and it is represented in the formulation of the national plan for higher education.
7.	Philippines	It follows a general policy of laissez-faire in which little is done to advance the public universities while the private sector is left to the market.
8.	Singapore	All higher educational institutions are public institutes.
9.	United Kingdom	The private institutions are exceptions, but they are engaged in all kinds of income generating activities.

Source: Cheng, 2009, pp. 52–57.

The federal funding for private institutions is manifested in case of Harvard University, which receives 30 per cent of its income from tuitions, 10 per cent from the private donations and 60 per cent from the projects, most of which are government projects. In Botswana, a new University is being established under PPP model wherein the state will provide substantial funding for capital expenditure, while the private sector will be responsible for operational expenditure. A similar venture is being created in Zambia at the Mulungushi University. In Bangladesh the Asian University for Women has been established by the AUW Support Foundation and owes its existence to both private and public donations. The Bangladeshi Government allocated land and provided infrastructure to the campus (ibid., pp. 57–58).

It is relevant here to take a look at the case of Melaka-Manipal Medical College, which is the first Indo-Malaysian joint venture in private medical education. An agreement in the presence of Prime Ministers of India and Malaysia was signed in 1993 between the Joint Venture Medical College Corporation (JVMC) Malaysia and the Manipal Academy of Higher Education (MAHE) India to offer a twinning programme leading to the MBBS degree. This PPP initiative is recognized by the Malysian Medical Council, WHO and Sri Lankan Medical Council. However, it is not recognized by the Medical Council of India as it is a twinning programme between two countries. The partners in this PPP model are state government of Melaka, Manipal Group and members of the Indian Diaspora (Nagra, 2005).

An overview of the select international practices in higher education reveals that public-private partnerships are on the rise in many countries. However, the model of PPP and the distribution of responsibilities between the public and private vary from country to country. These range from the system which is basically a public system but allows private participation in certain domains to a system wherein there is a basic division of labour between the public and private sectors. These arrangements have been chosen depending upon the form of governance, policies being followed by the governments, level of economic development and availability of resources along with the expertise with the governments as well as the private sector in the respective countries.

V
PPP Model in School Education

The Eleventh Five Year Plan proposed setting up of 6,000 new model schools at secondary level by the year 2014, of which 2,500 are to be under the PPP model. These Central Board of Secondary Education (CBSE) affiliated schools are to be established in the backward and remote areas to give impetus to quality education in these areas. These schools will have wherewithal to educate 65 lakh students, including 25 lakh from the deprived sections. Under the proposed model chalked out by the Planning Commission in consultation with private sector, each school is to have 2,500 students, out of which 1,000 will be from the deprived sections. Amongst these students from deprived sections, half would be from SC, ST and OBC category, who will be charged a token fee of ₹ 25 per month and the other half will be from non-income tax paying families who will be charged a token fee of ₹ 50 per month. The union government will reimburse the rest of the costs incurred on education of these students to the concerned schools. These schools have been provided absolute freedom to admit anyone in the remaining 1,500 seats and charge any quantum of fee. Both corporate companies as well as non-profit companies with prior experience in education are eligible to establish schools under this model. This model has been criticized on account of promoting privatization and a high degree of commercialization and that too by utilizing funds from the public exchequer. It is observed that government shall have very less control over these schools especially with regard to the admission and fees to be charged in case of non-deprived section students. A contrast is also built here with an earlier model of government aided private school system, which was subject to all the government rules and regulations with regard to admissions, fees, scholarships, recruitment, salary structure, etc. (Tilak, 2010).

Two observations are in order here: First, there is a need to have clear and unambiguous policy pronouncement with free rein to privatization and commercialization.

In light of this initiative, the following observations are warranted:

First of all, Public-Private Partnership model in higher education needs clear and unambiguous policy pronouncements. The policy pronouncement regarding setting up of 2,500 schools under Eleventh Five Year Plan under PPP model have drawn criticism on the count of giving free rein to privatization and commercialization. Secondly, an effective regulatory framework is vital for the growth of PPP model. The regulatory framework should ensure that not only the interests of all the partners are protected, but more importantly consumer interest is placed at the centre of it all. The role of regulatory administration has been quite visible in various sectors like telecommunication, power, insurance, etc. and has been instrumental for ensuring quality, competition, lower prices and equitable growth of the respective sectors. It is felt that regulatory framework in PPP model may follow the same pattern. Thirdly, for PPP model to be effective, clear-cut division of responsibilities of all the partners needs to be laid down at all levels. This would avoid confusion and determine accountability. It would also ensure that one partner is not all the time carrying the others on its back and thus, defeating the potential synergies, which can emerge from such arrangements.

Fourthly, in the light of rapidly changing socio-economic scenario, the government needs to be flexible in its approach. The overview of the above mentioned Melaka-Manipal Medical College set up under PPP mode reveals that it is not yet recognized by the Medical Council of India as it is a twinning programme between two countries. It is pertinent to mention here that the agreement for this joint venture was signed in the presence of Prime Ministers of Malaysia and India and the World Health Organization recognizes it. Our regulatory institutions also need to consider such cases in the right spirit.

Lastly, PPP mode can become successful only if it lays adequate emphasis on access and equity aspects. The PPP mode has been ushered in the domain of higher education, more importantly as the government sector alone was finding it challenging to increase the access and usher in inclusive growth. If PPP mode also travels on the path of more autonomy to private partners and commercialization aspects, it may lose its objective. The equity concern mandated in the above policy initiative at the school level should also apply to higher education.

References

Anand, Abhay. 2012. 'Public-Private Partnership, the Best Foot Forward for Higher Education'. *India Education Review*, February 16, retrieved from: http://www.indiaeducationreview.com/features/public-private-partnership-best-foot-forward-higher-education, last accessed on 27 April 2013.

Chaudhary, Chadra Prakash. 2012. 'MoU Signed for Two PPP Mode Engineering Colleges'. *The Times of India*, October 20.

Cheng, Kai-ming. 2009. 'Public-Private Partnerships', in Svava Bjarnason et al., *A New Dynamic: Private Higher Education*, World Conference on Higher Education, Paris: UNESCO, pp. 51–69.

currenteventsworld.com 2012. '20 New IIITs Across India Through PPP Model'. July 25, retrieved from: http://www.currenteventsworld.com/categories/details/career-and-education/20–new-iiits-across-india-through-ppp-model.html, last accessed on 28 April 2013.

E&Y and FICCI. 2008. 'Leveraging Partnerships in India's Education Sector'. FICCI Higher Education Summit, November.

——. 2012. 'Higher Education in India: Twelfth Five Year Plan 2012–17 and Beyond'. FICCI Higher Education Summit.

Government of India. 2010. Approach Paper on Defining Public-Private Partnerships. Discussion Note, Department of Economic Affairs, Ministry of Finance, February.

——. 2011. *Consolidated Working Group Report of the Department of Higher Education for Twelfth Five Year Plan on Higher Education, Technical Education and Private Sector Participation Including PPP in Higher Education*. Department of Higher Education, Ministry of Human Resource Development.

Indalytics. 2012. 'These Companies are Best Suited for PPP in Higher Education'. February 23, retrieved from: http://indalytics.com/2012/02/these-companies-are-best-suited-for-ppp-in-higher-education/, last accessed on 28 April 2013.

Mahadevan, G. 2008. 'Private Partnership in Education Mooted'. *The Hindu*, September 9.

Nagra, J.S. 2005. 'Public Private Partnership: A Case Study of Melaka-Manipal Medical College'. *Kathmandu University Medical Journal*, Vol. 3, No. 4, Issue 12, pp. 451–54.

Planning Commission. 2002. *Higher and Technical Education, Volume II: Sectoral Policies and Programmes*. Tenth Five Year Plan 2002–07, Government of India, New Delhi, December 21, pp. 53–66.

——. 2012. *Committee on Corporate Participation in Higher Education: Report of NR Narayana Murthy Committee*. Government of India, New Delhi.

——. 2013. *'Education' and 'Employment and Skill Development', Volume III: Social Sectors*. Draft Twelfth Five Year Plan 2012–17, Government of India, New Delhi, pp. 47–123 and 124–63.

Tilak, J.B.G. 2010. 'Public-Private Partnership in Education'. *The Hindu*, May 24.

University Grants Commission. 2008. *Higher Education in India: Issues Related to Expansion, Inclusiveness, Quality and Finance*. November.

——. 2012. *Higher Education in India at a Glance*. February.

Vats, Rohit. 2011. '20 New IIITs on PPP Model are About to Set-up Soon'. *India Education Review*, March 22, retrieved from: http://www.indiaeducationreview.com/features/20–new-iiits-ppp-model-are-about-appear-soon, last accessed on 28 April 2013.

14

Industry-Institute Partnership

A New Paradigm in Technical Education

S.K. SHARMA

Building of a strong and dynamic economy in the era of globalization requires sound policies for science and technology. Pure scientific research may be relevant for understanding the mysteries of nature but may have little relevance towards fulfilling the needs of society and creating national wealth. It was felt by the purists that in case there is a greater interaction between institutes and industry, institutes will be forced to neglect fundamental research and education which is regarded as their primary function. On the other hand, industry is also apprehensive about the capability and usefulness of the research being carried out in the institutes. This is a sort of chicken and egg situation regarding interaction between industry and institutes. Decline of Britain after second world war prompted Maurice Goldsmith to state, 'It was easier to accept why the educational purists of the past, in such a cloistered, cultivated atmosphere, had been able to contribute to Britain's slow decline in industrial efficiency by insisting on the separation between the university, Technology and Industry". This is further amplified by the fact that in eighties, economy of Japan was galloping, while that of America was declining. It was observed by Americans that the Japanese companies had purchased maximum number of patents of fundamental scientific discoveries from the US and built innovative products using these cutting edge technology patents. Studies on the role of technology in development show that the long-term economic growth is technology-based, as technological capabilities of a nation have a direct bearing on its international trade. The shining example of this is the economic revolution brought about by Information Technology in India, which made Indian service sector as a pivot of economic resurgence of the country. Earlier, technological inputs to agriculture brought about green revolution and made India self-sufficient in food products.

In view of this, there is a feeling among some sections of the society, that pure academic institutions are irrelevant for the economic growth of the country. However, there is an equally strong and balanced view, which says that academic institutions with strong linkages with industry could substantially contribute towards the fundamental research and economic development of the country. Silicon Valley and MIT are the shining examples of the strong linkages between academia and industry, which brought a new technology revolution in the world by the creation of companies like Microsoft, Apple, Google, etc. It not only transformed the American economy but also uplifted the economy of India and many other countries through trade linkages. Thus, the main emphasis of science and technology policy for promoting R&D efforts should be to generate commercially viable innovative products and processes. It has been estimated that 30–40 per cent of economic growth of a country is technology-based (1). Which means that in four years a country will be twice ahead economically due to technological advancement. The perceived advantage of low labour and material cost by the developing countries like India is also short-lived phenomena as innovative technological inputs in the developed countries can counter it in the long run. Germany did so in textile sector and China is learning it the hard way as the cost of manufacturing is increasing due to increase in wages over time, as a result of economic upturn and the increasing cost of imported energy and raw material due to spurt in international commodities prices.

Growth of Indian Technical Education

Figure 1 shows the development of technical education in India since 1790. Only British nationals were allowed admission in the Madras Survey School. The first technical institute set up with indigenous initiative was Hindu College Bengal. Roorkee Engineering College was set up in 1848 for developing the canal irrigation systems in India. The major initiative in quality technical education in India started in mid-nineties when a number of IITs were set up with the collaboration of foreign governments.

Figure 1 also shows that girl students were permitted to take admission in engineering institutes only after Independence. Only 910 women students were enroled in engineering institutes in 1970 and this number increased to 2,64,370 in 1995. Since then, there was an increasing trend in the share of women students in technical education. Percentage of women students in Bachelor programme in 2001 was 22 per cent, 16 per cent and 17 per cent in B.Tech, M.Tech and PhD, respectively. In order to further encourage women students, AICTE has allowed additional women engineering institutes to be established in the existing engineering campuses.

Figure 1

Growth of Engineering Education in India

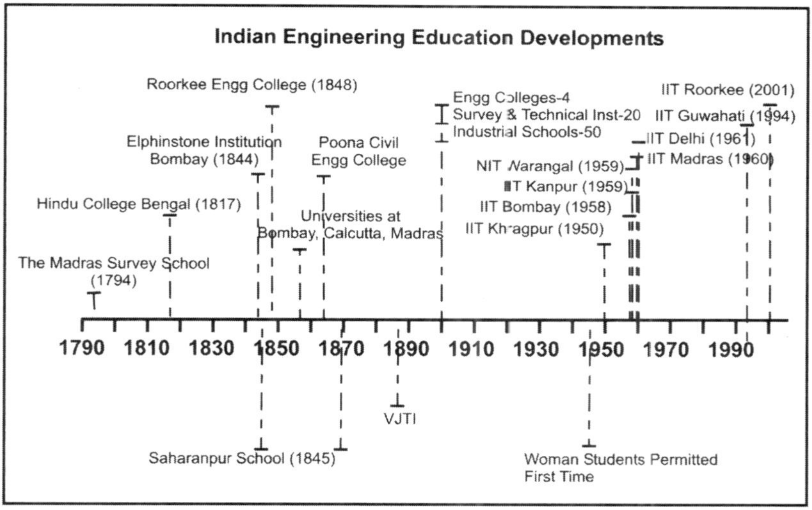

Growth of technical manpower is given in Figure 2. It shows that enrolment was virtually static till 1970 and then it started growing at a fast pace. The real exponential spurt in the growth of technical education came in the nineties with opening of Indian economy. It was recognized that technology is the prime mover for increasing efficiency, productivity and accelerating economic development, which is essential for bridging the gap between developed and under-developed sections of the society by providing basic amenities to the deprived sections.

Technical education is the bedrock of technology. Keeping this in mind, the Government of India through MHRD and AICTE embarked upon a programme for the exponential growth of the technical education in the country.

It can be inferred from the above figures that in pre-liberalization period of 40 years between 1950 1990, intake in undergraduate engineering institutions increased from 3,700 to 66,600. On the other hand, there was an exponential growth in enrolment from 66,600 to 653,290 in the post-liberalization period of 17 years between 1990 and 2007.

Figure 2

Growth of Sanctioned Intake of Graduates 1947–2007

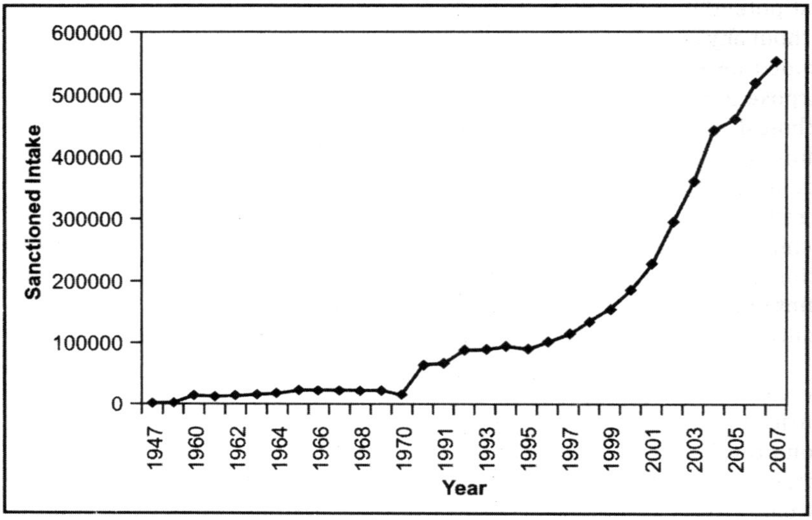

Figure 3

Total Output of Engineering Graduates 1947–2006

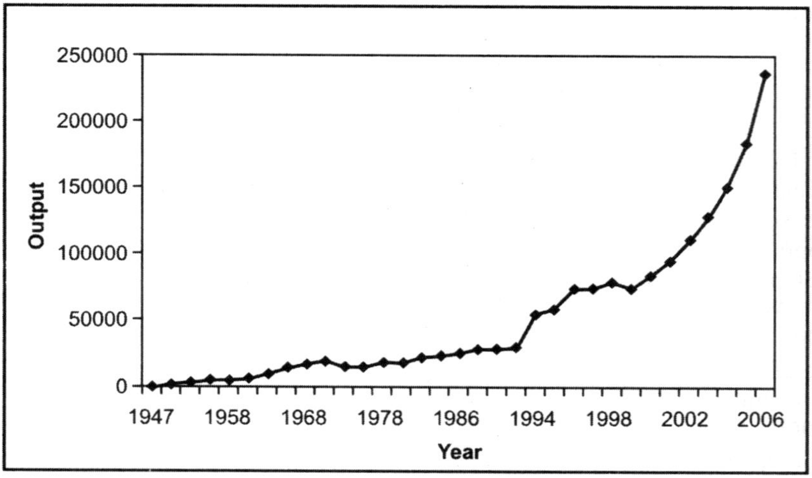

Due to limited resources of the government, a model of privatization in technical education was developed, so as to provide technical/professional manpower for the fast developing economy of India, which is growing at an unprecedented rate of 9 per cent per annum. Looking at the vast potential of technical education, a large number of business people, without any experience in the field of education and technical background, jumped on the technical education band wagon, purely for commercial purpose to make quick profits. There was a race to open more and more technical institutes, as a result of nexus between politicians, administrators and educational governing bodies. This can be judged by the fact that in one year (2008–9), the enrolment in engineering colleges increased incredibly by 1,66,710 seats. No thought was given by the MHRD, AICTE, Technical universities and college managements about the availability of technically trained teachers and proper technical infrastructure for maintaining quality. Output of M.Tech students, which is essential for faculty positions, increased from merely 30 in 1947 to just 20,000 in 2006.

A large number of MNCs at this juncture entered the Indian market due to opening of economy. They started paying astronomically high salaries to their technical staff as compared to the existing low remuneration prevalent in the country. As a result, there was a deluge of students for taking admission in technical institutions to reap the benefits of huge pay packages being offered by the MNCs. This is evident from the fact that total number of seats in technical institutes in the northern states of Punjab and Haryana increased from less than 10,000 in the year 2001 to 97,000 in 2011. A large number of technical institutes without adequate infrastructure and qualified manpower reaped a windfall in the form of capitation fee in collusion with the monitoring agencies by admitting students with low percentage, in the form of management quota. Thus, in spite of impressive quantitative expansion of technical education, quality and training suffered substantially. There was an imbalance between the curriculum and the skill set required by industry and business sector. Infrastructural facilities in most of the institutes were pathetic and there was severe shortage of qualified and trained faculty. As a result, the dropout rate of undergraduate students in technical institutes was as high as 50 per cent in 2006, as shown in Figure 2 and Figure 3.

As a result of the twin effects of oversupply and steep fall in the availability of jobs due to slowing down of national and international economy, lure of technical education faded over the years. Like the equity bubble, the technical education bubble also got burst. Only 7,696 seats out of 43,000 offered in affiliated colleges of the Panjab Technical University could be filled during academic session 2011–12 during counselling. Fate of technical institutes in Haryana is rather worse. Haryana State Counselling Society could fill only 4,377 seats out of 54,000 offered. Situation is the same or worse in other states of the country, especially south and south-west which account for 50 per cent of the seats in all institutes in the country. There are a number of institutions, where not a single student has taken admission. There is need to take urgent measures so as to stem this land slide in technical education. The main reasons for this catastrophe are the improper technical manpower planning, deficiency in skill set being provided to the students and absence of linkages with user agencies.

Technical educational institutions in India have no proper linkages with user agencies such as industries, R&D and design organizations and the development sectors of the economy. They are functioning in isolation. The situation has become so pathetic that industrial associations and professional bodies are openly admitting that the fresh technical graduates are unemployable primarily due to the outdated curriculum and lack of proper skill set acquired by them. A survey done by McKinsey Global Institute shows that multinationals find only 25 per cent of Indian engineers employable.

Technical Manpower Planning

Based on the historical data (Figure 2 and Figure 3) of Indian technical education, a relationship between the number of engineering graduates (E) with the population (POP) and GDP was developed by Banerjee and Muley shown in Figure 4 and is represented by equation

$$E/POP = 51.034 + 0.81\ GDP/POP$$

The R^2 value obtained is 89 per cent and the model is not rejected based on the t and F statistics.

Figure 4

GDP/Population

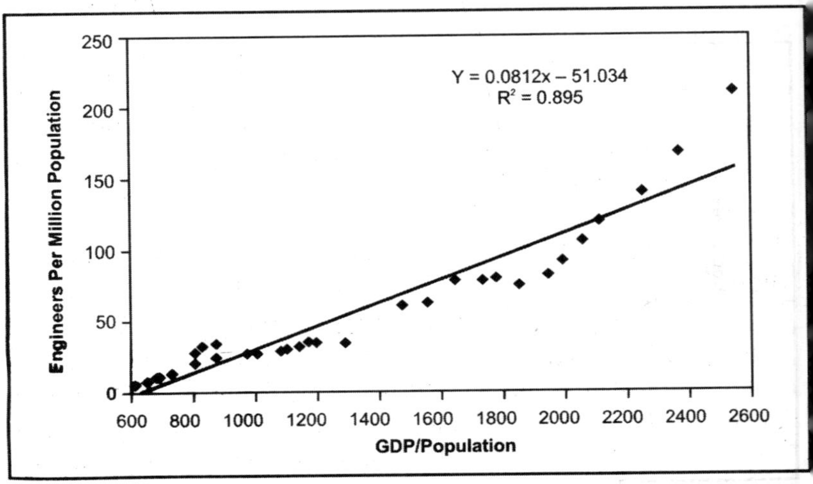

The future projections of the number of engineering graduate students, as per this model, are given in Table 1.

Table 1

Projection of Technical Graduates as per Model

Year	*Number of graduates*
2006	2,86,704
2012	4,48,067
2017	6,60,842

The projections can also be made on the basis of historic trends in the growth rate of the enrolment of students. Based on the values of AGR of 12.5 per cent, 7.5 per cent and 6.1 per cent for B.Tech, M.Tech and PhD respectively, their projections have been given in Table 2. Total faculty requirements have also been calculated based on the student-faculty ratios of 9:1 for the IITs and 15:1 for other institutions.

Table 2

Projection of Technical Graduates as per AGR

Year	*Population Millions*	*Graduates*	*Masters*	*Doctorates*	*Total Faculty*
2006	1,112	2,37,400	19,900	1,030	79,500
2012	1,223	4,81,300	30,700	1,465	1,59,270
2017	1,324	8,67,400	44,100	1,970	2,38,840

Figure 5

Engineering Doctorate Degrees Awarded in India

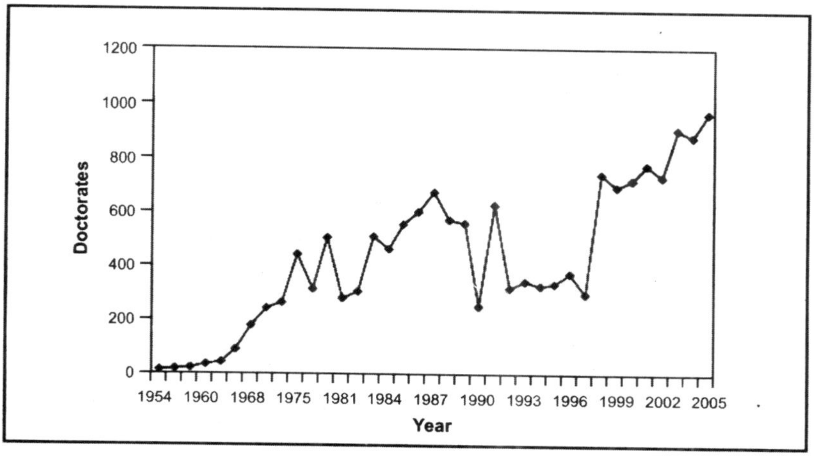

However, for realistic projections, the growth of the industrial and service sector should also be considered, as slowing down of the economy will generate lesser number of jobs.

Bridging the Skill Gap

NASSCOM reported that there will be a shortage of 500,000 knowledge workers by 2010. The U.R. Rao Committee had earlier projected that over 10,000 PhDs and twice as many M.Tech degree holders will be needed in India for meeting its R&D. However, the output is much less. Figure 5 shows the number of PhD degrees awarded during different years in India. Total number was less than 1,000 in 2006.

Industry – Academia Interaction

Our economy in the coming years will require innovative and properly skilled professionals, as industry will be exposed to domestic and global competition. High level of skills and cutting edge R&D has to be achieved so as to maintain productivity and innovation at par with the world standards. Our technical manpower will have to be conversant with frontier areas of knowledge which will dominate and determine the course of the present century. Technical education and research in the country needs urgent reorientation. There is an urgent need for a new initiative in proper regulation of technical education in terms of modernization, quality, manpower planning and training, relevance and above all, a robust industry-academia interaction to stem this rot of technical education. A strong industry-institute partnership programmes in the country is essential.

A holistic model of Technical Education is given in Figure 6. The chart gives input-output parameters and linkages between society and industry. The model shows that input/output model without linkages with industry and society will not be growth oriented and sustainable.

Engineering Education

There was a lack of interaction between industry and academics since Independence. They stayed in their respective cocoons. It has been aptly depicted by the statement that 'Indian science and technologies is busy finding answers to questions which industry is not asking, while industry is thriving without innovation and imported technology'. The main reason for this dichotomy was that academic institutes never felt the need to communicate with the industry, so as to find their needs and problems. They rather waited for the initiative to come from the industry. They concentrated on publishing their work in academic journals on the topics either not relevant to industry or just reinventing the wheel. Even in the

Figure 6

Technical Education Model (6)

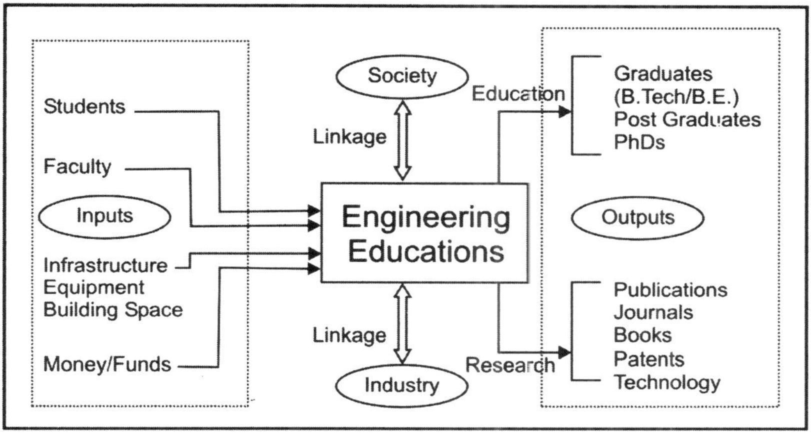

sphere of academics, performance of the faculty is also dismal. India claims that it has one of the largest pools of scientific and technical manpower in the world. However, the impact factor of its publications is dismal at international level. There are only couple of institutes of higher education which figure in the list of top 500 institutions in the world.

Table 3 shows that the productive output of the premium Indian institutes is much lower as compared to institutes in the US and China. Tasinghua University has higher bachelor student to faculty ratio than IIT Bombay, but produces more than 10 times the research papers produced by IIT Bombay. Even the combined output of research papers of all IITs, with 2,400 faculty members, is only 60 per cent of the papers published by one Chinese university (Tasinghua University), having half the number of faculty members and the same student to faculty ratio. This shows that Indian technical education has failed to make any mark in generating knowledge or technologies. The performance of higher learning institutions in the area of patents is more dismal. Ratio of patents produced to scientific and technical manpower is pathetic. In contrast to India, China has developed its technical education sector at a much rapid pace. China has produced more than 5,000 PhD holders per year compared to 1,000 in India. Instead of constituting committees, we should learn from the experience of China in area of scalability of technical education. India has opened large number of new IITs and NITs. It needs to be seen as to how they are able to recruit faculty at par with the existing IITs and NITs. Otherwise, all the resources spent in creating this huge new infrastructure may go waste.

Table 3

Comparison of Indian Engineering Institutions with Select International Universities 2006

Institute/University	*Student Output*				*Faculty*	*B/F*	*S/F ratio*	*PhD/ Bachelors*	*Research Fund (million)*	*Papers*	*Research Fund in ₹ (PPP)*	
	Bachelors	*Masters*	*PhD*	*TED*							*Million*	*Lakhs/ faculty*
Massachusetts Institute of Technology, USA	578	745	135	1,458	372	1.6	8	0.23	US $234.5	3,129	1,876	50.4
Univ. of Illinois, Urbana-Champaign, USA	1,237	554	156	1,947	441	2.8	15	0.13	US S200.1	2,251	1,600.8	36.3
Purdue University, USA	1,238	461	144	1,843	309	4.0	19	0.12	US $112.3	2,648	898.4	29.1
Georgia Institute of Technology, USA	1,391	751	162	2,304	419	3.3	20	0.12	US $203.7	2,811	1,629.6	38.9
California Institute of Technology, USA	247	120	277	644	398	0.6	6	1.12	US $80.4	2,885	643.2	16.2
Imperial College, UK	695	600	160	1,455	291	2.4	15	0.23	UK £63.4	2,674	768.408	26.4
Tsinghua University, China	2,100	1,400	500	4,000	1,200	1.8	12	0.24	NA	6,590	NA	NA
Tokyo Institute of Technology, Japan	980	1,633	382	2,995	906	1.1	10	0.39	NA	3,993	NA	NA
Nanyang Technological University, Singapore	2,635	1,400	500	4,535	1,020	2.6	27	0.19	NA	2,564	NA	NA

Cont'd...

...Cont'd

National University of Singapore	1,402	570	119	2,091	288	4.9	20	0.08	S$82.5	1933	532.1	1.8
Pohang University of Science and Technology, Korea	306	329	134	769	305	1.3	11	0.44	NA	1259	NA	NA
Korea Advanced Institute of Science and Technology	755	731	390	1,876	418	1.8	18	0.52	NA	939	NA	NA
IISc, Bangalore	0	337	165	502	432	0.0	3		₹ 1,024	1,274	1,024	23.7
IIT, Bombay	422	581	56	1,059	401	1.1	12	0.13	₹ 520	568	520	13.0
IIT Total	2,316	3,449	262	60,627	2,400	1.0	12	0.11	NA	3,942	NA	NA
NIT Total	7,000	1,550	120	8,670	2,215	3.2	15	0.02	NA	678	NA	NA
Manipal (MIT, India)	751	81		832	280	2.7	13		NA	33	NA	NA

B/F: bachelor output per faculty, S/F: student faculty ratio.

In order to improve quality of faculty in the technical institutes, AICTE had initiated quality improvement programmes (QIP) with less than 200 seats for M.Tech. and PhD each. Teachers from private institutes can enrol at prestigious technical institutes under this programme. With more than 50,000 engineering faculty without doctoral degrees, this initiative is like a needle in the hay stock. A large number of participants join this programme simply to get a certificate for their promotions. In the absence of any post course evaluation, the continued improvement and motivational aspects are lacking. There is an urgent need to strengthen this programme in terms of numbers, quality and industrial orientation.

Industrial Environment

Since Independence, industry was sheltered from external competition by quota raj, till the opening of economy in early nineties. They thrived in an insulated economy and never felt the need for modernization and innovation. Consumers were at the mercy of the manufacturers, who had monopoly in their respective domain and had no alternative option and had to be satisfied with whatever was available in the market. Consumers even had to wait for the delivery of the product at the convenience of the manufacturers. Industry never showed confidence or inclination in the indigenous technology developed by technical institutions and preferred to import technology from abroad. With the strengthening of IPR system, globalization of economy and demise of quota raj, Indian industry also needs to reorient its inward thinking process. This is the only way to withstand the onslaught of MNCs and the international competition due to globalization and WTO norms. Industry-institute partnership will be an elixir to survive in this competitive world, as a result of discerning and well-informed purchaser, in the era of internet marketing. Industry must be vigilant about imported technology trap, as no technology is universal and shelf life is also short. To overcome the short obsolescence period of technology in the fast changing international industrial climate, there is a need for simultaneous/continuous engineering. This requires teams working as one unit and having persons with innovative ideas and knowledge of production system, design and marketing. Industry also lacks engineering, information sourcing, standard procedures and documents and quality control. Institutions can contribute substantially in these areas.

Industry-Institute Partnership

We need to look at strengths and weaknesses of industry and institutes for a successful partnership programme and to create synergy between them. Some of the important characteristics of these are presented in Table 4.

Table 4

Characteristics of Industry and Institutes

Industries	*Academic Institutes*
Specific experience	Theoretical and general knowledge
Organized teams	Individuals or number of small groups
Tight time schedule	Open ended time schedule
Products and services	Ideas, innovation and reports
Focused routine work	Dynamism and exuberance
Prone to status quo	Ability to take risk
Commercial and market aspect	Science and technology aspects

There are a number of flaws in the management system of educational institutes. These include:

(i) Hierarchical management system which slows down decision making process

(ii) Individualistic traits of the employees, which is difficult to control

(iii) Little knowledge of business environment.

On the other hand, industry's prejudice and apathy towards institutes is making them less competitive in the global market due to lack of certain critical inputs, which can be provided only by the institutes. Some of these include:

(i) Out of the box thinking of young students in the institutes, who are not constrained by the stereotype thinking, contrary to myopic thinking of the in-house personnel's in the industry.

(ii) It is easier to absorb jointly developed technologies than imported technologies.

Flow chart for linkages between industry and institutes to develop a technology is given below.

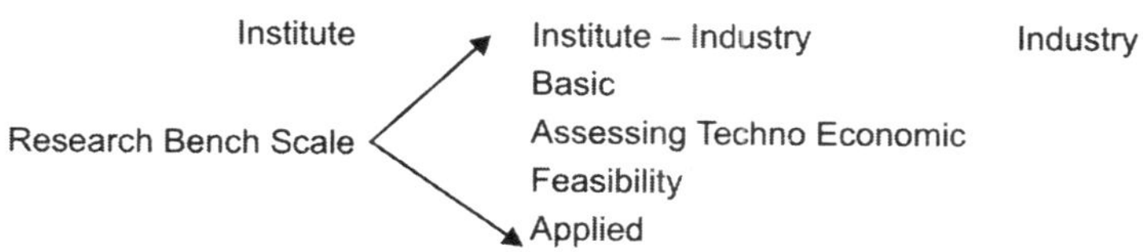

Ways to Promote Linkages Between Institutes and Industry

Institutions need to focus on the following areas:

- Curriculum adaptation with changes in industrial environment;
- A cohesive relationship between industry and career advisors;
- Skill development efforts in the shortage areas to create employment opportunities;

- Developing joint Academic–Industry Degree Models;
- Development of research-based teaching material;
- Setting up broad-based and dynamic Alumni network;
- Capacity building of the faculty, students and the industries through mutually enabling processes; and
- Creating endowed Chairs through industries in specific areas of management.

Modes of Robust Interaction Between Industry and Institutes

Following activities are important for sustained interaction between industry and institutions:

- Round tables with industry to identify areas of cooperation and generation of consultancy projects
- Consultancy: institutional, retainer and research-based
- Industrialists' lectures to students
- Preparation of state-of-the-art reports on technology for industries
- Joint student projects on the topics relevant to industry
- Training and registration of staff from industry for higher degrees
- Organizing technology appreciation programmes, technology requirement programmes, library and information services and short-term courses for lifelong learning.
- Adjunct faculty from industry to institute
- Participation in technology development missions
- Simulation and modelling
- Quality control and system design
- Joint development and operation of sophisticated facilities to leverage investment
- Focus and accountability in research work and resource utilization.
- Involvement of industry in framing syllabi for technical courses. At present the focus of the curriculum/education system is on analysis and mathematical formulations. Students often do not get the hands-on experience of engineering components/systems.
- Confidentiality of industrial data

Operational Mechanism of Industry-Institute Co-operation

A number of studies have been carried out all over the world on the essential linkage mechanism between institute and industry to facilitate above mentioned joint issues. Two universally recognized mechanisms are:

(a) Industry Liaison Cells/Industry-Institute Partnership Programme (IIPP)

(b) Technical Business Incubators/Science and Technology Entrepreneur Park

Setting up Industrial Liaison Cell/IIPP in the Institutes/Technology Transfer Offices

It is a single window facilitation point. The main function of this facilitation point is to organize contacts between institute and industry for research contracts, consulting agreements, affiliate programme and research consortium. This cell will also organize contact meetings, look for potential technologies useful to industry, bring contracts for academics, look for potential patent, organize human resource development programmes and organize technology transfer programmes. Stanford and MIT have opened such Technology Transfer Offices.

Setting up of Science and Technology Entrepreneur Parks (STEP)/Business Incubation Centres

This is an infrastructural facility which provides shared services in terms of office space, management, consultation, marketing and technology transfer for high-tech start-ups. In addition, it provides access to the technical facilities and human resource capital of the institute in terms of infrastructure and technical advice on attractive commercial terms. The main aim of the business incubator is to create value added jobs and services, creating technology-based new enterprises, transfer of technology, and commercialization of R&D outputs, inculcating entrepreneurial and innovative spirit and providing low cost specialized services to small and medium industry. This is a new concept of economic development facility for creation of employment, commercialization of new innovative concepts, development of local economy and improvement of the economic health of the institute.

Three kinds of incubators can be established:

- Government sponsored,
- Business-based incubators, and
- Public-private partnership (PPP) incubators.

PPP model is becoming more popular as no free services are provided and return on investment is favourable.

These incubators/STEPs are not only technology innovation hubs, but can also help in strengthening university-industry linkage by nurturing high tech start-ups and harnessing the innovative potential of young researchers. These centres will also enthuse the faculty and the students to improve their skill set and making them more relevant to the needs of society for creating wealth and job avenues.

National Science and Technology Entrepreneurship Development Board (NSTEDB) of DST India is supporting STEP through grants and support from All India Financial Institutions (Industrial Development Bank of India (IDBI), Industrial Finance Corporation of India (IFCI), Industrial Credit and Investment Corporation of India (ICICI). 15 STEPs so far have been established in different parts of the country. Each STEP has been established as an autonomous registered society having an independent legal status, which is external to the administrative structure of the host institution. However, progress is slow due to inherent systemic bottlenecks.

Incubators of various types are operational in the world. National Business Incubation Association (NBIA) estimates that there are about 7,000 incubators worldwide; 1,000 are in Asia (548 in China), 1,400 in North America, with 1,115 in the United States, 900 in Europe and close to 400 in Latin America. Silicon Valley and Oxford model have demonstrated the role of incubators to innovation system of the respective countries and produced present day technology leaders such as Microsoft, Apple, Google, face book and many others.

Department of Science and Technology, Government of India, has initiated promotion of Technology Business Incubation. During the Eleventh plan there are provisions to establish 25 Business Incubators per year at a cost of nearly 16 crore per year. Total number of incubators to be established during the Eleventh plan is 100 at an out lay of 66.50 crores. Nineteen Technology Business Incubators have been established in the country. Against this, Torch Center incubator of China's Ministry of Science and Technology has an area of 19,699 thousand square metres, with 40,639 enterprises and a total income of 213.32 billion Yuan. According to the Eleventh Five Year Plan of China, Technology Business Incubators(8), by the end of 2010, the number of incubators in China will increase from 500 to 1,000. Total area will reach to 25,000 thousand square metres. It will harbour more than 50,000 companies and create over one million job opportunities.

There is an urgent need to recalibrate Indian Technical Incubation Programme and take lessons from Chinese programme, so as to make Indian TBI programme more potent.

Conclusion

The technical education is at cross roads and there is an urgent need to restructure it, so as to make it responsive to the needs of the society and the industry. Otherwise, it will be a major handicap for the growth of the country and our ability to face the global challenges. Inefficient and non-responsive technical education system will create an army of unemployable youth, who may pose a challenge to the basic fabric and economic well-being of the country. It will also shatter the dream of India becoming a super power of tomorrow. There is, therefore, an urgent need to make technical education responsive to the needs of the industry by promoting greater interaction between institutes and industry through various mechanisms such as industry liaison cells and technical business incubators. This will help faculty and students to improve their professional skills and usher a spirit of innovation and entrepreneurship. It will make industry more competitive to face the challenges of globalization. In the process, it will create wealth for the country and the academic institutions and create jobs for the fast growing young population of the country.

References

Aggarwal, S.P. 2002. 'World Scenario on Technology Business Incubators'. Proceedings of Workshop on Technology Business Incubators, Noida, India, August.

Banerjee, R. and V.P. Mulay. 2008. *Engineering Education in India*. Report on Review Sponsored by Observer Research Foundation, December 16.

FICCI. 2006. 'Industry – Academia Convergence: Bridging the Skill Gap'. Federation House, New Delhi, November 23.

Jain, Ravi. 1995. Proceedings of the Regional Seminar on Planning and Management of Technical Education in India. Editor: S.K. Sharma, Panjab University, Chandigarh, March 22–23.

Liming, Wang. 2007. 'Business Incubators Help SMEs Entering in Industrial Chain'. Shandong Province Natural Science Project No. Y2007H21.

Menon, P.K.B. 2001. 'Technology Business Incubation Systems in India'. Paper Presented at the First International Workshop on Technology Business Incubators in India, Bangalore, January 29–31.

Rao, U.R. 2005. *Revitalising Technical Education*. Report of the Review Committee on AICTE.

Soni, V.K., V.K. Khare and V.P. Wani. 2009. 'Analysis of Total Factor Productivity: Change and its Sources – Indian MSEs'. *Industrial Engineering Journal*, Vol. 2, No. 6. pp. 21–25.

15

Academy-Industry Interaction

A Case Study of Engineering Colleges in and around Chandigarh

NAMITA GUPTA AND RAJIV GUPTA

Need and Significance

Knowledge has been recognized as the key driving force in the 21st century. India's ability to emerge as a globally competitive player will substantially depend on its knowledge resources. This calls for a systemic transformation that seeks to address the concerns of the entire knowledge spectrum. Such a massive endeavour involves creating a roadmap for reform of the knowledge sector that focuses on enhancing access to knowledge, fundamentally improving education systems and their delivery, re-shaping the research, development and innovation structures, and harnessing knowledge applications for generating better services. Such a knowledge revolution that seeks to build capacity and generate quality will enable our country to empower its human capital, including the 550 million below the age of 25. Our unique demographic dividend offers a tremendous opportunity as well as a daunting challenge which requires creative strategies for a new knowledge-oriented paradigm.[1]

Globalization has posed the challenge of quality improvement in higher education. At present, the graduates from institutions of higher education are not only having opening for their careers within the geographical boundaries of their own country or state, but also at global level; thereby, putting a lot of responsibility on institutions. Globally competitive students have to acquire skills to be effective to perform in different settings, to manage changes and transitions, to manage work force diversity, to be able to learn and transform knowledge and to form adventures and alliances. The institutions of higher education have to evolve mechanisms to incorporate the above traits in their curricula in order to prepare students to meet the global demands.

In the modern competitive corporate world, when the business houses are expanding their wings over the Global Nest, there arises the need to produce a quality talent pool which possesses the skill set and the calibre to match the requirements of the employers. A student graduating with a professional qualification has many expectations in terms of a good job, learning atmosphere, work environment and, above all, the remuneration. The dream with which he takes up a specific qualification cannot be fulfilled unless and until the student is equipped with the desired skill set which is required in the relevant field. This creates a gap between the academia and the industry. The endeavour, thus, remains to make the student employable in addition to evolving his skill set. Thus, the institutes have to adopt and incorporate new mechanisms to make the teaching programmes more relevant, tailor the programmes to meet the global needs, upgrade the programmes and courses as per the changes in techniques and technologies, and promote programme diversity so as to make them suitable for inter-disciplinary and multidisciplinary units. For this, there is a need to develop strategic partnership between educational institutions and industry, institution and R&D labs and among institutions to develop cooperative research and teaching programmes in close collaboration with industry.

Every enterprise needs to have a system to check whether the raw-materials it uses, the product it makes, or the service it provides reach minimum pre-defined, threshold standards. The raw materials of a higher education institution are its students, teachers, researchers and its curriculum. The products of an educational institution are its graduates and the competencies they have acquired (examination results and employment destinations) or the new knowledge generated by research.

The educational institute produce the human resource, i.e. man, the most vital of all the M's of Business, i.e. Man, Money, Machine and Material. In order to produce quality man power for industry, the need of the hour is to promote ever greater academy-industry interaction.

The UNESCO Task Force report on Technical and Vocational Education also recommended encouraging institutions to conduct contract research and undertake joint projects with enterprises, business, social organizations and other branches of private sector. The report also laid emphasis on making higher education practical and relevant to societal and market needs by linking university with industry and society.[2]

The liberalization of trade and technological progress has increased the speed of change in the world of work. In developed and developing countries non-competitive industries cannot rely anymore on being safeguarded by the protective measures of domestic governments. The resurgent India sees wealth creation as a great equalizer amongst all sections of the society. In such a scenario, a knowledge worker who can work at the cutting edge of technology, add value to the bottom-line, and provide competitive advantage to industry, has become a hot commodity to acquire. India is one of the youngest nations today that holds the maximum number of employable youth with average age of around 23 years. For the coming three to four decades, the situation will continue to remain the same.

The growth of technical education before Independence in the country has been very slow. The number of engineering colleges in 1947 was 44 with an intake capacity of 3,200 students. Due to efforts and initiatives taken during successive Five Year Plans and particularly due to policy changes in the eighties to allow participation of private and voluntary organizations in the setting up of technical institutions on self-financing basis, the growth of technical education has been phenomenal (Table 1).

Table 1

Growth of AICTE Approved Engineering Institutes in India

Year	*Number of Engineering Institutes*
2006–07	1,511
2007–08	1,668
2008–09	2,388
2009–10	2,972
2010–11	3,222
2011–12	3,393

Source: AICTE, *Approval Process Handbook*, 2012–13 p. 18.

The number of engineering institutions has more than doubled in the past five years. Though the quality of education is not the best as compared to international standards. Employment in high growth sectors such as telecommunication, IT, health care and pharmaceuticals, etc. is forecasted to increase almost three-fold (from 15.2 Mn to 40 Mn) in the next 10 years in India. Therefore, there is a need to meet the requirements of the future job market, for which improvement in technology and innovation need much attention.[3]

The National Knowledge Commission (NKC), constituted in June 2005 to prepare a blueprint for reform of our knowledge related institutions and infrastructure, has also emphasized on the significance of academia-industria interaction: 'Industry and trade involvement should be enhanced not only at the internship stage, but also at the time of examinations and placements. Curricula should be constantly monitored and updated'.[4] Similarly, Yashpal Committee Report has also noted that there is a lack of adequate linkages between universities and research laboratories on the one hand and universities and businesses on the other.[5]

It is in this context that the Planning Commission constituted a Committee on 'Corporate Sector Participation in Higher Education', in January 2012. The Committee's mandate was to examine and provide recommendations on the potential and modalities for corporate sector participation in higher education and models for industry-institution interaction to act as catalysts of innovation and sustainable and inclusive economic and regional development. The committee stated: 'The corporate sector is a key stakeholder in higher education. It can play a pivotal role in improving India's current higher education system as well as in meeting future aspirations. Corporations can collaborate with the academia in several ways, with varying funding commitment, ranging from direct ownership and management of institutions to collaborating with the higher education institutions in research, faculty development, infrastructure creation, student scholarships, and governance.'

Objectives

The present paper attempts to explore how engineering colleges and universities can work closely with industry, study the dimensions of academia-industry partnership, and identify possible areas where industry's contribution to academia would be most effective. The primary research has been taken up with the objective to identify the areas where academic institutions include industry participation and to assess the perceived benefit accrued from this partnership in specific areas.

Methodology

Primary data has been collected from the administrators and faculty of four Engineering Colleges and Universities in and around Chandigarh. Two of them were government-funded and the other private institutes. The administrators of these colleges and universities were sent across a structured questionnaire as also personally interviewed. They were asked to rate the extent of their university/institute with industry on 8 listed areas on a scale of 1 to 5. (1 being the lowest level of collaboration or the benefit accrued and 5 being the highest degree of collaboration or benefit accrued). The mean of the responses was taken to get degree of collaboration and the perceived benefit in specific areas.

II

Modes of Interaction

The engagement models for the corporate sector can be several – from being a passive provider of capital to the most active in terms of directly owning and running an institution. Various modes of interaction between academia and industries can be discussed as below:

(1) Interchange of Resource Persons

It is one of the most important modes of industry-institute interface. It can be a two-way process. First is the guest lectures by executives to students. Second is the expert lectures by teachers in industry. Special expert sessions for students delivered by company officials give a deep insight into the core industrial concepts, latest developments and technologies in use. It also helps the students to explore their potentials through innovative methodologies.

(2) Practical Training/Students Internship

Partnership through training and internships of students is another common mode of interaction. Industry gets a first hand feel of students. Students benefit from an early introduction to the real world of work by becoming aware of what is going to be expected of them. Their prospects on the labour market rise as a result of practical work experiences. The attachment of the students to industry provides live practice which supports the theory learned in the classroom and laboratory situations.

(3) The Inclusion of Executives in the Governing Councils and Board of Studies

The objective of having industry representation in the Governing Councils and Board of Studies in engineering institutes is to benefit from their work experience and perspective. This may also enhance the image and recall value of the institution, which not only attracts prospective students, donors and other stakeholders but also work in favour of these institutes during ratings and rankings. Besides this, the interaction between faculty and relevant company officials to draw up result oriented attachment programmes and monitor the implementation of the same ensures the maximum benefit to the students. This can be done through – involvement in Research Degree Committees (RDCs), Board of Studies (BOS), other committees for inspection, monitoring, participation in project evaluation, panel discussions, faculty selection and alumni affairs related activities in colleges/institutions, etc.

(4) Training Programmes for Working Executives

The engineering institutes may offer part time training programmes for the executives and personnel of industries. Such initiatives may attract industry's interest to collaborate by assisting them in development and training its human capital.

(5) Integrating the Industry's Views into Their Curriculum

The mismatch of curricula in technical and vocational education with the needs of the enterprises is a key issue world-wide. The relevance and appropriateness of the curricula for preparing students for the world of work needs to be reviewed on a regular basis. Hence, the engineering institutes needs to slowly integrate the industry's views into their curriculum. Many engineering institutes in India have been inviting suggestions from industry to update their curriculum and include the topics of present day relevance. This is done with a view to imparting the knowledge and skills set needed by graduating students in constantly changing global business environment. This can be done by conducting seminars and training sessions for the faculty, to give them an industry perspective to enable them to design industry-oriented topics. Industry inputs can be included for improving the quality of output of engineering institutes and making them competent of surviving in rapidly changing business environment.

(6) Consortium R&D Project

Consortium R&D project in mission mode are considered to be an effective mode of not only cross-branding but also strengthening the academic relationship between engineering institutes and the industry. The exchange of knowledge and know-how, and the joint undertaking of research and development projects also have potential for promoting productivity. It is one of the most important aspects of engineering institutes research. It not only adds to current knowledge pool but also enhances the learning experience of students. Formal relationship between industry and academia can definitely add to the research and knowledge generation. Industry may help the institutions generating knowledge by funding academic research. Confederation of Indian Industries (CII) has collaborated with many engineering institutes to support both academic and applied research initiatives. Though this is one of the best ways of collaboration, engineering institutes need to take more steps in this regard.

(7) Technology Transfer: Field Trail of a New Technology

Large-scale industry has the resources to invest in new technology development initiatives, but it often tends to rely on bought out technologies, generally from the overseas. Academic intervention may be required in minor technological innovation/modification. In the case of medium and small-scale industry, the needs are primarily oriented towards problem solving, with support required in the areas of design, process improvement and plant and machinery performance, etc. In small-scale industry, problem solving may simply amount to product testing and production enhancement in terms of quantity and quality. There can also be offer of special equipment/machinery to technical education institutions by the industries for an agreed period for training purposes. For instance, IBM has set up its research centre in collaboration with IIT Delhi and Roorkee under its IBM's Shared University Research (SBU) initiative. Here the company awards equipment to universities to promote research in areas of mutual interest, besides connecting the research and researchers at the university with personnel who are interested in the research from the IBM research, development and solutions provider communities.[6]

(8) Faculty Training by the Industry

The shift from conventional, primarily a theoretical educational process to a research and theory-based process will require not only constant innovation to incorporate new findings about learning but also faculty and staff professional development necessary to support this innovation. In order to improve the quality of faculty researchers, many prestigious institutions have started conducting faculty development programmes. The focus of such programmes is on enhancement of quality of teaching and training in India, knowledge in functional domains and educational skills. For example, there is the Indo-US Collaboration for Engineering Education (IUCEE), which has been set up to improve the quality of engineering education in India by bringing the best practices from US university education to India. Pan IIT, an organization of the alumni and faculty of Indian Institutes of Technology, has provided a strong foundation for building this collaboration between American Society for Engineering Education (ASEE), along with academic and business leaders from leading US and Indian universities.[7] Such initiatives can be replicated in other institutes/universities as well.

III

Perceived Benefits of Such Interaction: A Case Study

The case study consists of primary data collected from administrators and faculty of engineering colleges and universities in and around Chandigarh. The cases were identified where academic institutions include industry participation. The efforts initiated by these institutes are discussed below.

(a) PEC University of Technology

The PEC University of Technology encourages its faculty to undertake consultancy work through which the faculty contributes toward the industrial growth, strengthen institute-industry interface and enrich their professional experience. The Research Planning and Development acts as a liaison between the institute and industry/government bodies to undertake projects with specific problem, which are generally of short duration.

The institute has well-established norms and standards for in-house research projects. The objective of the in-house research proposals for internal funding is for creation/enhancement of facility, which is useful to research students (M.Tech and PhD) as well as to the needs of the industry. MoU has been signed with industrial giants such as: NJIT, USA, IBM, ALSTOM, Intel, PECOSA, ESIGELEC (France Collaboration), Philips.

Collaborative programmes and interaction among faculty, students and industry is encouraged. Sponsored projects, in-house projects, consultancy and collaborations with industry and academia are important modes through which institute contributes towards knowledge and technology. Financial assistance is provided to faculty and students to present the outcome of their research projects in national and international conferences in India and abroad. Besides this, short-term courses as well as training programmes for industry, institutes and organizations are conducted. Office of Dean Research, Planning and Development provides administrative and managerial support for the operation of sponsored research, in-house projects, consultancy and other RPD activities of the institute. It promotes and manages institute-industry interaction and provides help in establishing collaborative programmes of interest to Institute and Industry.

The faculty of the institute undertakes research in the field of science and technology through sponsored projects. At present faculty along with research scholars and research fellows are engaged in sponsored project of 2 to 5 years duration funded by government agencies. Some of them are Department of Science and Technology, Department of Information Technology, Indo-French Centre for the Promotion of Advanced Research, CSIR, AICTE, SASE and Chandigarh Administration.

(b) Panjab University

In Panjab University, Chandigarh, there are two engineering institutes – University Institute of Engineering and Technology and University Institute of Chemical Engineering and Technology.

University Institute of Chemical Engineering and Technology (UICET)

Internships and training in industry is compulsory for the students in their VII and VIII semester. The internship is of around 6 weeks and most of the time it is done during summer vacation so that it does not disrupt their classroom studies. Though there is no periodic arrangement for the visit of executives from industry to the institute, frequent seminars and conferences ensures the academia-industria interaction as executive from industry participates in these conferences. Besides this, there are certain industrial groups such as Petro-LNG which visit to the institute. The faculty also goes to the industry on an invitation to attend some training programmes and on sabbaticals which is generally once or twice in an year. As far as participation of industries in Board of Studies or Governing Council of the institute is concerned, there is no systematic arrangement for the same. However, industries are informally consulted while the revision of the curriculum is done. The executive from industry are welcomed for the higher studies in the institute, i.e. PhD; however, no short-term courses have been introduced to make this interaction more effective. Several faculty members of the institute have been actively involved in rendering consultancy to industrial organizations in the region. The consultancy activities include preparation of feasibility reports, development of pollution control technologies, energy auditing of industrial units, development of alternative and more economical technologies for industrial units, development of new products/processes of laboratory scale and recovery of chemicals from agro-based effluents. The institute has well-equipped research laboratories in some front-line areas and a number of sponsored research projects have been successfully completed. Some of the research projects amounts from ₹ 10 lakh to ₹ 74.5 lakh and are for the time of three to five years. The strong alumni of the institute occupying higher positions in the industry have also facilitated better academia-industria interaction.

University Institute of Engineering and Technology (UIET)

UIET has a well-established mechanism of training and internship of the students. The internship is compulsory for the students of II and III year during summer vacations. The VIII semester students are given option to take internships with those industries who have already selected them at the time of placement. This gives opportunity to the students to be able to understand the industry well before joining it after the completion of the course and also to the industry as they get more time to orient the student with the industry much before that student formally enters into the place of work. For better interaction between industria-academia, the provisions have been made for sabbatical leave to the faculty for 6 weeks so that they can go to industry and help industry in certain projects. MoU has been signed with Infosys, IBM and others. Besides this, there are certain short-term training programmes, including soft skill training programmes conducted by the industry for academia to make them aware about the requirement of the industry. This faculty then further trains the students for their future assignments in the industry. This training also facilitates the faculty to make changes in the curriculum according to the requirements of the industry. Though there were no short-term courses for the executive in the institute; the higher studies in the form of PhD was allowed to the executive from the industry. Various R&D projects have been sponsored by the industry in the institute. The collective R&D has been done through MoU signed with different industries. Besides this, consultancy services are also provided to various agencies such as training of the technical staff of Dr Reddy's Lab. Similarly, students of Electronics are working on the Automatic Parking of Sector-17 with Chandigarh Administration. To further enhance the industry-institute partnership, a Fun Conclave has been organized by the institute where industry executives can directly contact the students.

Centre for Industry-Institute Partnership Programme (CIIPP)

With a view to bridge the gap between theory and practice and to sensitize the university towards needs of the industry, CIIPP was set up in 1996 as a separate entity as a self sustaining centre on strategic business unit concept. It creates awareness about the industry-institute programme and devises strategies for the promotion of synergistic interface with industry and to develop methodology for creation of endowment funds and promotion of consultancy/technology transfer to cater to specific needs of the industry. Besides this, it recommends need-based courses to industry and prepares learning materials relevant to industries. CIIPP has rendered valuable services to various public and private sector institutions/departments. The CIIPP clientele includes: Ministry of HRD (Government of India), Department of Finance (Punjab), IISc (Bangalore), Dr Reddy's Lab. (Hyderabad), Gujarat Ambuja Cement Ltd., etc. CIIPP has also created Intellectual Property Right Cell (IPR Cell) in collaboration with Patent Information Centre and Punjab State Council for Science and Technology, Chandigarh. IPR Cell provides information orientation and facilities to scientist and researchers of Panjab University and its affiliated institutions for protecting the products of their intellectual powers. The cell also guides and advices researchers on how to obtain and sustain patents, facilitates routing of patent searches to Patent Information Centre and getting the necessary clearances from the competent authorities in the university while filing patent specifications. The Centre has generated revenue of ₹ 40.42 lakh during the financial year 2009–10.

(c) Rayat and Bahra Institute of Engineering

Rayat Bahra Institute of Engineering has initiated a comprehensive training programme which aims at producing quality human resource. The institute has collaborated with top IT giants in the market to evolve students as pool of trained manpower ready to deploy in the market as per the industry needs. Keeping this picture in mind the industry giants have 'adopted' the engineering students right from the entry level and are trained over 4 years along with their academic sessions.

Besides inviting Top MNCs and Corporate houses for Campus Placements, the Department of Career Development and Placements (DOCDP) of the institute closely works with the leading business and industry organizations. Special expert sessions for students delivered by company officials give a deep insight into the core industrial concepts, latest developments and technologies in use. In addition to this, direct practical experience on the work is provided with the help of industrial visits.

Modular in-house training workshops are conducted on regular basis to improve soft skills of students studying in all the disciplines such as business etiquettes, learning language functions, foundation course (for new entrants), Induction courses, written aptitude (numerical and verbal ability), personal interviews, group discussions, CV writing, general awareness (including business awareness), etc. Rayat has a Skill Development Institution (Centre of Excellence), which in association with top industry partners along with government support provides knowledge and develops skills in students to meet industry requirements and secure jobs. Centre of excellence endeavours to bridge the gap between the outcome of general qualifications and specific requirement of the industry.

Infosys Campus Connect is another joint initiative of Rayat and Bahra Institute and Infosys, where the college curriculum is aligned with the industry's requirements. Under this initiative, seminars and training sessions are organized for the faculty to give them an industry perspective, enabling them to train the students accordingly; industry-oriented topics are designed, courses to students are provided along with the to-do projects and the sabbaticals for the faculty. Some of the 'trademark' programmes launched under this in the campus are Foundation Programme, Faculty Enablement Programme, Soft Skills Programme and Student Industrial Visit.

An automotive cluster has been set up under Centre of Excellence to establish and facilitate the 'Industry-Institute Interface'. Institute under Automotive cluster in Centre of Excellence has signed MOUs with the leading Auto Giants of India such as: Maruti-Suzuki India Limited, Volvo-Eicher Commercial Vehicles Limited, Volkswagen Group Sales India Ltd., Royal Enfield India Ltd., etc. MoU ensures knowledge transfer, technology sharing, training and course development services, academic guidance, career and placement and skill and employability development.

(d) Chandigarh Group of Colleges (CGC)

Chandigarh Group of Colleges has established a Microsoft I-Spark Centre. The main objective of this centre is to bring industry-institution to a common forum, thereby mutually benefiting each other through exchange of technology and other resources. This innovation centre helps in building and accelerating skills of the student community as the students work on different projects having practical applications enriching them technically. It also helps students in nurturing and harbouring their innovations and thus, implementing their ideas into products and fostering entrepreneurship resulting in financial gains also.

CGC has started a project named 'Earn while you Learn'. Under this project, the students of various streams not only financially support their studies but also gain hand-on experience which would stand by them in their later career. This helps the students to gain a firsthand experience of the corporate world and, thereby, develop their self confidence and personality. Accordingly, the students are encouraged to take up part-time jobs after completing their regular classes or during holidays which would enhance their career rating at the time of final placements. As a result of these encouraging efforts, TATA has already selected 52 students of Chandigarh Group of Colleges offering handsome packages for doing part-time jobs.

Institute Industry Partnership Cell (IIPC) and Corporate Resource Centre (CRC) of the institute work in tandem with the corporate leaders to develop a deep bond between CGC and the industry. Besides this, the Entrepreneur Development Cell (EDC) has been established with a view to provide fillip to the young and budding entrepreneurs. Regular programmes are conducted for the volunteer students to create awareness as well as to sharpen their skills which are absolutely essential for success in entrepreneurial ventures. Experts from academia and industry address the students to coach, guide and motivate them.

Management Development Projects (MDPs) are taken up frequently at CGC. These projects include training programmes conducted for the various companies, both at CGC as well as at their respective locations. These MDPs are tailor made to meet the specific requirements of the companies and delivered with the professional touch to ensure effectiveness. CGC has undertaken consultancy projects in the mould of Engineering and Information Technology. These projects have resulted in improved performance and production, efficient delivery and competitive pricing of the commodities/services by cutting down the wastages.

As part of its Corporate Social Responsibility, CGC has undertaken several initiatives towards the benefit of the society at large. Some of these efforts are: A Charitable School (Humara Bachpan) for unprivileged children; donation of computers for blind schools of nearby areas; free education to meritorious students from weaker sections of society; adoption of schools in interiors of Punjab for provision of quality and value-based education; beautification of allotted areas in Chandigarh; blood donation to needy emergency cases to save precious lives in PGIMER, etc.

Analysis

It was found that the highest perceived benefit accrued from training and internship of students (4.8). All these institutes had a Comprehensive Training Programme which aims at preparing every student to be the best human resource available. Interchange of resource persons from industry and institute is the second highest mode of interaction (4.2). Administrators regard these as great value addition to student learning. Special expert sessions for students delivered by company officials are conducted, which give a deep insight into the core industrial concepts, latest developments and technologies in use. Similar is the thought for Consortium R&D, with perceived benefit score being 4.0, indicating the effectiveness of this tool to build industry partnerships. However, both academia and industry leave something to be desired to make this kind of alliance work fully towards their mutual benefit.

Table 2

Extent of Perceived Benefit from the Partnership

S.No.	*Areas of collaboration*	*Average score*
1.	Practical training/students internship	4.8
2.	Interchange of resource persons from industry and institute	4.2
3.	The inclusion of executives in the Governing Councils and Board of Studies	3.5
4.	Depute persons for higher degrees to institutes	2.8
5.	Integrating the industry's views into their curriculum	3.8
6.	Consortium R&D project	4.0
7.	Technology transfer, field trail of a new technology	3.4
8.	Faculty training by the industry	3.0

Certain collaboration modes, scored quite fairly as far as their extent of collaboration was concerned. These are such as inclusion of industry in Councils and Boards of studies (3.5), integrating the industry's views into their curriculum (3.8) and technology transfer, field trail of a new technology (3.4). However, administrators have varying views about this kind of association. The remarks by respondents make it evident that this mode is effective when the executives actively contribute into institution's operations and development rather than playing a passive role of attending scheduled meetings and chairing important events.

Faculty training (3.0) and deputing persons for higher degrees to institutes (2.8) are considered among the least preferred modes. The engineering institutes and industries have their own policy and rules for training and deputation of faculty members. Outsourcing the entire course has been perceived quite low on its effectiveness. Academicians feel that this particular mode is not able to impart the conceptual underpinnings of the issue, as practitioners tend to deal with the issue at only the practical level from their own perspectives; thus, reducing the possibility of its general application across situation.

IV

Problem Areas

The interaction with the faculty and students, however, revealed certain problems as far as academia-industria interaction is concerned. Some of these problems have been discussed below.

(1) Lack of an efficient mechanism in planning for and managing the institutional and industrial linkage to foster effective training: The number of training places offered by industry is insufficient. Often students are exploited as cheap labour for work which does not offer them any kind of skill improvement. In other cases, the remuneration does not even cover the transport costs. When students receive this kind of treatment, their motivation drops. The existing linkages between training institutions and industries are weak and they largely occur through students' industrial training. This is partly due to: inadequate industrial training places for all students; weak interaction between industrial training officers in technical institutes and their counterparts in industries; absence of vetted industrial training programmes; absence of supervised industrial training programmes; absence of clearly articulated joint projects between universities and industries; negative attitude to industrial training by industries as they still hold on to a short-term commercial focus. Due to shortage of the industrial base, there are normally not enough places to absorb all the students during industrial training. The reason for this is number of students (all technical institutions and universities) is always larger compared to the available opportunities. Industries are also not willing to take on students when they are laying off workers, due to low economic activity. This leads to under-training and in some cases mismatch with the students' discipline.

(2) Low level of participation by industry in curriculum development: While companies complain about poor quality of students, their participation in curriculum development is low. Equally, educational institutions are reluctant to revise their curricula as per the requirements of the industry. They tend to stick to traditional teaching material and methods. Not many institutions have been able to work on the right method of including the industry's viewpoints into curriculum and structuring the courses for student and corporate benefit. The rigidities of central curriculum development, coupled with lack of adequate resources, further restrict institutions from attempting more innovative and flexible approaches to vocational instruction. The need is for setting up of mixed curricula review commissions and also for more initiatives to be taken by both parties.

(3) Gap between industry's needs and the academic community's aspirations: This gap appears to be considerably large. There exists a strong feeling, at least in the academic circles, that unless technology driven initiatives find a surer place in the industrial sector in this country, the academia-industry interaction is likely to remain confined to developmental activities with limited exploratory or research-based content.

(4) Lack of appreciation of the longer term benefit of industry academy interface: Enterprises generally view the issue of co-operation as a distraction – especially in light of an 'Employer's market' situation. Those

enterprises that do co-operate, do so half heartedly. Many others exploit the arrangement as a means of 'cheap' labour. There is inadequate follow-up by government agencies to encourage co-operation. There is a lack of well conceived and co-ordinated policy governing co-operation between universities and industry. Different institutions engaged in co-operative schemes use their own guidelines and initiatives.

(5) Reluctance in industry to invest in technology and R&D: In its interaction with the academia, industry's expected time frames are immediate, and investment is directed towards efforts that promise result-oriented solutions. The costing frames are typically guided by a reluctance to invest in technology R&D which has either long-term or unclear outcomes. For academicians, the primary focus of interest is invariably a problem that throws up an intellectual challenge. Technology development initiatives which involve understanding/exploration of a concept/phenomenon and alternative methodologies, etc. related to process and design improvement could be of considerable interest. Academic environments value the autonomy of the individual researcher and there is a strong preference for working towards creation of knowledge in specialized domains. Typically, academic interest in the multidimensionality of a problem leads to a tendency to explore a variety of options to arrive at a solution. Such activity consumes both time and effort and the result may often be inimical to what the industry would regard as a wholesome solution.

The above issues clearly indicate that the potential gain from the co-operation of academia with the world of work is not fully utilized. The problems stated above are not new, but they are becoming more compelling. The following section recommends certain measures for better academia-industria interaction.

V

Recommendations

The need for a strong link between the producers of trained manpower (educational institutions) and the users of such manpower industries is getting stronger world over. Intensifying co-operation between the two by developing multiple modes of interaction, considered to be the best solution. Up-to-date and comprehensive databases are the backbone of an informed technical and vocational education system. This would have educational institutes to plan their programmes in a rational manner.

The industry should cooperate with educational institutions to enable them to turn out high quality graduates by contributing positively towards, curriculum design, improvement in the quality of instruction through interaction with teachers in academic institutions, enriching the instruction by the participation of experienced professionals, and rendering support services, e.g. maintenance/provision of equipment/machinery for training purposes. An in-depth study of successful models of university/industry partnership in developed economies may be revealing in this regard. An appropriate model should then be researched and tried out in India, on a pilot basis, before nationwide adaptation.[8]

The educational institutions also have to devise programmes for the demand driven needs for short-courses relevant to the local conditions. They should also devise appropriate marketing strategies to sell these courses to industry. It should be recognized that the most valuable asset for all industrialists, next to financial capital, is time. Hence the need for time efficient courses. Educational institutions should also establish linkages with the informal sector of the economy, especially with the small-scale or medium enterprises which have tremendous potential as the main employers. Furthermore, students should be assigned problem-solving projects in the informal sector. With technology driven entrepreneurship coming up in the country in a big way, the academia should plan its programmes accordingly. Small and medium sectors, which are also going to be a major force in the fast growing IT industry should be given special consideration.

Key constraints on quality such as inadequate finances, weak information linkages with employment, fragmentation of training systems and constraints at the level of individual organizations must be addressed. Not all modes of partnership are equally beneficial to every engineering institute. They have to work on 'differential modes'. Each engineering institute needs to identify the areas where they can build an effective academia-industry relationship. They need to revisit their mission and academic model to be able to relate to industry. Engineering institutes have to move beyond the phenomenon of 'working with employers' towards the concept of 'working with partners'. The collaboration between the two, academy and industry, is dynamic and complex.

Compulsions of a global market are bound to force industry in general to look afresh at their R&D efforts. This process must be guided by a complete paradigm shift from a simple capital intensive trading set-up to a technology driven entrepreneurial one. Industry could set up research consortia with a view to encouraging research-driven technology developments either in-house or in collaboration with the academia. Simultaneously, if the academia could tilt the focus of basic research towards application its interaction with industry would receive further impetus.

'Whether we have to cover one step or a thousand, the first step always remain the first, the second step cannot be taken until the first has been taken'.

—Mahatama Gandhi

Notes

1. National Knowledge Commission. *Compilation of Recommendations on Education*, 2007, p. 18. Also available at: www.knowledgecommission.gov.in.
2. UNESCO's International Project on Technical and Vocational Education 'UNEVOC'. A Seminar for Key Personnel from Africa and Asia, Berlin, Germany, 2–12 May 1995. Also available at: http://www.unevoc.unesco.org/fileadmin/user_upload/pubs/iug005e.pdf.
3. Confederation of Indian Industry. 'Global Partnership: Towards Expansion, Excellence and Inclusion', Global Summit on Higher Education, 16–17 February 2010, p. 7.
4. National Knowledge Commission, op. cit., p. 25.
5. *Yashpal Committee Report of the Committee to Advise on Renovation and Rejuvenation of Higher Education*. 2009.
6. Confederation of Indian Industry, op. cit., p. 23.
7. Ibid., p. 16.
8. UNESCO's International Project on Technical and Vocational Education 'UNEVOC', op. cit., p. 25.

References

All India Council for Technical Education. 1996. 'Planning and Management of Technical Education in India'. Chapter 7: Management Education: Today and Tomorrow.

Draft Report of Working Group on Higher Education. Eleventh Five Year Plan 2007–12. Planning Commission, Government of India.

http://planningcommission.nic.in – Chapter 1: Education.

http://www.rbiebt.rayatbahra.com.

http://www.cgc.edu.in.

http://www.pec.ac.in.

http://www.uiet.puchd.ac.in.

http://www.cipp.puchd.ac.in.

Report of NR Narayana Murthy Committee. 2012. Committee on Corporate Participation in Higher Education. Planning Commission, Government of India, New Delhi.

Part IV

Other Facets of Education

16

Right to Education

Problems and Perspectives

ASHA SETHI

After six decades of struggle, Right to Education (RTE) became an Act in August 2009, with a provision that every child of 6 to 14 years shall have a right to free and compulsory education in a neighbourhood school till completion of elementary education. Some of the salient features and the broad objectives of the Act are:

- Better education for children to be provided free of cost by the government.
- The private schools to admit 25 per cent of the children from neighbourhood at entry level.
- Accreditation and recognition of private schools on the basis of quality of education.
- Curriculum to be consistent with the national curriculum.
- Infrastructure in schools to be provided as per norms laid down by the government.
- Teachers to be properly qualified with necessary academic credentials.
- Social responsibility: making parent or guardian responsible for providing opportunities for education of their children.

Eleventh Plan Targets of Elementary Education

Along with the objectives of the RTE Act, it is pertinent to have an overview of the Eleventh Plan Targets of Elementary Education which are as follows:

- Universal enrolment of 6–14 year age group children, including the hard to reach segments of population.

- All gender, social and regional gaps to be eliminated by 2011–12.
- Significant improvement in learning conditions with emphasis on learning basic skills, verbal and quantitative.
- All Education Guarantee School (EGS) centres to be converted into regular primary schools.
- One year pre-school education for children entering primary schools.

In view of the enormous scope of the RTE Act 2009, its implementation in 2010, and the targets of Elementary Education in the Eleventh Plan with similar goals, the question arises: will free and compulsory elementary education ever become a reality or it will remain just a dream for most children of disadvantaged groups of our society. The question is important because every objective of the Act or target of the Eleventh Plan is a challenge in itself from the point of view of achieving the goals. Although all the state governments claim to have provided a primary school at a distance of 1 km from the residence, but plight of the government primary or even elementary schools is pathetic and similar in respect of inadequate infrastructure, strength of teachers along with their non-academic engagements, dwindling enrolments of children, absenteeism among the children as well as among the teachers, apathy of the state or local government and also the community towards primary education. Under the circumstances one wonders what purpose is being served in these schools in the name of educating the children in the most vulnerable age group of 6 to 11 or 14 years. Will these children be proficient in basic verbal and quantitative skills? How many of the government primary schools will have provision of pre-primary education for 3 to 6 years of children? Is it possible to provide quality education, free of cost to all in the primary schools in their present condition? To what extent gender, social and regional gaps will be eliminated after the implementation of the Act. In this context an attempt is made to pin point the key issues and challenges of implementation of the RTE in Part A and Part B presents alternative measures to make the RTE a reality.

Part A

Key Issues and Challenges of Implementation of RTE Act-2009

Of all the stated objectives of the RTE and the targets of Eleventh Plan, it is the objective of Equity and Access to Quality Education in terms of free, compulsory Universal Elementary Education (UEE) or Education For All (EFA) which is the most challenging task before the government. Equity and access in education means schooling for all social, economic, religious, gender and caste groups. At the same time, explosions in population, knowledge and aspirations place a heavy demand on quality of education. Another challenge is that of inclusive education which calls for making provisions for good elementary schools in the neighbourhood not only in urban areas but also in remote villages, in far flung pockets of tribal belts, in difficult inaccessible terrains of hilly areas, in urban slums and harijan bastis. Is any of the state government or even the central government in a position to reach out to all the segments of population in the country and to provide quality education for their children?

Equity and accessibility in private schools: Besides the universal enrolment in government schools, the mandate of the Act of 25 per cent intake of children from marginalized communities in private schools in their neighbourhood is a problematic preposition.

This is so due to the following reasons:

(i) Lack of clarity in the concept of neighbourhood school *per se*.

(ii) Lack of proper definition of marginalized groups entitled to seek admission in a particular privately managed school.

(iii) Woes of the parents (in session 2010–11) whose children were denied the right to admission in the private school in their own neighbourhood because they were from better off socio-economic background. In the process, many children lost one previous year of academic career. Right to education of one child in private school in the neighbourhood at the cost of another child flouts the norms of equity and accessibility of the RTE Act itself.

(iv) Problems of inclusive education and integration. Privately managed aided or unaided schools are worried about enrolment of special children. Even if there is one or two of them from any of the differently-abled category, the problem is how to make provision for infrastructure, classrooms, curricular transactions, and teachers trained in special education. To top it all, how to meet the cost incurred on these changes to be brought in the existing set-up of the school.

(v) Another challenge before them is regarding how to bring the achievement level of special children and/or children from weaker sections at par with children of elite background, or at par with their grade and age in commensurate with their abilities because of immense inequalities. Adjustments with upper class children from affluent background as equals is yet another problem.

(vi) The main worry of the private schools is about higher fee structure. How will the government bear the higher costs incurred on special category children and children from disadvantaged section, and what will be the modalities of reimbursement of the finances by the government.

Enrolment of out of school children: To think that there is a primary school at a distance of 1 km of the residence of the child, the government primary schools have been facing the problem of enrolment of all the children in compulsory school age group. There are a large number of educationally deprived children (may be 50% at certain places) living in rural as well as in urban areas who are not enroled in schools. These children are:

(i) Differently-abled children, with challenges, or with ill-health due to malnourishment and/or inadequate health care facilities.
(ii) Hundreds of street children living in urban slums.
(iii) Those engaged in household chores, working for paid or unpaid jobs to supplement family income; or as child labourers. For the parents of these children working outside the classrooms and learning life skills are more useful and important than the classroom teaching.
(iv) Minority community girls who are deprived of education for customary reasons.
(v) Children whose parents have different perception of suitable age of their children to admit them in school; or they are ignorant/indifferent about their education.

Attendance, retention, and completion: A major issue particularly of government primary schools is that of attendance of the children who remain absent from school for days, weeks and months together. The prolonged absenteeism of children either due to ill-health or seasonal migration of their parents consequently results in frequent failures, and eventually dropping out of the system without completing five-year cycle of primary education.

Provision of Quality Education and Its Requirements

In addition to access, equity, enrolment and attendance, another issue is that of providing free of charge quality education by the government. In order to provide quality education, the entire system needs overhauling in order to bring about improvement in infrastructure, curriculum and teacher training.

Infrastructure refers to plant and equipment as per norms laid down by the government in the Act, i.e. building, classrooms, furniture, basic amenities, playground, compound wall and the equipment, teaching-learning material suitable as per requirements of the curriculum. Keeping in view the scenario of the existing primary schools run by the government anywhere in the country which have a dilapidated building, with one/two rooms/sheds, no toilets, or playground, how can quality be expected to attract the children to get education in these schools.

Curriculum involves academic activities such as subjects taught, methods or classroom transactions (pedagogy); evaluation of the learners' progress for the cognitive growth of the children; and the non-academic activities for physical, emotional and social growth through games and sports, recreations, music, dance, art and painting, etc. In the present system of multi-grade teaching, with virtually one or two teachers responsible for teaching languages, maths, science, and social/environmental science to all the five classes, the classroom routine is reduced to containing children for number of scheduled hours in the school rather than engaging them in teaching and learning activities. Under the circumstances, how can the teachers, even though trained in modern pedagogy, apply the techniques suitable to individual learning needs of first generation learners who otherwise also do not get any guidance from home.

The curriculum at the elementary stage is not related and relevant to the life of children coming from deprived sections. It is not user friendly. Except for the languages, sciences or maths, there is no provision of teaching vocational skills at upper primary stage which can prepare the children for fulfilling the basic needs of their life. Secondly, the state level regional languages taught in the schools are different from that of the spoken mother tongue of the child which affects adversely their comprehension level. The numerical skills are even worse, what to speak of science subjects. Most of the children are not in a position to acquire and exhibit minimum level of learning in any of the subjects and at any of the stages of elementary education because there is a mismatch between curriculum and the needs of children of heterogeneous backgrounds.

Methodology and Classroom Transactions: Under the prevailing conditions, where lot of emphasis is given on rote memory rather than understanding of the concepts, even the best of teachers trained in modern techniques of pedagogy, in the absence of teaching-learning material, illustrative aids as charts, maps, models, apparatus or even the blackboard in the classes, they cannot do justice with any of the subject in multi-grade teaching at primary level. In the process, the children resort to memorizing facts without understanding the concepts. Paying individual attention to tackle the learning needs of every child is out of question. There is a world of difference between the training the teachers receive and actually applying those techniques while teaching in primary classes. To add to these problems, the teachers do not have any autonomy to bring necessary changes in the curriculum to suit the requirements of learners from varied backgrounds. It leaves no scope for paced learning in case of slow learners. The rigidity in the system is responsible to a great extent for failures, drop-outs, and also dwindling enrolment among children.

Evaluation: Except the written tests given at the end of a quarter, half-yearly or annually, the concept of continuous comprehensive evaluation for all-round development of the child finds hardly any place in the curriculum at the elementary stage. Other than declaring the child either pass or fail, or causing anxiety and stress in the children, it does not assess the child's progress from one step to another, or diagnose their learning difficulties.

Requirements of Inclusive Education

For providing quality education and also integration of differently-abled children, the schools whether managed privately or by the government, will have to make special provisions for these children, which may require:

- Modification in building with ramps, specially designed classrooms, furniture, changes in the time-table and daily schedule of activities to suit the requirements of children with physical or cognitive challenges.
- Different offerings because of diversity of their circumstances, i.e. the type of education that nurtures their strengths for the maximum development of their potentialities.
- Teacher empowerment: Special training/orientation programmes for the teachers proficient in classroom transactions and making provision for teachers trained in special education to cater to the learning needs of children with exceptionalities in respect of their abilities, challenges, and background.
- Provisions for adequate teaching-learning materials and apparatus for special need children like visually impaired, the deaf and dumb, and mentally challenged.

Constraints and concerns of the private schools: In the last decade and a half there has been an unprecedented growth of private schools be it in urban, semi-urban, or rural areas. Leaving aside the centuries old established schools of British period, out of about 20 per cent of private schools in India, some in the name of famous Saints with medium or high budget, others such as low budget English medium schools whether aided or unaided, have been attracting clients even from lower socio-economic groups. Most of these schools are not in a position financially or otherwise to fulfil the requirements of inclusive education. Their major concerns are primarily financial and these are as follows:

(i) With no aid from government, how to enhance their financial position, in view of the RTE Act that prohibits capitation fee.

(ii) How to bear the burden of 25 per cent admission of children from weaker sections, at the cost of loosing the financially better off children. If the fee structure is increased the parents from economically weaker sections will not be in a position to educate their children in English medium schools, which amounts to denying these children right to education in a school with better educational opportunities.

(iii) From where to pay the salaries of teachers in accordance with the Sixth Pay Commission in order to retain the committed and qualified teachers in the school.

(iv) How to compete with other reputed private schools that offer curriculum to prepare children from affluent background for international institutions.

(v) How to bring the level of achievement of first generation learners at par with children from better background.

(vi) How to recruit teachers trained for special need children with cognitive and physical challenges especially in view of financial constraints.

Loopholes in the Act

Apart from the key issues, there are some loopholes in the mandate of the Act itself in respect of:

Norms and Standard for a School

'All schools, which are deemed to have been recognized at the commencement of the Act (under Subsection 1 of Section 20), but did not fulfil the norms prescribed in the schedule at such commencement, shall do so within a period of three years, therefrom'.

This gives leverage to many a private school to function without fulfilling the norms. For maintaining quality, the recognition to private schools should be granted only when the norms are fulfilled before they start business of educating children. Three-year period is long enough for them to thrive without providing quality education.

Responsibility of the Appropriate (State Government) (Section 11)

There are no clear guidelines in the Act for:

The provision of financial assistance to be given to local authorities for implementation of Act (Subsection 2) (i), Establishment of additional schools as per requirement 2(iv); provision of building, teaching aids; and learning material to every state and fully-funded private schools 2(vii); adequate facilities for training of teachers to meet human resource requirement 2(x).

Responsibility of Local Authorities (Section 13)

Subsection 1 (i): To maintain the record of all children, belonging to disadvantaged, and weaker sections ... as may be prescribed. Till this day the concerned authorities do not have any such regulation.

(iii) Plan, budget and provide for additional schools ... as a result of gaps identified. Till today, the existing government primary schools have not been improved as per norms prescribed in the schedule, what to speak of providing additional schools and that too by local authorities.

Responsibility of the Parent/guardian (Section 15)

'It shall be the responsibility of every parent/guardian to enrol his child or ward in a school who has attained the entry age (6 year)'. Unless strict measures are adopted, such as penalty or punishment for the offenders, the parents of weaker section will go on ignoring the education of their children or force them to earn their livelihood and also supplement income of the family. These children will remain deprived of educational opportunities.

These are but a few of the drawbacks in the implementation of the Act.

Part B

Strategies for Making RTE a Reality

In order to enrol every child in 6–14 years age group in school, there is an urgent need to change the mindset of the entire community in general and the parents in particular who are indifferent towards the education of their children, or force their children to work to supplement their finances. The society in general is indifferent towards working children or street children, for whom survival is more important than education. For these children it matters little whether education is compulsory, free or paid or whether school is in the neighbourhood or at a distance. Thus, the access of education to all children is possible only if there is a general consensus among all sections of society, and also a legal force to make it compulsory for all. Whatever efforts are made, there has to be a missionary zeal to make education compulsory for all.

For Enrolment of Children in Schools

Awareness campaigns: In order to sensitize the parents whose children are out of school, the school children from senior classes may be involved to organize campaigns by way of enacting skits/plays in public places highlighting the importance of education, ill effects of child labour, and better earning capacity of the person by being educated and acquiring vocational skills. The rallies, candle light marches, 'Run for the cause of Right To Education' organized during festivals by the children has the potential to generate lot of interest among the poor/deprived section of the society. These activities can be organized as part of NSS programme. The special certificates for volunteers may be given in Annual function of the school, which serves the purpose of public recognition for children. In this way, through campaigns and other such activities to create awareness the message goes home with the parents easily and they think of sending their children to school.

Social support for parents who take initiative to educate their children as first generation learners, by commending and appreciating them publically by PRI's or any influential person in the locality. These parents, by setting an example, can be role models for others and can generate confidence in the poor to seek/demand access to education for their children.

Creation of Child's Rights to Education Forum: Such forms may be created by inducting educated youth, retired persons from government jobs as well as parents with a missionary spirit. They may keep track of parents whose children are not enroled in schools. They can motivate them to take steps in the right direction for the welfare of their children.

Role of Village Education Committees (VECs): The VECs can monitor and supervise the school as well as they can create awareness among the parents through dialogue and discussion, by reminding them of their responsibility of providing educational opportunities to their children. Likewise making teachers conscious of their duties to give a wider publicity about admissions in school at the beginning of the academic session. Secondly, during the session the teachers may be required to inform VEC about the absence of a child from school without permission, and the members of VEC can intervene by exercising their authority. They can act as agents of social change. Similarly, the school managing committee can monitor and supervise day-to-day school activities and functioning of the school so that children's education is not compromised.

Joint Venture of Anganwadi/Balwadis and Government Primary Schools: The teachers need to establish liaison with the Anganwadi workers to seek their support in enlisting the children at the completion stage of pre-school education. The efforts should be made to admit them in primary schools so that they are not lost because of their parents' ignorance, indifference or selfish motive of forcing them to work. As per the Act and the Eleventh Plan, the target of one year pre-school education for children entering primary school can be fulfilled only if the Anganwadis are equipped with the requirements of pre-school education in respect of curricular requirements and the workers are trained in providing pre-school education for 3 to 6 years of children.

Role of Panchayats: Capacity Building of BPL Women: In rural areas women in panchayats have a strong hold over women from lower and backward classes. The women Panches/Sarpanches can be trained in formation of Self Help Groups (SHG's) and vocational skills, to empower women folk to earn and save some money. In the process, the panches can take a pledge from the members of SHG, whose children are out of school, to divert some funds out of their kitty for their children's education. Once the earning capacity and financial status of the family is improved, the burden on children to work instead of being in school, will be reduced.

Responsibility of Local Authorities: As stipulated in the Act, the authorities are required to maintain record of children with special reference to the disadvantaged groups, in their jurisdiction, and to ensure their enrolment in an elementary school till completion and also to ensure sustained education of children of migrants, through bridge courses and remedial teaching, apart from budget to provide additional schools if required. To carry out this task, the local authorities can take the help of NGOs to provide bridge courses and can have liaison withy EGS and AIE centres to help the migrant children to get the benefit of RTE.

Alternatives to Improve Learning Levels of Children Leading to Success and Retention in Rural Schools

In rural areas, the bulk of enrolment is from backward classes and weaker sections. If enrolment in school is a challenge, a bigger challenge is to enable the children achieve minimum levels of learning leading to successful promotion year after year.

Modalities of Enhancing Minimum Learning Level: There can be a number of ways whereby the teachers may enhance their efficiency. All it requires is simple classroom techniques, such as the following:

- Paying individualized attention to slow learners by way of eye contact with every child in the class. This assures the child that teacher cares for him/her.
- Speaking slowly, repeating every word and sentence, explaining the concepts clearly to enable the children understand whatever is taught in the class.
- Model reading by teacher laying emphasis on stress and intonation by reading aloud and then asking children to read the text. It helps reading comprehension, which is an essential aspect of language learning.
- Paced learning: Teaching unit-by-unit based on the principle of programmed learning, and giving them enough time and opportunity to learn at their own pace to master the task.
- Asking questions for removing the difficulties.
- Encouraging and appreciating the slow learner at each successive success. It motivates the child to learn more especially in the acquisition and mastery of languages, science and of numerical skills.
- In rural primary schools, enlisting cooperation and support of educated boys/girls to share academic tasks of the teacher in class or in outdoor curricular activities by telling stories, playing games when the teachers are on government duty; or even to maintain STR pupil teacher ratio of 1 to 30 at this stage. Involvement of youth in teaching and learning makes them confident to handle responsibility of children's education. At the same time, children start enjoying because learning outside the class is much more meaningful to them.
- These strategies cost nothing. All they require is a little change in the mindset of stakeholders.

What Private Schools Can do to Improve the Achievement: In order to bring the level of achievement of first generation learners, and of children from educationally deprived and backward classes to be at par with the children of better educational background from upper strata of society who have better exposure and learning environment at home, following measures may be adopted:

Provision in the Time-table for Peer Tutoring: The special wings need to be set up where bright children can help the slow learners/low achievers or children with deficit mental abilities, assuming the role of a teacher. As surrogate teachers they are doubly gained. While teaching their peers and, thereby, gaining clarity about their own concepts, they also feel important in performing this role which enhances their self-image.

Adopt a Peer: The academically bright children can adopt a peer from disadvantaged group, or a child with some challenges. They can pull them through their difficulties, by rendering moral support and cooperation in learning. This will encourage equality and reciprocity among the children and reduce segregation to a great extent. For this they can be rewarded symbolically giving them certificate of merit for cooperative learning and team/peer teaching.

Talent Search programmes may be organized to nurture the talents of students from weaker sections, to enhance their confidence. Participation in cocurricular activities by all type or category of children will reduce segregation of class leading to integration.

Special Training and Remedial Teaching for Typical Children: The school is required to provide special training to teachers to handle children with special needs, and those from economically weaker background, in order to familiarize them to the new, changed educational transactional mode and also to cope with age appropriate class. It has to be strengthened with remedial teaching to be provided either during or after school hours to bring improvement in achievement which encourages to take a leap forward. Once their achievement levels are at par with those of others the social barriers are removed and children start mixing with each other as equals.

Teacher Empowerment: Changing the Mind-set of Teachers

In spite of training of the teachers for heterogeneous class of learners, what the teachers need to understand is that every child is special and capable of learning. All they need to do is to find out the uniqueness in the child to cater to their individual ways of learning and responding to newness in the environment. What is required is to shift from teacher-centred to child-centred approach, recognize their worth and then see the transformation in the child.

In order to set the ball rolling, rethinking is required about essentials of capacity building in teacher training programme. It has to be laced with teacher friendly approaches with emphasis on attitudinal training to develop positive attitude towards diversity in children to have faith in their potentialities, and to inspire the will in them to learn. With this type of pedagogy, the training inputs should also include development of creative thinking skills to enable the teachers to bring innovation in teaching strategies like 'a juggler' to suit the requirements of diverse needs of children.

Mentoring by senior faculty members to provide guidance and support to newly recruited teachers and to motivate them to accept the challenges of teaching, it has its own rewards.

Public-Private Partnership (PPP)

The implementation of RTE Act, depends on several factors. The most important being the proportion of financial burden to be shared by centre and state governments. As it is, most of the state governments have already expressed their inability to bear the expenditure on education for all. With investment in quality education that is accessible to all, the question arises how to enhance the public finances. In this regard, the only viable alternative seems to be to go in for public-private partnership.

Since 1990 with economic reforms, not only demand for private school has increased but there is a greater demand for quality education also. As a result, a number of private schools from International Baccalaureate (IB) Schools to English medium schools, whether aided or unaided, have sprung up in both urban and rural areas. With a mandate of the RTE of 25 per cent quota for children of marginalized section of society, the question arises what category of private schools and to what extent and manner they can be a partner with the government in providing education to children in compulsory age group.

Partnership Between Government and Private Schools

The literature is replete with suggestions of partnership between government and various agencies. With the RTE Act, the government can bank upon private sector in terms of delivery of education, infrastructure, support services, administration and supervision. The partnership can be between government and private sector, NGOs, industry, etc.

Contribution of for profit-private schools: The profit-making private schools of reputed standards can contribute by way of providing education delivery service; support services; and also supervision and management services.

Delivery of education service: The most recently opened private schools are catering to the elite and affluent class by providing curriculum of international standing (Baccalaureates) to prepare students for international institutions of higher learning. Making provision of education for children from deprived backgrounds in these schools becomes meaningless.

Then the 'Public Schools' in technical sense of the term, with residential facility established during British regime are located mostly quite away from urban localities, do not fit in the arena of neighbourhood school. These schools have been serving the uppermost strata of society ever since. These high budget schools even though admit children from lower strata, the curriculum is not related to their life. They are affiliated to national and international boards of education. By and large the type of education provided in these schools, thus far, has been suitable for preparing students for administration, defense, business, commerce or industry.

In the third category, the urban private schools of higher standing are mostly situated in elite part of the urban areas, catering obviously to upper strata of society. Again these are away from the reach of marginalized group for getting benefit of education provided in these schools because, these schools are not in their neighbourhood.

There is another category of English medium schools opened in urban, semi-urban as well as in rural areas providing State Board of Education curriculum. They also cater to the economically weaker sections. Then there are the denominational schools in almost every state with religious background and philosophy of education. These schools cater to all type of students, even the poor may hope to have access to education where the State Board of Education curriculum is provided as it is in government schools.

By and large, the private schools have varied standards and philosophy of education. They do have the potential to serve the society from varied socio-economic backgrounds. At the same time, very few of the these schools with comparatively lower budget, may be suitable for the intake of educationally deprived children. In spite of higher fees and costs, even the parents from economically weaker sections prefer to educate their children in these schools rather than sending them to government school.

With demand for education in English medium schools even from economically weaker segments of population, many low budget private schools have come up in cities, whether big or small, in urban or semi-urban areas, or even in far-flung rural areas. The quality in most of these schools is much to be desired, for in terms of curricular requirements and educational opportunities being provided to match with the fees collected from the children. The teachers may or may not have essential qualification, even as they are paid much less than the salaries drawn by the government school teachers. Yet they are committed because they are under the direct supervision of school management. The enrolment and attendance in these schools is never a problem, because: the infrastructure provided in private schools contributes a lot to satisfy outwardly the minimum expectations of the parents who are disillusioned with provisions made in government schools. These schools attract the children because they have adequate number of teachers and classrooms for every class. They have colourful furniture in classrooms, attractive uniforms, and good bus service for children and teachers commuting from distance. By comparison the enrolments in government primary schools are dwindling which do not offer such services. Though these schools are thriving financially, at least they are serving the society by providing education for all without making it compulsory. Even the poor children are being benefited, which is the mandate of the RTE Act.

Support services: Here the role of elite private schools that practice innovation, and experimentation with new ideas is of paramount importance. These schools can provide academic and professional support.

Academic support: These schools can render academic services in preparation of curricular inputs, a user-friendly curriculum that relates to the life of the users; software for teaching and learning which is age and grade appropriate, for the children provide suggestions/alternatives in evaluation of children with a focus on diagnosis of learning difficulties, and with a scope for remediation.

The professional support can be provided with the aim of preparing committed, motivated teachers who make children love their school, by making learning enjoyable experience for them. The elite and innovate schools can organize preservice/inservice training programme with a focus on innovations in curricular transactions to enhance the quality of teaching and learning in other private or state-owned schools.

Although, it is the responsibility of the government to argument teacher training capacity, in view of the large number of teachers required to provide compulsory elementary education for all, the government has to rely on the private institutions to provide Elementary Teacher Training (ETT) by increasing the units in teacher training institutions to be effective from the academic session 2012–13. Otherwise the requirement of the number of qualified teachers with academic credentials in schools may not be fulfilled even in the next 10 years, what to speak of 5 years, w.e.f. implementation of the Act.

Administrative and supervision of school system: Some of the unaided private schools are independent. Along with NGOs, they can assume the responsibility of strengthening the school management committee or village education committees, to monitor day-to-day functioning of the school in order to reduce absenteeism in teachers and students. The private schools managing the public (government) schools is another way of PPP.

Infrastructure: Although as per the Act, it is the responsibility of state governments to make provision for building, teaching learning material, the private sector (industrialists, business magnets, charitable trusts) can be explored to provide infrastructure for schools by way of constructing building with facilities required for schools; providing equipment and apparatus for labs; take up maintenance work of labs and school work and making provision for basic amenities and catering service also. This type of service provided by the private sector will be helpful in uplifting the standards of government schools. Since the Act has been implemented, keeping the constraints of time, the government should tap these sources to fulfill the requirements of norms for the schools.

Sponsorships: The corporate sector or philanthropic groups can help the government schools by way of providing scholarships, teaching-learning materials and illustrative aids, recreational equipment, and books for the library. In addition, they can provide educational assets, transport service, etc. To top it all the corporate sector can create employment opportunities for parents who force their children to work, instead of sending them to school.

Role of academicians/educators in the universities: Research and Development Wing: In the public-private partnership every stakeholder, every partner in education can contribute to improve the performance, enhance efficiency and ensure accountability on the part of the teachers. In this context, innovation and development are the key factors of profit or non-profit making private sector.

To enhance efficiency of delivery of education from the point of view of all round development of the child and making education relevant to the life skills required by the children, the universities need to set up special Research and Development Wings, where the teachers and the researchers are engaged in preparing innovative kits to make teaching and learning an enjoyable act. University Departments of Education can organize refresher courses or short-term summer courses to provide inservice training programmes to train elementary school teachers in user-friendly techniques of teaching. Secondly, the students pursuing their degrees at Masters and PhD level can take up research project experimenting with new techniques of teaching and learning based on the psychological principles of learning.

The collaboration and partnership of educational institutions with outside agencies, private and corporate sector for exchange of technical know-how, material, methods and resources, are the only mantra for successful implementation of the RTE Act in letter and spirit.

17

E-governance in Educational Institutions

Practical Challenges in Implementation

K. TANKESHWAR

In recent years, the Indian higher education system has seen tremendous growth with participation of private sectors in bringing up new universities. On the one hand, it gives more opportunities and option to students and, on the other hand, it poses challenges to maintain quality of these education institutions in terms of teaching, research and governance. Issues relating to teaching and research are certainly of greater importance than the management of institutions as being the backbone of any institution. However, we shall take up here the issues like e-governance and e-learning. For higher educational institution e-governance[1] is defined as:

'E-governance is the application of information and communication technologies (ICT) to transform the efficiency, effectiveness, transparency and accountability of informational and transactional exchanges within government, between government of states and managements of Universities and/or Colleges, citizens, employees and students, and to empower students through access and use of information'.

Government of its own has started activities like National e-governance plan. To bring the benefits of Information and Communication Technology (ICT) at the last mile to ensure transparent, timely and hassle-free delivery of citizen services, Government of India has initiated e-governance programme in country in the late 1990s. After that, Union Government has approved the National e-Governance Plan, comprising of 27 Mission Mode Projects and eight components 2006 to give a boost to e-Governance initiatives in India. The Department of Information Technology and the Department of Administrative Reforms and Public Grievances has formulated the National e-Governance Plan.[2]

Most of the higher educational institutions in India are managing the information through websites. But very few institutions have Management Information Systems (MIS) which is the key for the e-governance. What is lacking is the visionary leadership of such institutions who could understand its need and/or put efforts to evolve this change management. Developing software tools for educational institution is not an issue to developers of Indian companies.

Restructuring Education for National Delivery Using ICT

Education is about putting teachers and learners together. As we evolve into different stages of society, from agricultural, industrial, post-industrial, to knowledge society, its modes must change. Learners may be anywhere and educational service providers could come from everywhere. Even Gurukuls which followed traditional system of education are now transforming their education system by adopting IT.

The objectives of e-learning and e-governance in education are to meet challenges of:

(i) Accessibility and affordability
(ii) Scalability
(iii) Relevance
(iv) Quality

Accessibility and Affordability

With the help of ICT, education should reach out to the unreached areas. It should cross limits of regions, rural and tribal area. This could be done only if we have low power consumption and rugged devices. 'Aakash' is an achievement of Indian technological frontier. Another aspect is that education should cross limits of hours of classrooms. It should be accessible 24×7 throughout the year at will of candidate (not only 180 days a year).

Scalability

It should be scalable and should include the excluded. We have today isolated pockets of excellence. Expansion at high speed often leads to decline in quality. Scalability while maintaining quality is a challenge. National Knowledge network[3] is being established to link up all educational institutions for research and teaching.

Relevance

It should not be a mere lecture rather a creation of a learning event. It is not enough that a lecture was taken. The learning transactions are more important.

Answer to the following three questions can determine the relevance.

Did learning take place?

Did an interest in more learning take place?

Did the learner learn how to learn?

Quality

Providing high quality instructions and management is a greater challenge. Re-structuring and transforming educational processes shall be required. Learner relationship management needs to be strengthened. Enterprise resource planning and quality and Security Management systems are needed. Global e-sourcing of learning resources and expertise shall be made available. Learner facilitation system shall be required for bringing quality. We should now concentrate on producing quality lectures available at Sakshat and NPTEL rather than duplicating.[4]

Real Challenges

E-governance in higher educational institutions is a developing phenomenon, and requires a change in the mindset of one and all – teachers, students, principals, Vice Chancellors or the management. With the support of the Internet, the management processes defined by specializations can be made efficient, effective and student-friendly. There are many challenging issues lying ahead. Security of data is the main concern, and redefining rules and procedures, information transparency, legal issues, infrastructure, skill and awareness, access to right information, inter-departmental collaboration, tendency to resist the change in work culture, are the main concerns and challenges to institutions. Beside these factors, institutions need to make significant investments in areas such as process re-engineering, capacity building, training, change management, assessment and awareness

Assuming that an employee spends about 35 years of his life in an institution, the institutions of higher education can be put in three categories.

Category I. Institutions older than 35 years

Category II. Institutions older than 15 years but less than 35 years

Category III. Institutions up to 15 years older.

These e-governance and e-learning activities in these institutions depend on many factors like willingness of head of institution and its employees, infrastructure and change processes. These different categories of institutions behave differently in government and private sectors especially in change managements. Following is an estimate based on observation gathered through websites, on the ranking index of websites[5] of different categories of institutions and on the experience gathered over many years through interactions.

Category	*Willingness of CEO*	*Willingness for Training to manpower*	*Infrastructure facility*	*Funds availability*	*Compatible processes*	*Willingness to change processes by staff*
			Government/Aided Institutions			
I	Yes: 60% No: 40%	Yes: 25% No: 75%	Yes: 25% No: 75%	Yes: 25% No: 75%	Yes: 20% No: 80%	Yes:20% No:80%
II	Yes: 75% No: 25%	Yes: 50% No: 50%	Yes: 50% No: 50%	Yes: 55% No: 45%	Yes: 75% No: 25%	Yes: 50% No: 50%
III	Yes: 85% No: 15%	Yes: 60% No: 40%	Yes: 55% No: 45%	Yes: 65% No: 35%	Yes: 75% No: 25%	Yes: 65% No: 35%
			Private Institutions			
I	Yes: 70% No: 30%	Yes: 35% No: 65%	Yes: 75% No: 25%	Yes: 65% No: 35%	Yes: 40% No: 60%	Yes:30% No:70%
II	Yes: 75% No: 25%	Yes: 50% No: 50%	Yes: 60% No: 40%	Yes: 45% No: 55%	Yes: 75% No: 25%	Yes: 55% No: 40%
III	Yes: 75% No: 25%	Yes: 60% No: 40%	Yes: 25% No: 75%	Yes: 35% No: 65%	Yes: 80% No: 20%	Yes: 65% No: 35%

Clearly, private institutions have an edge in change process and as a result are inching towards e-governance. The only major constraint is the financial resource and government support.

Implementation

The change management requires the following:

(i) Willingness of officers involved.
(ii) Networking.
(iii) Training to staff.
(iv) Awareness of importance.
(v) Adaptability to changed processes
(vi) Will to work in changed environment.

Practically, it is observed that the higher the rank of officer, more difficult it is to involve him/her in the process of change. As they are generally senior employees and are not receptive to computer's working. The age is a big factor for these officers. In fact, those who had got their graduation/post graduation in the era of Personal Computer, i.e. >1985 onwards, they are found to be more computer savvy, with the exception of those who have been initiated and trained in computer learning. Training to other staff also has similar problems. Employees lose interest and start to follow conventional practices again if not constantly pressurized by the officer incharge.

Employees organizations/unions also played their own role. They will tell the authority to hire computer professionals for doing their jobs which a normal person can learn to perform. But these problems are all over now and the use of ICT has begun to be appreciated and accepted. This is more so in private educational institutions than in public sector institutions.

How smart classroom could be used? How lectures be recorded? How students can learn/relearn if missed out? These things are better managed in private schools than in public universities/colleges.

Nevertheless, beneficial impact of ICT and of e-governance on the educational institutions, their economy and quality of education is now widely recognized. National mission of education through ICT (NMEICT) is a step taken in right direction by ministry of Human Resource and Development.

Notes

1. Mrinalini Shah. NMIMS University, Mumbai, *India International Journal of Education and Development Using Information and Communication Technology* (IJEDICT), Vol. 3, Issue 2, 2007, pp. 125–37.
2. http://www.indg.in/e-governance/e-governance/egov-plan
3. Sam Pitroda. *Knowledge Commission Report and its Recommendations*, http://www.knowledgecommission.gov.in/downloads/report2009/eng/3_Recommendations.pdf
4. http://www.sakshat.ac.in/and http://nptel.iitm.ac.in/
5. http://www.alexa.com

18

The Role of English in Educational Development

JITENDRA SETHI

The role of English in educational development in India can best be studied if we first make an appraisal of its place in general in the country today. In this paper, therefore, I first dwell upon the importance and use of this language in India, and then move on to its role in educational development. While speaking about its importance, I also take into account its use as a medium of instruction since it strikes me as a relevant point. Also, discussed in the paper is the oft-worrying question of 'which English'. I conclude the paper by suggesting how to conduct the teaching of English through public-private participation.

Place of English in India

The place of English in India and its role in many walks of life are so well recognized that we don't need to rub this point in. Its demand has increased manifold over the last few decades. Witness, for example, the mushrooming of English-medium schools even in small towns. To these schools go the children of not only the well-to-do, but also those whose parents can hardly afford it. This trend is easily understandable: acquisition of a good command of English opens up the doors of a good many coveted careers besides enhancing one's position in society.

Not many among us know (or remember) that English too is one of the major Indian languages listed in the VIII Schedule of the Constitution of India. The name Central Institute of English and Foreign Languages (and now: The English and Foreign Languages University) at Hyderabad clearly recognizes that, in India, unlike in many other countries, English is not a foreign language.

Furthermore, English in India today is not just a status symbol; it is much more. There is hardly a sphere of everyday life in which English is not employed: be it administration, internet, outsourcing, travel and tourism, banking, trade and commerce, medical tourism, science and technology, industry, and higher education and research. Furthermore, expansion and development of education, as we shall see soon, depend heavily on English. Its importance can be measured negatively as well: witness, for example, the unhappy outcome of the near-banishing of this language over a long period in certain Hindi states under the guise of pseudo-patriotism.

My speaking so lyrically about English should not give the reader the impression that I am advocating the propagation of English for its cultural values or the humanizing effect that a study of its literature can produce. Such cultural values and humanizing effect can equally well be achieved through the literatures of other Indian languages as well. As for the occasional 'complaint' that a god command of English (especially spoken English) leads to the cultivation of elitism among its speakers (which is not considered desirable in a democratic society), our claim is that cultivation of elitism or a false sense of superiority is not our aim. At the same time, it may also be stated that such fear is rather exaggerated. The fact is that when a certain language is shared among a large number of people of all strata of society, it loses its air of superiority and elitism. The much wider use of English in south India is a case in point.

Now, granting that in India English is used for a wide variety of needs and purposes, our next concern must be how to make its use effective. This point we take up for discussion in what follows.

English as Medium of Instruction

If any language is required to be used effectively, then it follows that its users have to have a good command of it. And to achieve a good command of English, it is necessary that its learners receive a much greater exposure to it than is generally afforded by a mere 30 to 40–minute period a day in schools (of which much time is taken away by the teacher talking alternately in English and the local language). Since providing more time to English than to other subjects is often not acceptable to many, the remedy lies in employing English as a medium of instruction. This way learners' exposure to this language is increased manifold (without taking time away from other subjects of study), and this results in a higher level of proficiency in English – a fact amply borne out by a comparison between English-medium products and non-English-medium products.

An incidental, but definitely a rich, dividend of a higher level of proficiency in English is that it enables you to gather knowledge from more sources than just the textbook. Isn't it an observed fact that those taught through the medium of English are often more widely knowledgeable than others? Now, this is easily understandable: at a higher level if you are learning your economics or chemistry or anything through English, you have a comfortable access to a wide variety of useful articles through the internet and journals of national and international standing. You then learn not only that which was printed in your textbooks a decade ago, but also that which is the latest on the frontiers of knowledge in a given discipline. It is an accepted fact that an inevitable gap will always remain between the availability of the latest knowledge through English and its availability through translations into other Indian languages.

Educational psychologists hold the view that learners grasp a subject better and can develop originality in their thinking if they learn it through their mother tongue than through another tongue. I do not subscribe to this view. It is not corroborated by facts – at least not in countries such as India, where English is a second language, not a foreign language.

Role of English in Educational Development

Educational development remains a mere dream as long as standards of teaching and learning various subjects at the tertiary level remain low. They remain low for a vast variety of reasons, but our concern here is with one: low levels of proficiency in English among students. A general complaint voiced by faculties of even the most prestigious institutions such as the IITs and IIMs is that their students with low levels of proficiency in English (e.g. those who receive their schooling through a regional language) often fail to perform well because they fail to comprehend lectures and books well. Often this is not due to any serious deficiency in their grasp of the subjects taught up to the +2 level; it is due to their poor English (And admission tests do not test their English).

Now, if many students fail to draw the maximum benefit from lectures and prescribed books because of their poor English, then any measures to raise the standards of the courses (even in prestigious institutions) cannot succeed. It follows, therefore, that standards of higher education imparted through the medium of English cannot be raised unless the level of students' proficiency in this language itself is raised.

What is said above pertains no doubt to formal classroom teaching. But educational development is not a function of classroom teaching alone; many other factors also contribute to such development. Of these, participation in national and international seminars and conferences is an important one. Such participation leads on to interaction among professionals at a higher level, thereby encouraging and promoting research and development. And for us in India, this becomes possible only through English.

It is often complained that many scholarly papers written by our scientists are not published in international journals. They are duly acknowledged and sent back with the remark that the journal does not have adequate editorial facilities. What this means in simple English is that the English used in these papers is not up to the mark and is sometimes even confusing. This results in non-recognition internationally of many of our top-level professionals, their brilliance and originality notwithstanding. Besides, their peers and juniors remain deprived of the useful knowledge that they could have accessed if the seniors' papers had been published.

For any development in education, therefore, it is absolutely imperative that we devote attention to raising the level of proficiency in English. Later in this paper, I shall suggest some measures to do so, but in the meantime we need to decide which English to teach.

Which English?

This question was never asked until well after the British Raj. We used to take it that there was, for us, just one English – the English that the British had left us with. We woke up to the full realization of the existence of other-than-British Englishes only in the recent decades when our contacts with the US, Canada and, more recently, Australia grew up. In particular, with the US, our contacts in technology, trade, foreign relations and education reached a certain level when it became natural for people to ask why not teach American English. To appreciate the problem fully, a little digression at this point may be necessary.

There are two principal native varieties of English today. We can call them General British and General American. They differ from each other in respect of vocabulary, grammar and pronunciation. The differences in respect of vocabulary (e.g. 'elevator' for 'lift'; 'gas' for 'petrol'; 'railroad' for 'railway'; 'sidewalk' for 'pavement') are, however, not so formidable; they can be acquired easily. As for differences in grammar (e.g. 'He arrived already' instead of the British 'He *has* arrived already'; 'I left for Delhi Sunday' instead of the British 'I left for Delhi *on* Sunday'), they are not very many. And, moreover, even in the US many people use British grammar or at least understand it easily. The problem then remains mainly in respect of pronunciation.

At this point, for convenience of reference, I would like to introduce a useful term – 'accent'. The term, as used in the present context, refers to different varieties of a language when they are distinguished on the basis of differences in pronunciation. It is in this sense of the term that we speak of the American accent, the British accent, the Australian accent, and so on.

The rest of this section will deal with accent only.

Votaries of American accent in India do not realize that differences between General American and General British pronunciation are very many, especially in the vowel systems of the two varieties. Unless you acquire the General American vowel system in its entirety, and use it consistently, you may land up creating and confronting situations of utter confusion. If you pronounce the word 'class' so as to make it rhyme with the word 'lass', I shall expect you to use the American pronunciation elsewhere too. Therefore, the next moment, if you pronounce the word 'glass' the British (and Indian) way, I may think you are saying 'gloss'. And, if in American English I say 'Hir is my her', I am not sure you will understand it.

Demanding American accent is easy; granting it is not. Who is there in India to teach it? And is the stupendous effort and money involved in it worth its while?

As against the votaries of American accent, there are others who, enthused by their patriotic zeal, ask why not teach 'Indian English'. My simple answer to that would be: 'Fine, but where *is* it?' Whose English is 'Indian English'? An Assamese' English or a Malayalee's English or a Punjabi's English? Those who are regarded as good speakers of English in India, whose English is easily understood all over India and abroad, base their pronunciation largely on General British as defined in *Oxford Advanced Learner's Dictionary*, 7th edition. This accent is acknowledged to have a high degree of intelligibility all over the world. And we must remember that in today's world our use of spoken English is not meant for communication within our city, region, or the country only; it is meant for communication globally. Hence, no regional variety will do, and a pan-Indian accent simply does not exist.

In the light of the foregoing, my unhesitating answer to the question of 'which English' is General British – may be with a few minor adjustments in regard to a couple of vowels and the use of the sound (r) wherever the letter *r* occurs in the spelling. In adopting this accent (even with a few minor adjustments), we enjoy a great advantage: after all the foundation of our pronunciation of English is the British English, a few divergences from it over the years notwithstanding.

Teaching English through Public-Private Participation

After making a case for English, and after discussing which variety of it should be taught in this country, the question that arises most naturally is how to teach it effectively to the vast multitudes aspiring to learn it.

Time was when government institutions – both schools and especially colleges – were rated by parents as better options for their children than most of the private institutions. Such rating was not without reason: government institutions had qualified teachers, libraries, laboratories and playgrounds, which many of the private institutions did not afford. Of course, some private institutions, especially those run by altruistic and religious/denominational organizations, did shine out in their curricular and co-curricular activities. But that was the time when you set up a private school or college not *make* money but to *spend* it to educate people. Money came largely from philanthropic organizations and individuals voluntarily – not via 'extortion' of 'capitation fee' from helpless but ambitious parents.

Times have changed. Today, government institutions are rated lowest in the general public perception, and for good reasons. What with bureaucratic indifference, they are often not adequately staffed; their infrastructure is abominably poor, affecting the morale of the students and teachers alike; and there are no incentives for members of the staff to put in their best. As for private institutions, barring a fast-dwindling number of exceptions, they are today money-spinning shops. Cases are heard of many professional colleges in the private sector today where you just pay the demanded fee year after year and try your luck in the examination hall on your own. Many of them do not employ full-time faculty, but just make do with desperately low-paid teachers appointed on ad-hoc basis, and that too not in the right numbers.

The performance of coaching centres is no better. It's time they changed their names to 'poaching centres'.

What's the answer then? Imparting of education is too serious a job to be left in the hands of bureaucrats alone. And, at the same time, we have seen that private individuals and bodies have turned this noble cause into a profit-yielding industry. What's the remedy?

The remedy lies, I believe, in instituting public-private participation in imparting education. The public sector finances and the private sector runs institutions. To make both accountable, an independent body can be set up. This can comprise representatives from both public and private sectors. The public sector should nominate only those people who are sufficiently interested in education. The private sector should be comprised mainly of people of established reputation in the fields of education and educational administration. The said independent body will not only look after finances but also – and chiefly – monitor and regulate the task of imparting education. An incidental, but important, gain of giving the private sector its say will be that, unlike the government (which works under several political compulsions), it will not play fast and loose with English, thereby ruining the careers of many a youth. It will suffer from no false sense of idealism or political compulsion.

Summing Up

In this paper, I have expressed my view that for any worthwhile plan aimed at the development of education to succeed, it is imperative that we recognize the role of English in it. And for English to play this role effectively, it is essential that we devote attention to raising learners' level of proficiency in this language. For this to happen, I have suggested two measures: one, increase learners' exposure to the language by employing it as a medium of instruction from an early stage, and two, establish and run educational institutions through public-private participation.

Index